HOW TO FISH PLASTIC BAITS IN SALTWATER

BY CAPT. JIM WHITE

HOW TO FISH PLASTIC BAITS IN SALTWATER

BY CAPT. JIM WHITE

THE FISHERMAN LIBRARY
1622 BEAVER DAM ROAD
POINT PLEASANT, NJ 08742

PRINTED IN THE UNITED STATES OF AMERICA
Library of Congress Cataloging-in-Publication data
ISBN 0-923155-32-5

THE FISHERMAN LIBRARY CORP.
1622 Beaver Dam Road
Point Pleasant, NJ 08742

Publisher . . . . Richard S. Reina
Associate Publisher. . . . . Pete Barrett
Associate Editor . . . . Linda Barrett
Copy Editor . . . . Zach Harvey
Cover Photo . . . . Tom Migdalski
Cover Design, Layout and Production . . . . JNC Design Group, LLC

DEDICATION

I would like to dedicate this book to my beautiful wife of 28 years, Nancy. Without her patience, tolerance and love, I would not have been able to accomplish everything that I have so far. She has truly been my inspiration in all avenues of life. They say you are blessed if you find true love, and I am truly blessed.

I also would like to dedicate this to my grandson, Devon James, DJ, who will hopefully follow my son and me into the outdoor world and learn to love it as we have. He has become my life and my little friend.

To both—I love you dearly.

ACKNOWLEDGMENTS

I have been very fortunate to have had a father, grandfather and uncles who fished. Coming from a fishing family certainly has helped me over the years.

Thanks to Lefty Kreh for his advice and guidance over the years and Nick Curcione. They provided the confidence boost I needed to tackle such a project as this. Lefty's endless advice over the years has made me not only a better angler, but a better person as well.

Pete Barrett of *The Fisherman* made a place in The Fisherman Library series for a book of this type. He quickly saw a big hole that has never been filled or tackled in this manner, and he took the time to listen to my ideas.

I'm indebted to Bob Pond, former owner of Atom Lures, and founder of Stripers Unlimited and pioneer lure maker for his endless supply of striped bass knowledge and his guidance over the years. He made me ask those basic questions about fishing: Why? How come? What now? Where? And more. He is a very special man and a dear friend.

Frank Woolner took the time forty years ago to talk to a 10-year-old kid with a Penn Squidder, 9-foot bamboo rod, 36-pound Ashaway line and a burnt thumb. He gave his time and advice, and shared his knowledge with someone so young. I have never forgotten it.

It was my good fortune to have a father who loved to fish. It was also my good fortune to have grown up in a time when so many special men made such big contributions to the angling world, such as Jerry Sylvester, who owned a bait and tackle shop in Narragansett, Rhode Island where we would stop, have coffee and chat. Charlie Murat built most of our rods. Art Lavallee, Sr. of Acme Lures was an inspiration, as was Lester Boyd, outdoor columnist of the *Providence Journal*, and many, many others who became legends in the northeast saltwater fishing scene. All had a vision and a passion for fishing that exceeded all others and all were willing to share it with a young skinny kid. I have and will be forever grateful to have known such men.

INTRODUCTION

This book came about after many years of fishing and experimenting with soft-plastic lures as a recreational angler and professional guide. Soft-plastic lures are the new wave of saltwater fishing and new innovations are fueling a big boost in tackle shop sales. More than just a pretty new face, soft plastics are fabulous fish catchers and the recreational fishing community is cheering on new developments and new techniques.

This book is a broad representation of the soft-plastic fishing world. There is a plastic bait to meet almost any possible fishing situation, and the manufacturers list at the back of this book is extensive and growing.

The techniques within these pages will be a good starting point to help you think of your own new ideas to find more new ways to use these very effective lures. Soft plastics lend themselves to all kinds of new ideas and rigging.

In my winter-season seminars, I tell the audience that saltwater anglers could learn a great deal from their freshwater counterparts. Freshwater anglers are light years ahead of most saltwater anglers simply because they study, pick apart, try, change, poke, cast, make, break and adapt to a wide range of fishing situations. Professional bass tournaments drive them to be more creative and inventive than saltwater anglers ever thought possible. Salty brethren would do well to find that extra edge that tournament anglers use to discover refinements, ideas and tactics that help us all catch more fish.

The overlap of freshwater techniques into the briny world is extensive, such as drop-shotting. Just as Carolina rigging, Texas rigging, slip bobbers, split shot and other tricks work their magic in freshwater, so these same techniques work with tremendous effectiveness in the salt.

What makes soft plastics so attractive to fish and fishermen? Price is one advantage. They are inexpensive to buy when compared to the rest of the lure market. They are manufactured in an infinite selection of styles, shapes, weights, colors and scents. The soft texture means a fish is more likely to hang on longer once it bites. That extra split second of hold-on time can mean the difference between hooking and landing a nice fish or having him swim away laughing at you. As we all get older and reaction time slows in setting the hook a bit, any help that we can get is a great boon to our day on the water. Let's face it, I am not as quick on the trigger as I was when I was 25 years old and I bet most of you aren't either.

Soft plastics also have a very life-like appearance and action in the water that is tough to duplicate with solid wood or hard-plastic baits. As good as they are, hard lures just don't flip, hop, twist, jump and dive like soft plastics will. You can also carry a wide array of shapes, styles and colors with very little room being taken up in your boat, beach buggy or tackle bag.

I hope to have made this book as complete and as informative as possible. It is by no means the last word on fishing these lures, because new techniques are constantly being discovered. Fishing is a constant learning process and no one ever learns all there is to know. Those who think they know it all soon fall to the back of the pack and will no doubt catch less fish than those who keep an open mind. Accepting new ideas is your greatest tool to catching more and bigger fish.

Jim White

TABLE OF CONTENTS

This book is about fishing with soft-plastic baits, including selecting, rigging and fishing them so you too can catch trophy-size gamefish like this big striped bass.

CHAPTER ONE

HISTORY OF SOFT-PLASTIC BAITS

Discovering the history of soft plastics was a tall order, but it's the best way to start this book. Much of the early history is sketchy and more than one company claims to be the "first." Despite the lack of comprehensive documentation, there's enough background information to piece together an interesting story.

Nick Creme is generally credited with inventing what was considered to be the first soft-plastic worm in 1949. However, delving into other records, I discovered that DeLong Lures in the Midwest, laid claim to pouring the first plastic eel in 1945, a full four years before Creme poured his own worm design.

During those early years, there were very few companies trying to gain a foothold in this new area of the fishing tackle industry. Skeptics believed the concept of soft-plastic lure manufacturing would not survive, and that soft-plastic lures had no place in the tackle arena. Today, the soft-plastic portion of the tackle industry's total sales is immense and covers freshwater, back bay and inshore saltwater, and there's a growing following in the offshore market.

In my attempt to find information about other companies that were in the industry in those beginning years, and after spending nearly a year researching this topic, I still found very little to chew on. I am sure there were a few mom-and-pop operations during that time period that I've overlooked. The fact is, several of today's larger lure companies began their road to success by manufacturing lures in a basement, garage or very small shop.

Over the years, many manufacturers came and went for one reason or another. Some probably made an inferior product, while others fell victim to bad timing and not being in the right place at the right time. The attempt here is to document those companies that made a big and lasting contribution to the industry, and to document those companies that survived, grew and went on to become examples for others who followed.

If I left someone out, I apologize. The fact is, an entire book could be written just on the half-dozen or so industry leaders and their own contributions to sport fishing. Unfortunately, that would leave less space for the vital how-to information, and that's why you bought this book in the first place—to help improve your fishing.

As you read through the following chapters, you'll see that almost all of the original soft-plastic lure companies began as freshwater manufacturers with the exception of the Alou Tackle Company and the Boone Trout Tout. The Alou Bait Tail was designed in 1960, primarily as a new type of plastic lure for striped bass. Meanwhile, the Boone Trout Tout quickly became popular with Florida's speckled trout fishermen, and soon after, with northern weakfish fishermen. I don't believe they had any idea of how far ahead of their time they actually were.

I can recall my own first encounter with soft plastic. It was a Burke night crawler worm with a double-hook rig, a spinner and a few beads at the head, and wire guards to fend off pesky weeds. I paid 59 cents for it and the first time I used it, the older men at the lake laughed at the young inexperienced kid. They laughed until that kid hooked and landed a 5-1/2-pound largemouth bass. The very next day, they were in the bait shop looking to buy a plastic night crawler.

To be fair, we'll place the beginnings of soft plastics in the mid-to late-1940s. If DeLong Lures had the first soft-plastic lure, it was Nick Creme's attempts, starting in 1949, that began to popularize plastic worms. This avid Ohio fisherman created a substitute for live night crawlers. At the time, live night crawlers were hard to come by and he felt there had to be a better way. Today, soft-plastic worms not only dominate the freshwater scene, including big-money largemouth bass tournaments like B.A.S.S., but have swept into the saltwater arena as well. Their influence and importance in the salt chuck is growing every year by leaps and bounds.

The Alou Bait Tail and Alou Eel were two of the very early successful soft-plastic baits in saltwater. Al Reinfelder's *Bait Tail Fishing* is long out of print, but is still read by avid striped bass fishermen.

Since that trend-setting soft-plastic worm popped out of a homemade mold, other inventors have taken this material, as well as newer space-age materials, to new levels of creativity. Soft plastics can be molded into almost any conceivable shape, size or form. Just look at what is on the market today. There are soft-plastic lures that are so realistic it's getting harder to tell them apart from the real thing!

It's A Plastic World

The first soft plastics were poured into crude molds made of plaster, wood, brass, iron, cardboard or any other material that lent itself to easy shaping. The first batches of plastic goo were melted down in an old cooking pot on a pot bellied stove or camp stove and probably stunk up the house.

Today's soft plastics are much more sophisticated and there are many different processes for making soft-plastic lures. Most of them are highly guarded, top-secret chemical concoctions that manufacturers are nervous to even discuss. Although there is some basic similarity in all the soft-plastic lures, the individual blends and formulas for each manufacturer are probably known only to the chemists who mix the compounds—and are carefully guarded by each company.

The production process is similar for all plastic baits; they are either hand poured into molds or injection molded. The hand-poured process allows some added creativity to blend color schemes, but it is time consuming. The basic injection-molding process uses specialized machines to melt the plastic at a specific temperature into a liquid form. Once it's liquefied, metal flakes, flavors, scents and any additional coloration can then be added before the melted plastic is injected into the molds.

Additional external coloration can be added to enhance the bait's lifelike appearance by an airbrush process after production. This is a vinyl paint that adheres extremely well to the finished product.

Many plastics are molded to be tough, while others are manu-factured to be soft and supple. According to the angler's preference, there are times when the softer bait is preferred, and other times when a tougher, harder bait is the best choice. Generally speaking, the tougher baits last longer and can be used to catch several fish before they are no longer useable.

Almost all plastic baits are made from polyvinyl chloride (PVC), the same material used to make PVC pipes in your home. The addition of other chemicals after the melting process gives soft baits their flexibility, texture, suppleness, color and fishing attributes. Softeners added during the injection process help to retain lure shape and a longer shelf life at the tackle shop or in your tackle box.

When compared to the new generation of so-called super plastics, PVC has a longer molecular chain than the plastic being used in the super-stretch baits like Cyber-Flexxx, a new material known as a crystal gel compound. It's strong and durable, stretches amazingly and won't break or tear. It's also more buoyant and contains no toxic substances.

Berkley, a division of Pure Fishing, has added another new material to the selection. Technically not a plastic, Berkley's Gulp! baits have the look and feel of plastic so they earn their place in this book as a "plastic" bait. Actually, Gulp! is a completely natural substance that is 100-percent biodegradable and poses no environmental threat. Plus, its scent dissipates into the water 400-times faster than any other known material.

Another type of plastic used today is Plastisol. According to the RPM Lure Company, extensive research in the past ten years by a committed group of manufacturers looking for a new type of supple plastic led to the discovery of Plastisol, a material that is softer, more durable and amazingly non-toxic to fish. To change its chemical composition, different chemical agents are blended with Plastisol to make it either harder or softer, whatever the manufacturer desires.

The one thing you should avoid is mixing dissimilar plastic baits together in the same package or tackle-storage system. If you mix them, a serious chemical reaction will take place as the plastics dissolve into a horrible mess.

The qualities of softness or firmness will dramatically affect a plastic bait's ability to catch fish. Suppleness affects how it moves through the water. It affects how the lure reacts to casting and the distance it can be cast. It can also influence how long a fish is willing to hang on, how easily the hooks push through the lure to strike the fish, and how well the hooks and jigheads remain in place inside the lure's body while fishing.

I'll bet that never in a million years would you have thought about how much time, science and research went into making a simple soft-plastic lure. As with everything these days, there is always a trade-off between the lure's durability and how soft it is. In my own

Berkley's Gulp! baits are 100% natural and took many years to develop. They disperse scent rapidly and trigger strikes from virtually all saltwater gamefish.

17

experience, a softer lure allows better hook penetration when you set up on a fish.

The Jelly Worm

The next significant breakthrough in soft-plastic baits came from Mann's Bait Company. Started by Tom Mann in 1956, the company today is one of the largest soft-plastic lure manufacturers in the world. Mann's Baits are used in all 50 states and in over 50 countries around the world.

In the salt, they became famous for their 9-inch and 12-inch flat-tailed Jelly Worms that became extremely popular back in the mid to late 1970s for weakfish and striped bass from Cape Cod to Cape Hatteras. Southern anglers used them for seatrout, redfish, cobia and snook. After some initial skepticism, anglers began to prefer the plastic imitations because they worked just as well as the real thing.

Alou Bait Tail

In the early 1960s, the Alou Bait Company was created in New York, where two friends, Al Reinfelder and Lou Palma, fashioned a soft lure with an eel-tail shape and lead jigheads to match. The new lure was so simple that many felt it wouldn't appeal to the general fishing public. On the contrary its simplicity was what made it so effective.

The Alou Bait Tail's only action was imparted by the angler. Once slid onto the shank of the leadhead, it was up to the angler to make the plastic lure dance and dart seductively. After its introduction, the Bait Tail accounted for numerous species along the coast, and in freshwater as well. It was extremely effective for fishing bridges at night, a popular striped bass method in New York during those years.

It wasn't long after the introduction of the Bait Tail that the Alou Eel came into production. The two inventors found softer plastic and molded eels from 6 to 14 inches, and rigged them on lead squid heads to make them swim like real eels. For a time, they were so popular that numerous charter captains used them in place of real eels because they worked so well.

Two-Tone Plastics

Culprit is generally credited with popularizing the two-tone plastic worm, similar to today's two-tone shad bodies that were mass-produced on a regional level until they went nationwide. Up until that time, almost all the plastic worms were one solid color. The design was classic, and is still used to this day. Culprit offers plastics from 4 to 12 inches, in many unique color combinations.

Classic Fishing Products has been a privately held company since 1979, and has grown to be one of the industry's top producers of soft-plastic lures. They employ over fifty employees who make, assemble and ship products from their 34,000-plus square foot facility.

Classic Fishing Lures has over twenty high-tech machines that produce, on average, one million pieces of soft plastic per month. Specialized injection machines produce custom lure molds, machined with precision detail. They hold patents and trademarks each for many products including Culprit, Rip Tide and others. Their products catch striped bass, bluefish, weakfish, fluke, seatrout, redfish, snook, tarpon, and many other species. Rip Tide is an official sponsor of the Redfish Tournament Trail.

Boone Bait Company

One of the early companies to specifically target the saltwater market was Boone Bait Company. Its famous Trout Tout lure was designed to fool southern gamefish such as redfish and spotted seatrout, jacks and snook. It made a very big splash with inshore fishermen in Georgia, Florida and the Gulf states. Snowbirds visiting Florida during the winter months soon discovered the lure's fish-catching prowess and brought the lure to more northern climes just in time for the big weakfish explosion of the 1970s.

The Trout Tout was equally at home in the waters from North Carolina to Rhode Island, and quickly developed a large following of inshore and back-bay anglers devoted to catching weakfish and schoolie-size stripers.

The rounded head shape of the Trout Tout and the position of the hook eye made the lure dance nicely. The painted leadheads were available in a limited assortment of painted head weights, and with

Tiderunner weakfish eagerly take a variety of soft-plastic baits, like these beauties taken by the author and his daughter, Ashley.

a good variety of tail sizes to match. The most popular colors were pearl white and hot pink. Although there are many new innovations, the old-time Boone Bait Company Trout Touts still catch fish. It was one of the trend-setting lures that opened the doors to soft plastics in the brine.

Mister Twister Tails

Mister Twister began in a small northern Louisiana town by using an old-fashioned pressure cooker to melt the plastic. Once melted, the soft, hot plastic was poured in molds for curing. Mister Twister is credited with the development of grubs and worms with a curly-tail shape in 1972. Prior to that time, most worms and grubs were straight in design and had little or no built-in action. The Curly Tail changed all that into a soft plastic that now had tail action, and sales of this type of plastic skyrocketed. Other companies took close notice, and saw they could now compete with the hard baits on the market.

In 1982, Mister Twister introduced the first Sassy Shad. Once again, sales took off along with a new following that developed and emerged into the twenty-first century.

In 2000, Mister Twister created the Exude line of lures, which virtually explode with scent when they hit the water, oozing a slime coating of scents, minerals, proteins and amino acids that attracts strikes. The exact process and chemical make-up is secret, as are most chemical make-ups of plastic molding.

Making Good Scents

In the early 1980s, Berkley Fishing Tackle Company was emerging as a leader in monofilament line technology and today is one of the leading manufacturers of soft-plastic baits as part of the Pure Fishing Tackle Company. Berkley's founder, Berkley Bedell, actually began this giant corporation in his bedroom, tying flies for friends. From there, it grew to one of the largest outdoor fishing corporations on earth, and is now headed by his son, Tom Bedell.

Berkley scientists and engineers developed Power Bait, an additive for their soft plastics that remains quite popular to this day. Open a bag of Power Bait and you'll quickly see how it got its name.

Berkley recently introduced a new product called Gulp!. The scientists at Berkley claim that Gulp! is four hundred times more potent with scent release than any scented lure previously made. It is 100-percent biodegradable and made of 100-percent natural ingredients. It leaves a scent trail that is said to attract fish and trigger them into striking. One of its more amazing qualities is that during head-to-head field-testing against live bait, Gulp! won the contest.

Berkley has been testing Gulp! for almost twenty years. They employed chemical engineers, fish behavioral specialists and experts to perform tens of thousands of hours of lab testing and research. When the group was finished, the result was the development of Gulp!. It out-fishes live bait because the scent trail is so intense that fish sense it from a greater distance and follow it to the source.

Gulp! is water-soluble, so the scents and flavors are released four hundred and twelve times faster than oil-based plastics. If the bait is lost, it will dissolve totally in nine months or less if left in the water. A finished bait is the result of thirty-six hours of processing.

Wild Actions

Steve Marusak founded Cotee Bait Company in 1983. An enthusiastic angler and design engineer, he went on to create jigs and soft plastics that have survived the test of time. Today, Cotee is dedicated to pushing the threshold of research and manufacturing technology to make the best possible fishing lures that can be made.

Cotee's contribution to soft plastics was the development of the corkscrew-falling jig, or spiral jig. This innovation revolutionized the way soft-plastic worms, grubs, curly tails and shads could be fished. The patented Liv-Eye corkscrew fall triggers vicious strikes from gamefish. Their newest innovation is the Reel Magic lure, a soft weedless Zara Spook type lure, and the JigNLip jighead. It's actually a jig with a built-in swimming lip like a crankbait. When rigged with a soft piece of plastic, it adds unbelievable action to the lure. I tried the 1-ounce size on a 9-inch Slug-Go and the results were amazing.

Slugfest

In 1985 the introduction of the Slug-Go from Herb Reed, owner of Lunker City Fishing Specialists in Connecticut, sparked the biggest revolution in saltwater soft plastics that the industry had witnessed since the invention of the plastic worm itself. The Slug-Go forever changed the way plastic lures were designed and fished, and the concept is now utilized by dozens of manufacturers across the country.

Prior to the mid-1980s, there was really no such thing as a soft-plastic stick bait, or soft-plastic jerk bait, as they are now called. Back then, Lunker City Lures was based in Herb Reed's garage, where he made custom spinner baits and rubber jigs for a small group of local anglers fishing the tournament circuit. The soft stick-bait concept came about when Reed made a few common observations while largemouth bass were feeding in front of him.

He reasoned that predatory fish exhibited a strong preference for long, slender, baitfish, and the more erratically the lures were fished, the more violently the fish would attack them. That led Reed to reason that the erratic, random motions of the baitfish were a natural trigger for gamefish and would cause them to attack.

Reed then set out to design and construct a lure that would mimic the long, slender prey the fish were looking to eat, and could be fished on heavy tackle and in heavy cover. He also wanted his lure to be easy to rig, and could be fished from the top to the bottom and everywhere in-between. That's a tall order for one lure. And consider this: the original design of the Slug-Go concept was made in wood. How's that for a piece of trivia?

When his design and testing were finished, he began to use his artistic background to create color patterns that would mimic common baitfish better than anything else that had been poured in soft plastic. The results were amazing, even beyond his high expectations.

The Slug-Go didn't fit the common worm or grub mold, and established a whole new category and a whole new way of fishing, imitating an injured baitfish with an action like nothing else before its arrival. The Slug-Go design has been copied an infinite number of times since its introduction, but few if any have matched its success.

It wasn't long before Reed followed up with another new design and concept in soft-plastic lures, the Fin-S Fish. This was a baitfish-shaped soft piece of plastic with a forked twin tail end. It also featured a built-in slot so the hook could be placed inside for weedless applications. The Fin-S Fish was another design that did not exist anywhere and changed the way anglers fished with soft

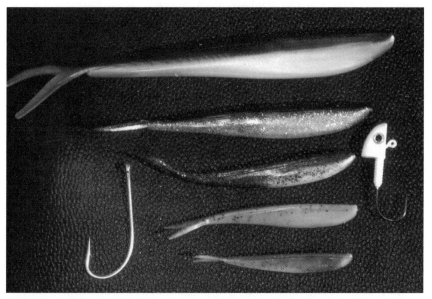

Herb Reed's Fin-S Fish has become a popular soft-plastic bait used from Texas to Florida to Maine, with an enticing action that gamefish find hard to resist.

plastics forever.

Both these baits have been imitated in every way, shape, form and color—a testament to their ability to produce fish on a consistent basis.

Super Cyber

Strike King Lure Company was started in 1966 by Charles Spence and is credited with introducing silicone products to the industry, which at the time were new and unheard of. In 1998, they began researching a new product and introduced the Cyber-Flexxx soft plastic in 2003. Strike King lures have been around for quite some time in freshwater, making spinner baits and a few other lures. Their jump into the soft-plastics market is a recent thing. However, their introduction of this new material is going to have a big impact.

Cyber-Flexxx, a proprietary crystal gel compound now covered by four U.S. patents, has been in development for over three years. Strength and durability is what led to this development and Strike King claims that the next 3X line is not only incredibly strong, but are durable and soft as well. You can stretch one out many times its length and it won't break or tear, always returning to its original form. Its advantage lies in more time fishing and less time rigging.

This new generation of 3X plastics is also more buoyant, so they float higher in the water with more action. It is a substance known in the automotive industry as crystal gel polymer, and contains no toxic substances whatsoever. They are 20 percent lighter than water, eliminating slide-downs and pop-outs when baits are rigged.

One thing you can't do is to mix these baits with other soft plastics or put them in trays where other plastics have been, as a serious chemical reaction will take place. You need to store them in their original bag or start a whole new storage system for them alone.

Terminator and SPRO Corporation have introduced their own versions of flexible, tear-resistant plastic lures into the market. The Terminator brand is called Snap Back that also employs the durable, tear-resistant, elastic material known as Cyber-Flexxx. Snap Backs truly float on the water's surface, providing a more natural presentation to the fish. SPRO offers a similar shad-body line with stretchable plastic lures that are said to withstand the bites of bluefish and other toothy critters.

WildEye Shads

One bait that gained a huge following in recent years is the Storm WildEye Shad. Its salt-impregnated body is rigged with VMC hooks, with a holographic swimming flash foil inside and features an internal leadhead weight for casting. The lures are poured from a strong PVC material with added blocking agents to make natural colors. The rigs come in sizes ranging from 2 to 9 inches. Their Rippin' Swim Bait has a built-in rattle chamber, is 6 to 8 inches, and has a treble hook below in its belly.

The Bimini Bay Performance Products line of swim shads and similar baits is marketed under the name Tsunami and offers a complete line-up of soft baits. Based on Mustad Signature Series hooks, they come in a variety of shapes, sizes and tail actions.

Storm's WildEye Swim Shad started the swim shad craze, a selection of lures that is used in surf and bay, for deep jigging and many inshore fishing situations.

Yum, Yum Good

The last plastic we'll cover is the YUM scent lures from Pradco Industries. YUM is a formulation of biological ingredients that triggers strikes from fish. YUM is composed of organic, non-toxic food and pharmaceutical grade ingredients. The product is biodegradable, non-corrosive, non-flammable and safe on non-porous surfaces. It is available in garlic scent and shad.

Plastics For Striped Bass

Striped bass are considered to be one of, if not the premier, inshore gamefish from Maine to the Carolinas. Its long stripes and greenish/black back and silvery-white coloration caused men to fight over its existence since the early 1600s. The first laws concerning conservation were enacted on behalf of striped bass by the Pilgrims who passed laws that it was illegal to use them as field fertilizer. Monies from the sale of striped bass built the first school in the new world.

Striped bass can be found in a wide range of areas and situations; back waters, rivers, streams, coves and harbors, and deep ocean rips, over wrecks, sandbars, rockpiles, strong river currents, deep holes and even shallow sand flats. They will eat almost anything they can get into their mouth and their diet varies from menhaden, herring, small baitfish, eels, other small fish species, and lobsters, crabs and shrimp. Stripers are not all that fussy when it comes to eating.

The striped bass lends itself to many different fishing situations and applications. It is the fish that we have pursued most and tested most of the soft-plastic baits. If it's made of plastic and can be cast, then most likely a striper will eat it under the right circumstances.

Stripers grow to over 70 pounds, but the usual size range is maybe 12 pounds or so. Bigger fish of 15 to 30 pounds are common in deeper waters along the oceanfront, and the larger bass of 30 to 60 pounds are usually taken at night. Some are also trolled during the day with live baits or huge lures such as the foot-long shad bodies that have become extremely popular. During the spring, when alewives make their annual spawning runs up to freshwater streams, they are usually followed by big stripers looking for a big meal.

We have taken stripers on almost every soft plastic described in this book at one time or another.

The largest striper that we have taken on a soft-plastic shad has been 43 pounds, a respectable fish in anyone's circle. It came in the spring of the year while trolling a 12-inch white shad body in less than 10 feet of water.

Stripers will eat large plastic worms, plastic eels, tube lures, shrimp, crabs, and all types of fish imitations, and twister tails.

Bluefish Basics

Bluefish are loved, hated, despised and acclaimed by fishermen. It seems it's hard for most people to make up their minds about bluefish. When they are plentiful, most anglers hate them; when they are scarce, everyone wants to catch one. However you feel, the bluefish is one of the strongest, hardest-fighting inshore gamefish. Pound-for-pound it will out-hit, out-fight, out-run and out-jump any other fish, and will still try to bite you before it dies. Revered by some, reviled by others because they tear up so much gear, the bluefish is still a terrific inshore predator and gamefish.

In my own humble opinion, Narragansett Bay, Rhode Island has to be the premier area for catching bluefish when they are plentiful in both numbers and sizes. My opinion comes after hosting thousands of anglers from all over the country and the world that have experienced a "Narragansett Bay bluefish blitz." It's nothing short of amazing to witness.

Bluefish come in all sizes and shapes from small snappers in back coves to big gorilla blues that grow into the high teens and low 20-pound range. A fish over 20 pounds is a real trophy. Bluefish have a mouth full of razor sharp teeth with jaws that are almost as powerful as a shark's. Just try to open the jaws of a 10 or 12-pound bluefish.

Bluefish also have excellent eyesight, which many anglers tend to forget. They can see just as well out of the water as they can in the water. Try this sometime: take a bluefish and hold it upright and facing someone, then have that person move right and then left. Watch the eyes follow that person in front of him very closely. What more can you possibly ask of a fish that is willing to fight to the death? I believe they get nowhere as much respect as they truly deserve.

Bluefish can be found from shallow water flats to deep offshore rips. In shallow water, they will leap and jump and run with the best of them. When taken on plugging, baitcasting or light to medium spinning gear the fight is second to none.

It's long been assumed that a bluefish will eat anything you toss into the water, with or without hooks. The assumption is that this makes them totally stupid. Nothing could be further from the truth. Depending upon what they are feeding, bluefish can be just as finicky as any other fish (sometimes even more so). They can be extremely selective as to size, shape, color, speed and depth of the lure. Sometimes they won't eat at all.

Many fishermen might say, "Hey, if I feed plastics to bluefish, they will eat it all or tear it to shreds." Yes, that is true, but isn't the idea to catch the fish in the first place? Using a soft-plastic lure that costs just pennies is much better in my opinion than losing or ruining a $15 plastic or wood lure. Do you realize how much soft plastic you can buy for $15?

Tiderunner Weakfish

The northern weakfish is also known as the gray trout, tiderunner and squeteague. The word squeteague is a Narragansett Indian word meaning "a fish of many colors," and once you see one, you will quickly see how the fish got that name. They display literally every color of the rainbow and are quite possibly one of the most beautiful fish in the sea. With distinctive yellow fins and purple, greenish backs, the weakfish is a work of nature's art. It has the same predominant canine teeth in front as its southern cousin, the spotted seatrout.

The fish average 2 to 5 pounds and 12 to 22 inches, but can grow well into the teens. The International Game Fish Association world record catch weighed 19 pounds, 2 ounces. At one time, they were one of the most abundant species in inshore waters, but weakfish are cyclical in nature and have periods of abundance and scarcity. When commercial over-harvesting is coupled with those down times, the species can be depleted very quickly. Presently, the weakfish is being managed by the Atlantic States Marine Fisheries Commission.

Weakfish respond very well to soft-plastic lures. In the 1970s, when there were good numbers of large weakfish available in coastal bays, the fish were suckers for a Mann's strawberry jelly worm of 9 inches. Fished on a jighead or drifted beneath a float in the current, the worms would draw vicious strikes, sometimes out-fishing the real worms that were much more expensive.

In more recent times, lures like the Killer Diller Shrimp, Power Shrimp, Fin-S Fish (especially in yellow or bubblegum colors), and small, thin, shad bodies have taken fish all along the coast. Weakfish are suckers for anything that is yellow, chartreuse or pink, though other colors will work also, depending upon the conditions.

Weakfish are called tiderunners for a reason. They love moving water. Find a sandbar or mussel bar that is adjacent to or close to deep water and that has good tidal movement and some baitfish, and you've got yourself a good weakfish hole to fish over.

The best times are just before sunrise and after sunset into the late evening. Once the sun gets above the 10 o'clock position, they usually head for deeper water of at least 10 feet deep or more.

Flounder Action

Summer flounder, also known as fluke, are one of the most popular coastal species—even surpassing the striped bass at some points in the season. It's readily available to both surf and boat fishermen from Cape Cod to central Florida. It was once believed that fluke could only be taken in water of 30 feet or less once they made their annual migration inshore. Now it is well known that summer flounder can be caught in water up to 60 feet or even deeper.

Known as the left-handed flounder, they have the ability to assume the color of the bottom they inhabit, including spots and lines. They average between 16 to 24 inches and 2 to 4 pounds with many now going over the magic 10-pound mark. The summer flounder is one of the most aggressive species of the flounder family. They will

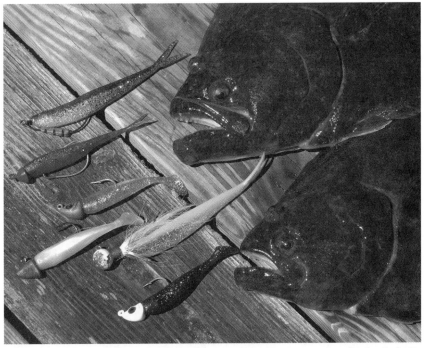

Bottom feeders, such as summer flounder, aggressively attack soft-plastic baits and can up the score of any angler looking to take a few of these tasty fish home for dinner.

readily chase artificial lures and rise off the bottom in a very fast burst of speed to capture their prey. Besides their fine eating qualities, anglers like the way fluke will readily attack a lure or bait.

Fluke will take jigs that have trailers attached to them. A popular trailer of soft plastic is the Mario's Squid Strip from 4 to 7 inches. This is a plastic bait with a split tail design giving it "legs", a very heavy hook-eye at the forward end of the bait to help keep the hook in place and to keep the bait from tearing off the hook when a fluke hits. The best colors are white, pink, yellow, red and chartreuse.

Plastic squids also work great as teasers fished above a jig or bait. Luhr Jensen B-52 squids are very productive as are the JT squids. Cabela's has some squids sold as salmon teasers that work quite well in saltwater as well. Mister Twister tails of 6 inches or more are also good choices.

Inshore Speedsters

The little tunny and Atlantic bonito are superb gamefish to catch on plastic baits. In many coastal ports, the little tunny is known as false albacore or albie, but in Florida it's referred to as a bonito. Whatever you choose to call it, the little tunny is one of the finest gamefish that swims. It's difficult at times to catch, is capable of super-fast acceleration once hooked, and makes long, powerful runs. It's built for speed, and puts smiles on anglers' faces.

All along the Atlantic Coast, anglers will go to any length to find and catch this ocean-roaming speedster, though many feel its food value is virtually non-existent. Even Florida anglers are discovering this terrific gamefish, which many use to think was nothing more than a "trash" fish.

False albacore are commonly confused with the Atlantic bonito, also called the green bonito. The little tunny has a rounder head, whereas the green bonito's head is more elongated. The bonito has a mouth full of teeth and the albacore doesn't. Long horizontal lines extend along the bonito's sides and back from head to tail, while the albie has a wavier pattern on its back and several pronounced dark spots under the pectoral fins. Both fish will occasionally display vertical striping on their sides.

Both species are regarded as being at the top of the list when it comes to light tackle angling. In my opinion, the little tunny or false albacore deserves to be right up there with the bonefish and permit in terms of difficulty to catch and an amazing fighting ability once hooked.

Light tackle anglers can use a variety of soft plastics to take both species. Old-timers claimed both species had a penchant for anything yellow. They would advise that an angler's first choice for lure color should be yellow, with yellow as the second and third choices! Small-size, 3-inch Fin-S Fish, Mister Twister tails, Slug-Go baits and Sassy Shads are excellent choices for these tuna tribe members.

Jigheads should be small in profile and light in weight, such as 1/8 to 3/8-ounce sizes. Besides yellow, try pink bubblegum, chartreuse, white and black. The swimming jigheads are also very good for tunas with small, long and thin plastics attached to them. Some trollers are rigging shad tails with a small skirt draped over them. The shad tail provides a wiggling action and color, and the skirt enhances the overall appeal.

Red Drum, For Sure

More commonly known as the redfish, red bass, puppy drum and channel bass, this great gamefish is a member of the croaker family. In recent years, commercial over-harvesting has been curtailed and brought under control, and redfish have made a remarkable recovery in many areas of the country. The recovery is so strong that mid-Atlantic states, such as Delaware and New Jersey, are beginning to see a few fish taken each season, much like the fishing of fifty years ago! In the south, full-blown fishing tournaments are held in many areas, modeled after the popular freshwater B.A.S.S. events.

The redfish's range is quite wide, with its northern extreme in New York down along the coast to the Florida Keys then over into the Louisiana Gulf Delta area and into Texas. Occasionally, it is taken in New England, but not all that often. We did catch one in 1997 around 20 inches long in East Greenwich Bay on a fly while fishing for weakfish.

The largest of the species is taken along the open oceanfront well offshore like other ocean dwellers. The smaller fish are found in bays, rivers, estuaries and anywhere there is rock, grass and shellfish present to feed on, as they eat all types of crustaceans such as shrimp and even small baitfish. Almost all redfish are actually more bronze in color than red. The one common thing they share is they have one or more black spots on their tails.

Redfish are usually eager to take soft plastics, such as shads, the jerk-style tails, plastic worms, shrimp, crabs and split-tail baits. Many tournament pros squirt their lures with special bait scents to "juice up" the baits with squid, shedder crab, menhaden or shrimp oils.

Snook Are Special

The snook is an important southern gamefish species seldom found north of Georgia. It's a fine, sporty fish that is usually found in mangroves, around piers, in the surf, up inside rivers and around docks, bridges and pilings.

Snook were once very scarce due to commercial over-harvesting, as its meat is excellent. If you like mild fish, like flounder, you'll like snook. With restrictions placed on commercial and sport fishing catches, the snook stands as a true testament to what sound, intelligent management can accomplish.

The snook is capable of long runs, with some aerial acrobats thrown in for good measure. Like the striped bass, they head for any obstruction once hooked, just itching to bust off the angler and free themselves from the line. They are justly famous for hanging out on the edge of a mangrove or bridge piling, and once hooked they try to dart right back to the security of those tree roots or pilings.

One of Florida's favorites, the hard-charging snook is an ideal candidate for soft-plastic lures cast near mangroves or bridge pilings.

Snook average about 3 to 15 pounds, with trophy-size fish tipping the scales at 20 to 30 pounds. Big snook can be found in rivers and in the mouths of inlets where the current is strong. Again, they like the same things striped bass do and behave in a similar fashion. Bouncing a 6 to 10-inch shad body near the bottom will usually catch a big bruiser. Use a jighead heavy enough to keep the shad body deep, allow it to drift back in the current, jigging the shad as you let the lure bounce bottom. The Optimum Swim Baits are excellent for this purpose as are the Storm Series of swim baits, the Tsunami soft lures, and Mann's big Mannhaden bunker baits.

Backcountry and shallow-water snook will hit a wide variety of soft plastics fished with or without a weight. In back waters, the popper combination such as Capt. Mike's Flats Candy popper, popping corks, or cork poppers with jerkbaits fished on a single hook, work well.

Spotted Seatrout

The spotted seatrout is also known as trout, speckled trout, speck and spotted weakfish, but should not be confused with the northern weakfish that is usually somewhat larger than its smaller southern cousin.

Spotted seatrout are probably one of the most popular and most sought-after gamefish species in the southern Atlantic, Florida and around the Gulf Coast along Louisiana and Texas. The spotted seatrout is a beautiful fish with two canine teeth in its mouth, beautiful coloration and a sleek shape, enhanced by its great eating qualities. This trout averages about 1 or 2 pounds with 4-pound fish being common. They do grow to over 10 pounds and the world record is 17 pounds.

Found in grassy bays, rivers, and flats as well as near oyster bars, shell bars and sandbars, they head for deep water when the weather turns cold. Light spinning gear is usually used for spotted trout, as is fly tackle and light bait casting gear. The fish respond very well to soft plastics, especially the shrimp-type lures like Creme's Killer Diller fished beneath a popping cork, one of the most popular rigs. Scampies, Power Shrimp and Shrimp Tails and the D.O.A. shrimp are other excellent lure choices.

Specks will also take Fin-S Fish, jerkbaits, plastic worms and thin shad bodies. Anglers probably haven't experimented enough yet with all the available soft plastic that is now on the market.

Tarpon On Tap

Once you have tangled with a tarpon, you'll never forget the experience, and most anglers who catch one believe it's the best angling experience of their lives. The fight is beyond belief and it puts most other fish to shame. With gills flared, they cartwheel, tumble and re-enter the water with thunderous splashes. Tarpon guides often say that only one in ten fish hooked is ever landed.

Tarpon like pinfish, mullet, crabs, shrimp and squid for live baits and are known to take a variety of artificials including flies. Small tarpon of less than 10 pounds will hit a lot of different lures. Jigs tipped with twister tails; large shad bodies both in the wide and thin-bodied versions will also work. The H&H Kokanee Minnow and the Berkley Power Mullet, Fin-S Fish up to 7 inches and jerkbaits like Zoom flukes, Slug-Go tails and Bass Assassins will also take fish. Fish these lures on light plug casting or spinning gear in back waters and rivers, beside channel edges of mangroves.

Tarpon can be taken near coastal fishing piers and in marina basins by jigging soft plastics along the bottom. The larger fish will strike larger lures and jigs readily. Soft plastics are a way to coax them into striking a bait they probably don't see too often. Tarpon are also taken during the night by lighted bridges, piers, and lit marinas. In such areas, you need to use heavier tackle to muscle them away from the snags that are present.

Bonefish Surprise

Bonefish are known as the speed demons of the flats. They are extremely wary and can be hard to catch, especially in heavily fished areas where it's a challenge to find and hook them.

Will they take small plastic tails? You bet! Bonefish will hit small jigheads with small soft-plastic tails attached. The D.O.A. plastic shrimp imitations are good choices and so are the new D.O.A. crabs. Try Mister Twister tails and the 3-inch Slug-Go and Fin-S Fish.

When fishing with very light spinning gear and 6 or 8-pound test mono, bonefish can be taken relatively easily on small soft-plastic lures.

An incoming tide, when a foot or more of water is covering the sand, is best on the flats. Bonefish will move in on this tide to feed on crabs, shrimp and small baitfish. Bonefish can be located near

Shrimp imitations are extremely realistic and they work on school stripers, weakfish, sea trout, snook and more.

areas known as "muds." The water appears milky-white in color and usually indicates bonefish are feeding and rooting out crabs and shrimp from the mud.

They can also be found by their tails and dorsal fins sticking out of the water when feeding, or making a telltale V-wake along the surface. As with most species of fish, you will find the smaller ones schooled together, while the larger ones are usually solitary or in groups of only a few fish.

Once a bonefish is hooked, most anglers will hold their rods high to keep the line away from coral, sharp grass and other bottom obstructions. That is when a 7-1/2 or 8-foot rod comes in handy. Bonefish also use the deeper channels of the flats to move from one spot to another.

Cool Cobia

Cobia, or lemonfish as they are sometimes called, are great sport fish. They fight like mad and are very strong contenders. Cobia are sometimes mistaken for small sharks because of their dark brown coloration and long slender bodies, but the long head and lack of teeth are the most obvious differences.

Cobia are mostly found around wrecks, oil platforms, mooring buoys, near piers and sometimes cruising along the edge of the surf. They generally make their homes in tackle-busting structure, but they also like to move around a lot and will venture onto shallow water flats, especially the smaller ones and into bays and rivers as well. Several years ago, one of our clients caught a cobia right inside Narragansett Bay in New England. A very rare catch indeed, but they do wander up this far and are occasionally caught even further north. New Jersey and Delaware sometimes enjoy steady cobia fishing when the summer weather is very warm; but the best action is from Virginia south to Florida and into the Gulf of Mexico.

Cobia will readily hit a variety of soft-plastic lures including six to 12-inch shad bodies jigged on 2 to 8-ounce jigheads, or bucktails tipped with long twister tails of 6 to 8 inches or more. The larger size jerkbaits such as the Slug-Go and Ledge Runner eels also work when the fish are cruising the surface. Recently, it has been discovered that they really love those big 10 to 16-inch soft-plastic eels by Felmlee. They can be cast or trolled for exciting action on light trolling or casting gear.

Delicious Pompano

The pompano is the little brother of the permit. This fish rarely exceeds 2 or 3 pounds in weight, but still makes a good account of itself on light tackle. Those who eat this species claim it's the best inshore fish there is, but that subject is always open to debate.

Pompano can be found in tidal bays, river mouths and river systems, and along sandy beaches in the surf. They usually follow the tide both in and out when feeding. Pompano can be taken by a number of fishing methods including trolling, casting, bait fishing and even drifting. On deep drops—around oil rigs or deep-water wrecks—heavier tackle will be necessary.

Pompano prefer lures with lots of action. This makes D.O.A. Terror Eyz, Fin-S Fish or shad bodies good bait choices as they lend themselves to this type of retrieve. So do some of the silverside imitations that are available. Don't overlook the new crab or shrimp look-a-likes which feature lots of built-in action.

Amazing Amberjacks

The greater amberjack is one of the ocean's strongest, toughest fighting fish. It resembles a huge bluefish, but it's the largest member of the Carangidae family of fish known collectively as "jacks." With a back of blue/black shading downward to silver, distinctive shades of yellow, and a big forked tail, this pirate of the deep looks mean and nasty.

The amberjack is found on deep ocean reefs along the edge of the Gulf Stream as well as around oilrig platforms, over wrecks, and in other deep-water spots. It does often come to the surface around weed patches as mahimahi do.

Big adult amberjack are rarely caught north of Virginia, but juveniles are taken along weed lines in the summer months as far north as Montauk. Its most common haunts are found in Florida and in the Gulf of Mexico. Each spring, amberjacks move into coastal waters to spawn and can be targeted with lighter tackle.

Amberjack are serious, tough fighters that will strike at almost anything that swims including a bluefish. With an amazing average weight of 25 to 30-pounds range, they will eat big swim baits of 6 to more than 12 inches fished on 2, 3 or 6-ounce jigheads; rubber eels, big Fin-S Fish, giant Slug-Go's or Ledgerunner baits have all taken their share of big A.J.'s.

Curious creatures, amberjack will respond to chum and sound, so many anglers will "lure them in", then hook up casting plastics. Their cousins in the jack family include the crevalle jack, yellowtail jack, roosterfish, pompano and permit, along with some other fifty smaller species. All will hit some type of plastic lures presented properly.

The Mighty King Mackerel

Also known as kingfish, the king mackerel roams the waters all around Florida, along the Gulf Coast and south to the Caribbean and Mexico waters. Its northernmost range includes Delaware and New Jersey, and the Carolinas are especially productive. If you've never caught a kingfish, you are missing out on one of the sport's greatest gamefish. My son and I tackled some big kings in Cuba on light

Yep, toothy critters chew up plastic baits, but the slashing strikes and sizzling runs are well worth it. Plastics can be trolled or cast into a chum slick.

tackle, and they proved to be a major challenge. After two days, they had broken two rods and burned out three light-tackle reels. We enjoyed ourselves and were impressed with the superb fighting qualities of king mackerel.

Kingfish are very fast and strike with a ferocity not seen in many other species. They also fight extremely hard and will not give up for one moment. Considered relatively easy to catch, or hook-up, because of their aggressive nature, they provide great sport.

Kings and their smaller cousins, the Spanish and cero mackerel, can be taken on many types of plastics. Be advised that their teeth will tear up a lot of baits; even the newer, super-tough baits don't stand much of a chance. Some of the larger plastics such as the squids and Mario's Squid Strips as well as Mann's Ballyhoos will work great. Be sure to use strong wire leader as they will make short work of almost any size mono.

Kingfish can't resist shad bodies reeled quickly—the faster the better. Even plastic shrimp can be used when following a shrimp boat around. These boats draw the fish in for a free meal, and you can toss in your imitation with high odds for success.

Spanish mackerel will make their way up to the northeast Atlantic Coast during the summer months and will eat 3 and 4-inch shad bodies, jerkbaits, twister tails and more. Spinning gear is fine for these smaller mackerel.

Challenging Permit

Permit are hard to catch even under the best of conditions. There isn't an awful lot of evidence that points to the effectiveness of plastics on the elusive permit, but they do occasionally strike jigs and small lures of 3 inches or less. Red and white, yellow and white, brown, pink and tan are the best colors. Jigs with Fin-S Fish that are 2-1/2 inches, small Slug-Go tails or Ultimate minnow series would certainly be worth trying on permit with small jigs. The D.O.A. soft-plastic crabs have also taken permit.

Permit are so difficult to catch that Lefty Kreh told me he had made casts to probably a thousand or more fish in his fishing career before he actually hooked one. Need we say more?

Great Barracuda

The great barracuda, in my opinion, is one of the most underrated gamefish that swims. They strike savagely, fight like Tasmanian Devils, run hard, leap incredibly high and jump in arches measured in feet, not inches. What more can you ask of any fish? Like the bluefish, because of their ability to tear up even the strongest tackle, they are shunned by many anglers.

Barracuda are recognized by their long bodies, black blotches on a silvery body and a long snout that is full of razor-sharp teeth. Barracuda are found from Cape Hatteras to southern Florida and will frequent the flats, bays and offshore areas where they may grow as large as 80 pounds. Just imagine an 80-pound barracuda that's hungry. The northern barracuda, called a sennet, is sometimes mistaken for the southern species, but it only grows to around 18 inches. This fish has been found locally, leading to more than one misidentification.

Barracuda will hit soft-plastic lures, such as shad tails and large (long) bright-colored plastic worms and eel imitations. Look for colors such as bright red, orange, fluorescent yellow or green—anything that is bright in color. The rig usually has a treble hook in the rear of the tubing and a small egg sinker is placed in the head for ease of casting the light plastic.

Here's a nice redfish that smacked a soft bait cast along a marsh sedge. Many inshore fishermen swear by soft baits for these bronze warriors.

Let's Review The Files

Soft-plastic lures have been around for about a half-century and their fish-catching abilities continue to expand. Their value as saltwater lures is no longer questioned. The future looks bright as new plastic formulations, new scent additives, new molding and manufacturing techniques, and new designs continue to improve these already terrific lures.

Virtually any fish that swims can be taken on a soft-plastic lure. I've covered the most popular in the preceding pages, but other popular gamefish such as winter flounder, croaker, sharks, snappers, tripletails, school bluefin tuna, white marlin and sailfish, cod and pollock are all taken on soft-plastic creations.

If there was ever a universal, catch-'em-all lure, the huge family of soft-plastic lures must surely near the top of the list.

Selecting tackle that enhances the lure action and retrieve, while providing maximum sport, is critical to experiencing success with plastic baits.

CHAPTER TWO

TACKLE CHOICES

After many years of using soft-plastic lures in all different sizes and shapes, and for many different species of fish, I firmly believe that just one rod will not get the job done. As much as I wanted to, and no matter how hard I tried, it was apparent that by only using one or two rods, I was being held back from getting the most from these great lures.

This seems to be a very basic mistake, if not the biggest mistake, anglers make when fishing plastic baits. It is their insistence, as it was once mine, that they can fish all methods with just one rod. The outcome of choosing this path is total frustration, complete confusion and little or no success in experimenting and catching more fish.

What is actually needed is at least three rod-and-reel outfits of various actions ranging from light to medium action, on up to heavy-duty tackle. This can be expanded even further if you do more than just cast and retrieve, because trolling requires another set of rods and reels.

When fishing by myself, I usually bring as many as five or six different rod and reel combinations so I can cover every fishing situation. You may say I'm crazy for suggesting that many rods. After all, that could add up to quite a chunk of change, but after we finish this chapter, you'll see the advantages.

You don't have to take out a second mortgage on the house to become well equipped. If you purchase all high-end models, then I suppose it would be expensive to get rigged up with more than one or two outfits; a better way is to buy one really good rod and fill in the gaps with less expensive models.

Let's take a look at what you need to build a well-rounded tackle system for fishing soft-plastic lures.

Tackle Choices

Decide on what rod and reel you use most frequently, and then spend a few extra bucks to get the best you can afford. A well-designed, quality rod and reel will provide years of good service and be well worth the price.

Graphite is at the top of the line, and its reputation for extreme sensitivity is well deserved. Graphite sticks offer great casting power, fish-fighting abilities and light weight, which is a big plus if you fish for many hours at a time. There are also many excellent composite rods on the market today. These blends of both fiberglass and graphite offer added durability and strength without sacrificing too much sensitivity, and they are priced more economically.

It's most important that you feel comfortable with the rod and reel you choose. Most tackle shops will let you mount the reel on the rod to see how the outfit feels in your hands. Some even let you make a few practice casts, though that's not the usual situation. It pays to check out what your fellow local fishermen are using, and perhaps try a few casts with your buddy's rod to see if you like it. The point here is that it's not really the rod that makes you a good fisherman, but how you use it. The skills you learn, the specific tactics and techniques that you use, is what catches the fish. The rod and reel are just part of the "tool bag."

Here's how I determine what rod and reel I need for certain situations. I gauge rod selection as follows: for what I consider finesse fishing, lures from 1/8 ounce to 3/8 ounce, such as Slug-Go's and small floating poppers, select a rod of 6-1/2 to 7 feet with a light action. That is perfect for that style of fishing. For heavier jigs in the 1/2 to 3/4-ounce range and baits from 4 to 6 inches, for general all-purpose casting situations, a medium-action rod will do nicely. For those big, heavy mommas, like the largest Fin-S Fish, big plastic eels and shad bodies or other heavier types of plastic lures, you need to call on the big guns to get that job done.

Spinning Vs. Conventional

I like spinning rods for all-round fishing situations and for those days when the wind is blowing hard. In windy conditions, keep the baitcaster racked in its holder. There are very few anglers who can

Plastic baits can be cast, jigged or trolled, so a variety of tackle can be used. Spinning and baitcasting rods with a fast action make casting a pleasure, while deep jigging and trolling usually call for stout tackle. Reels should have a smooth drag system.

use a baitcasting outfit in a stiff breeze—and even if you can, who cares and who wants too? Give yourself a break: toss lures with the spinning rod and reel, and relax. This is supposed to be fun, not work!

For heavy tackle, I prefer casting, or conventional gear, not spinning. A good example is the St. Croix 6-foot, 9-inch muskie rod that can really jab a hook into the maw of a big fish. In fact, I even use it to fish live eels at night from the boat. Load up a Penn 965 baitcaster with 17-pound line and you're ready to go.

Any rod less than heavy action when using the bigger plastics is almost totally useless. After making a long cast, if the fish hits at the end of the cast, you need lots of power and muscle to recover that amount of line and get a solid hook-set. Using braided line enhances the hook-setting power of the heavy-action rod. If you were using a rod with a light action tip, you would lose more power the more the rod tip bends. A rod of medium or heavy action can also be used for jigging or trolling as well, so you can get double or even triple duty from that one rod.

Trolling Tackle

There are basically three types of trolling tackle choices available for fishing soft plastics—heavy, medium and light. Okay, that seems pretty obvious, but how you handle these three outfits is what will make you a successful troller. Let's take a look at what you'll need.

An example of heavy tackle would be a wire line outfit that can handle 300 to 400 feet of stainless steel or Monel wire line on a Penn 113H reel and a trolling rod fitted with carboloy or ceramic guides to withstand the wear and tear of wire line use. This outfit has its applications, especially in deep water or where strong currents make getting down deep a difficult proposition by any other method. Many anglers today do not like using wire line outfits as they feel they are too heavy and difficult to use, and therefore not all that sporting. This may be true, but the fact remains trolling wire line is an extremely effective and efficient method of taking many different types of gamefish along the entire coast. Just as in other forms of angling, it was invented for a reason. It catches fish when used under the right circumstances. It may not be for everyone, but it is an effective method of trolling. Keep in mind that wire is "heavy," but because it has no stretch, you feel every headshake of a big striped bass that got hooked on your soft bait.

Fish on! A trolled double header can be controlled with a rod having plenty of backbone to handle big fish.

Wire is used more in the northeast and mid-Atlantic than in other parts of the coastal United States, but it will work anyplace it's necessary to fish close to the bottom in 20 feet or more of water. Wire is an inexpensive alternative to costlier downriggers.

Wire line rods are usually short in length, usually around 6-1/2 to 7 feet in length, with fairly stout actions. Reels like the Penn 113H or Jigmaster, or the Okuma Convector stainless steel spool CN-55-SS are used for holding the necessary lengths of wire plus the backing. When using the wire outfit for jigging, there is usually a break in the wire every 50 to 100 feet at which point either Dacron or heavy mono is spliced in so the jigging motion is on the softer spliced-in line. If you jig on the wire line itself, it will eventually kink and break. It's useful for trolling large size shad bodies, plastic eels, tube lures and more. For every 100 feet of wire line in the water, the lure will go down about 10 feet.

Medium trolling tackle will handle monofilament, braid or lead-core line. To get good line capacity, the reels can be similar to the heavy tackle selection or downsized slightly. Rods are usually 6-1/2 to 8 feet in length with a lighter tip action than the heavy-duty tackle.

Lead-core line comes in different color-coded lengths. Each length is approximately 27 feet in length. The accepted rule of thumb is that each color of lead core will take your lure or plastic down about 5 feet deep. Now you need to factor in your boat speed, tide, currents, wind direction, lure weight and more to achieve the proper trolling depth. There really is a science to it to be effective.

Many anglers will fish large leadhead soft baits on the troll with super braid outfits, such as the Penn 320LD, Shimano TLD15, Okuma Convector or Quantum Cabo CNW30. If you don't like wire, try 100 yards of 50-pound super braid with a 4-ounce drail ahead of an umbrella shad rig. It's deadly on stripers and blues.

Light trolling tackle provides the ultimate in trolling experience, especially when dragging soft-plastic baits. This method uses long, very flexible rods and light lead-core or braided line to troll soft baits. I use the Penn 320 LD levelwind reel and a Shakespeare 9-foot Ugly Stik with a so-called salmon/steelhead action, and have taken striped bass up to 43 pounds with this outfit.

Fishing with light tackle accomplishes several things. First, the light rod has a lot of flexibility, and tends not to tear a hole in the fish's mouth as happens with the stiffer traditional trolling rods. The rod's flexibility is very forgiving when a big fish runs and surges, so fewer fish are lost at boatside where many manage to escape. Second, you never fish a "dead line" due to seaweed or grass or other debris that gets caught on the hook or the rig as you are trolling. You instantly know by looking at the action of the rod tip that you have junk on the end of your line. Third, the rod's long length and light action allows you to use heavy pressure to wear the fish down quickly. If Great Lakes anglers can land 30 to 40-pound king salmon on this tackle, coastal anglers can catch the same size stripers. Another advantage is this tackle is more fun when you've hooked a smaller striper. Even schoolie bass will give a good account of themselves.

I like the braid lines in springtime and fall shallow-water situations because the braid's thin diameter cuts the water easily when trolling. Like wire, the braids have no stretch, so you must rig a shock leader at the end to avoid break-offs.

Trolling Aids

Let's take a look at several trolling aids that will help you catch more fish. Some of this stuff comes from the freshwater arena, but it works great in saltwater. I can use very light tackle with flexible rods and light line, and get my lures deep without using wire line, lead core, downriggers or huge reels to do it.

Most of these ideas come from the Pacific Northwest and Great Lakes salmon and steelhead fishery, where they have been used successfully for many years. Along the Atlantic Coast when dealing with strong currents, time your fishing to coincide with the slack water periods of high and low tides. The water begins to slow down then and you will get your rigs deeper as resistance to it will be greatly diminished. Contrary to widely held beliefs and old wives tales, big fish can and are taken at low water tide periods.

DIPSY DIVER: Luhr Jenson Company of Oregon makes them in three sizes; the number 3 dives to 20 feet. Size O dives to 35 feet and size 1 can reach depths of 50 feet. There are vertical and lateral adjustments so the angler can make one lure angle to the left and another to the right to get added distance between the lures to prevent tangles. You can also fish two additional lines straight back in the normal fashion as the first two rods are out and away from the boat. As long as you run accurate trolling patterns you will never tangle any of the lines. The devices can be set and adjusted in degrees so you can fine-tune it to correspond to changing fishing conditions and where the fish are laying within your trolling pattern.

Planer boards offer an effective, easy-to-use option to make the trolling pattern wider. The added width and distance places the trolled lures in front of a broader area and gets more strikes.

By adding what is referred to as a snubber, either behind or ahead of the device, it will absorb the shock of a heavy, violent strike and keep the fish from tearing a big hole in its mouth and keep the line from snapping on impact. Try that with 300 feet of wire and a 3-ounce parachute jig.

These devices can also be used with what is known as a "dodger", which is nothing more than a polished piece of metal that has swivels on both ends and wobbles violently in the water. Some have reflective tape on them and some have a hammered finish that reflects light. This works great for bluefish and other fish attracted to big schools of baitfish. Fished just ahead of a big 9 to 12-inch shad body it can have the same effect as a big bunker spoon does on bass. It works, it's just that not many anglers are using them because they either believe they are strictly for freshwater or they may feel that their buddies will laugh at them if they are seen using these items. When you hold up some big fish, I have found that usually stops the laughing and they now want to know how to do it themselves.

JET DIVERS: Another Luhr-Jensen product, the Jet Diver dives to a specific depth when trolled, but returns to the surface when at rest. The size 10 dives to 10 feet, the 20 to 20 feet, the size 30 dives to 30 feet, and so on with different sizes to reach 50 feet.

FISH SEEKERS: These planer devices are capable of taking a 4 or 5-inch shad body rigged on a 1/2 or 1-ounce jighead down to 70 feet or more. Follow the directions to select the right attachment hole to achieve the needed depth. The planer is small enough to fit in the palm of your hand and it easily stores on any boat.

Fish Seekers can be fished on mono line, but many sharpies are now using braided lines because of their smaller diameter. Cabela's sells Fish Seekers in their catalog.

DEEP SIX DIVERS: Another Luhr-Jensen trolling aid, these devices have an automatic trip mechanism built into the unit so that when a fish strikes the lure, the mechanism trips and causes the device to rise to the surface and turn over so you fight only the fish and not the planer as well.

The size OOO dives to 40 feet, size 001 dives to 60 feet and the size 002 dives to a staggering 90 feet of water depth.

SIDE PLANERS: Instead of diving down, side planers "dive" to the side and stay on the surface. The largest planers have a visible red flag so their movement can be tracked. Rattles that are built into the body add sound. Side planers also have a mechanism to release the lure and line after a strike, so the fisherman fights the fish unencumbered by the side planer.

The Hot Shot Side Planer is a favorite of mine because it allows me to fish lures up tight and shallow against banks, rocky shorelines, drop-offs and flats. Being able to stay a distance away from the targeted gamefish can be a sure-bet fish catching strategy.

Snaps And Swivels

There are several excellent choices for snaps, snap swivels and swivels. The time-tested Duolock style is handy when you need to change lures frequently and don't want to re-tie each time. Another excellent snap is the Crosslock, but because they don't fit easily into the eye of small leadheads, this snap is best used when trolling and with large baits.

Some plastic baits will cause line twist after an hour or so of casting, retrieving and fishing. You have only two choices. Either find a way to cut down on the line twist by checking the lure to be sure it's running true, or just forget about using those types of baits. Personally, I prefer to use solution number one. It cuts down on the line twist as these baits account for far too many fish, so choose answer number one.

You'll get less line twist if you learn the skills required to fish with a narrow-spool baitcasting reel. Because of its narrow-spool design and the way line comes off the spool and goes back on again, there is less of a tendency to get line twist. Spinning reels have a natural tendency to twist line, so with this type of tackle, I like to use a good ball-bearing swivel. Don't waste time skimping on the quality of the swivel. The better the swivel, the fewer problems you will have with line twist. Use a mono or fluorocarbon leader of approximately 14 to 20 inches with the barrel swivel at the top end and a snap at the other. There is more on this in the chapter on how to rig Slug-Go baits.

My favorite swivel is the SPRO. They are high in quality, small in size, extremely strong and never fail. They cost a bit more money than inexpensive swivels, but they will never let you down.

Storage Options

One major advantage to fishing with soft plastics is they take up very little room in a boat, beach buggy or surf bag. You can cram quite a few soft plastics into a relatively small area. Keeping them separated and organized is another matter.

Since we will be dealing with many different sizes, shapes and especially colors, storage will be a big factor. The chemicals used in making soft plastics will often cause a chemical reaction between two different types of plastics. Besides having colors bleed into one another, storing two dissimilar plastics together can actually cause them to breakdown and dissolve. Over the years, I've had some pretty strange looking pieces of plastic when two, three or more baits came in contact with each other.

You want to keep them separated, dry, and out of the sun. You also shouldn't store them wet. Lures that were used should be dried before placing them back into storage. Wet or damp plastic will fade and loose its coloration quickly.

When spraying your baits with any type of fish scent, only spray and package as many baits as you think you'll need for a day's fishing. At one time, I would package them and let them soak for weeks, but I don't anymore. After spraying them, place them in a Ziploc. Some baits will last a long time after being sprayed or soaked, and some won't. A lot depends on how the baits were manufactured.

Over the years, I've tried just about everything there is to store my soft plastics so they are fresh, clean and dry and ready for use. If you do it properly, you will also save yourself time and money. Even though soft plastics are relatively inexpensive, all things considered, if you toss ten away here and twenty pieces away there, it can add up over the course of a season.

I like Ziploc and Glad bags. I've used so many of them I may actually be mentioned in material they send out to shareholders. These companies would get a much bigger bang for their buck by sponsoring saltwater fishing guides and captains instead of wasting all those millions of dollars on television commercials. The big money is in fishing, guys, not in TV! Seriously, Ziploc bags are very useful for storing soft plastics.

When selecting storage alternatives, think about how you fish. Do you trailer a boat, or fish on a friend's boat, store your tackle in the

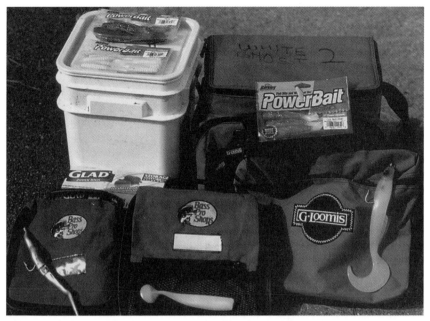

Plastic lures can be stored in a variety of buckets, pouches, tackle bags and zip-closure plastic bags for quick access while fishing.

garage, or leave some on the boat in between trips? Do you trailer your boat home each time, or keep it in a garage? Do you empty it after each trip as many anglers do? If so, you can probably use almost anything out there made for soft plastics. If, however, your boat is moored or at a slip most of the season, that presents a different set of storage options.

The sun is going to be your worst enemy. Never leave plastic exposed to direct sunlight for long periods of time. Store them away from sunlight and from areas where lots of heat is likely to build up.

Tackle satchels offer excellent carrying capacity and ease of transport for your plastics. Soft-sided systems like Tackle Logic or the systems from Bass Pro Shops or Cabela's work great as well. They allow the fisherman to categorize lures by size and color. You can pack a lot into a very small, lightweight package. They also give you the ability to mix and match for any specific type of fishing when taking a trip. Now if you're going to leave them on a boat for an extended period of time, it's time to check out other options.

Here's what I do. Keep in mind that as a full-time guide, I need to carry a lot of soft plastics to be sure my clients never run out of the hot color, size or action on any given day. I buy freezer Ziploc bags in the quart and gallon sizes in quantity so I get a good price. All colors and sizes are separated into individual bags and then categorized by fishing categories such as weakfish, spring stripers, summer stripers, bluefish, fluke, bonito, albies, southern species, etc. By doing this, we don't have to carry five tons of plastic when only one ton is needed.

The two best methods I've found for storage on the boat for long term is a Rubbermaid container or a plastic pail with a screw-on lid (the type pool chemicals come in). Both of these products are going to give you as close to dry storage as you are ever going to get. The buckets that come with chlorine tablets from swimming pool supply outlets are great, and come in several sizes. If you have an outlet nearby, just ask the owner if he'd save a few for you. They are usually more than willing to do so, as it saves them the trouble and probable expense of disposing of empty containers. It's a win-win situation.

You can keep the buckets on the deck ready for use and keep the contents dry and out of the sun all at the same time. The screw-on lids lock out all spray, water, rain and sunlight. For storage below decks in a compartment or hole, I prefer the Rubbermaid containers or something similar since I can stow them in compartments that won't accommodate buckets. The small rectangular containers are really nice if the lid snaps on tight. The containers can then be marked with a permanent marker so you know exactly what is in each box. This saves time and aggravation when the bite is hot and you need a specific soft bait in a hurry.

As your Ziploc bags become worn, torn or damaged during the day or over time, make sure you change them. There is always an extra box of plastic bags on board of each size stuffed in the console of my Triton just for this purpose.

To store additional accessories like jig hooks and weights, nothing beats the traditional Plano 3700 boxes or small plastic containers. You can dedicate one for hooks or jigheads. In another, put the swivels, snaps, small weights and almost anything you need to make or construct rigs. In a third box I place all the different size jigheads.

I also use 1-gallon buckets to store scent bottles, dyes, tools, lead weights and pre-tied rigs ready for use. Again, each Plano box and each container is marked so we know exactly what is in each and can find it fast.

Some soft-sided coolers have plastic inserts, plus a convenient carrying strap, and zippered front pocket. Some models have side pockets as well. These are great for fishing out of small boats, taking your gear to your buddy's boat, or traveling to distant destinations. They are relatively dry and require little maintenance.

No doubt there are other methods of storage, but this is what I've found to work and be relatively affordable. Keep in mind that I fish as a professional guide and captain so I need to carry a lot of gear. You can modify what I've described to suit your own needs. There are many tackle bags that will fit the needs of many fishermen. Keep your gear dry, readily accessible and easy to find, and that will allow you more time to catch more fish.

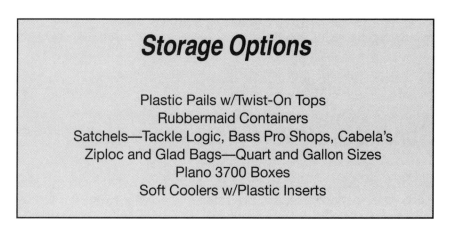

Storage Options

Plastic Pails w/Twist-On Tops
Rubbermaid Containers
Satchels—Tackle Logic, Bass Pro Shops, Cabela's
Ziploc and Glad Bags—Quart and Gallon Sizes
Plano 3700 Boxes
Soft Coolers w/Plastic Inserts

Fish Grippers

There are several fish grippers that I like to use. Some have scales, some are just grippers, but they are all handy to have on board.

Boga Grip: The Boga Grip is made from stainless steel, won't rust if given a little bit of care, and works every time I've used it. I've had mine almost nine years and it still looks and works like it did brand new. You cannot only grab and hold fish with it, but weigh them as well on a scale that can be certified by IGFA if you send it to them at 300 Gulf Stream Way, Dania Beach, Florida 33004. Boga Grips have a reputation for being very accurate.

It's a good idea to wrap the lanyard around your wrist so you don't lose your grip. I added a small lobster buoy on the lanyard so the whole thing floats on the surface if it goes overboard. I've already lost two, so I know from experience that it can happen. Watching a hundred bucks sink to the bottom is an awful feeling.

Lip-Grip Tool: A great tool from Berkley that is 28-inches long, has a powerful spring-action jaw, a non-slip foam handle and a lanyard wrist strap. It does not have a built-in scale like the more expensive Boga, but it shines when trying to grab a big fish from a boat with a lot of freeboard.

Rapala Lock & Weight: Also 28-inches long, the Rapala model has the added advantage of being able to weigh a fish up to 125 pounds. Made of stainless steel, it features a padded handle and wrist strap for holding onto.

Special Tools And Accessory Gear

There are certain things all anglers need to carry with them to make fishing easier, more productive or safer on the water. Nothing is worse than running into a problem on the water, and not being able to deal with it or fix it on the spot.

As a professional guide and captain, I need to be ready for a lot of pleasant and not so pleasant situations on any given day. Each time I go out on the water, I never know what is going to happen on my boat, so I'm a firm believer in being prepared for anything. The following listing is a brief summary of the items I've found useful over the years. Some are only for fishing situations, and some are for emergencies.

Lindy Fishing Glove: This dual-purpose item is great for grabbing fish and can save your hands from nasty cuts when handling a fish. The glove is puncture-resistant and great for handling lures with trebles attached or toothy critters like bluefish or barracuda. The glove is also good when filleting fish, cutting bait or chumming, as it will protect your hand and fingers very well. Its non-slip palm surface makes grasping items easy, even when the gloves are wet.

Fish grippers are a handy accessory when boating fish you intend to release. Several types are available and some of them include an accurate scale.

Pliers: No one should be on the water fishing without pliers. Yet, every year I run across someone who has a hook in his hand and can't cut the fish free or cut the hooks from the plug or lure. I like to have two types of pliers with me at all times. The first is a long 6 to 8-inch needle nose for reaching down inside bluefish that are hooked too deep for the shorter pliers.

Second is a good pair of cutting pliers to cut hooks or wire in a hurry. I've snipped a lot of trebles from fishermen's hands over the years. They easily open and close hook eyes or split rings, remove hooks, close sinkers or split shot, and handle a hundred other chores while fishing.

Keep your pliers well oiled so they don't rust, and store them in a sheath that will retain oil within itself. All you need to do is squirt or spray some oil inside the holder and place the pliers inside. They will remain looking like brand new for the entire season.

Hook Hones and Files: Everyone who fishes should have a good hook hone and file with him at all times. It's one of the most important pieces of equipment that you can carry. One of the best I have found is the Luhr Jensen hook file. It will sharpen almost anything, especially hook points. Its nice wide handle makes it easy to grip, and it won't break the bank.

I like to have a heavy-duty file for bigger hooks, and a smaller diamond stone type for touching up hook points on smaller hooks and fly hooks. It's also a good idea to have a good sharpening stone for your fillet knife if you intend to keep fish for the table. There is nothing worse than trying to fillet a fish with a dull knife.

Fillet Knifes: I've had so many that I've lost count. My most recent knives were purchased as a kit with two fillet knives, a bait knife, a small cutting board, and a steel sharpener. It sold for around $25, and kept clean, it's lasted several seasons. The best fillet knives usually have a flexible, long, thin blade that makes the filleting job go easier. A serrated knife isn't a good choice.

Gerber Tool: I'd be lost without my stainless multi-purpose Gerber Tool. I carry it wherever I go because it does so many different jobs. I like the way the blades and attachments lock in place and don't come back on your hand when cutting, screwing, holding, pulling, or filing. I've had mine for over 10 years and it's like brand new—a tool worth every penny I paid.

Deep Hook Removers: There are many good hook removers available, including special tools with a squeeze handle, long stem and small jaws to grab the hook.

The tool I've used for most of my career is simplicity in itself, and many times that's the best solution to a problem. Make your own from an 18 to 24-inch length of wooden dowel, such as an old broom handle section. At one end cut a vee notch in the center, and then cut the edges at a 45-degree angle on both sides of the notch. Don't cut so much that you form a point. You want it to taper evenly on each side of the notch.

Next, wrap the top of the stick with some heavy cord for a handle and then bring the cord back underneath the wrap like you would when wrapping an eye on a rod blank. Drill a small hole in the top to hold a lanyard, then apply a good coat of wood preserver. I've had the same one for over 16 years and only changed the handle wrapping last season.

To use it, simply follow the line down to the hook inside the fish's mouth. Hold the line tight against the handle and with one fast, quick movement, shove down and lift out. This hook remover will dislodge the deepest of imbedded hooks in a fish's throat. The best thing of all is that the fish will not bleed or be injured from removing the hook. I have removed hundreds maybe thousands of hooks from fish and few if any bled even a drop. It's fast, easy and clean.

WD-40/Silicone Lube: Both of these products are great to have on board or in your truck for a variety of small jobs. It's a small investment to use on tools, reels, gear, motors, electronics, connections, for rust removal and lots more. There is also a belief that the odor of WD-40 appeals to fish and makes them strike. I can't attest to that claim first hand, but who knows? Stranger things have proven to be successful. Rust-Off and Corrosion Block should also be considered, as they help in more heavy-duty situations.

Flashlights: Always carry at least one flashlight. I have three different flashlights on board. One is the long Brinkman type constructed of aluminum that uses "D" batteries. This particular light has a very bright beam and is adjustable from spotlight to flood. Then there is the smaller version that is so popular with both boaters and surf casters. This light takes two "AA" batteries. Both housings are made of aluminum so they won't corrode. The third is the new Ray-O-Vac headlight that goes over your head or cap. This light fits easily on your head and has a bright white light, a duller almost fluorescent light and a red light beam for nighttime fishing so it doesn't interfere with night vision. This is a great light for night fishing and I have four on board for my charters to use. The red light won't spook the fish.

The new INOVA light system, manufactured in Rhode Island, consists of LED light or Diodes. This model is called the 24/7 and has eight different modes: SOS, Hi-Beam, Low-Beam, strobe, pulse, red, white, yellow lights, and can be seen from 2 miles away. It is waterproof and runs on one lithium CR123 battery. This light comes with a headband or in a kit with a lanyard, headband, screw-in mount, or a magnetic mount for boats. Other models include the X-5 and X-1. The X-5 has five LED lights, is waterproof down to 150 feet, crushproof to 2,000 pounds of pressure and is also great for diving. The X-1 comes in three different colors: white, blue and green, which can be seen the farthest away, and in red for night vision. These are some of the best fishing lights available on the market today.

Windex Spray: Get a few 5-ounce spray bottles from your local Dollar Store and fill them with Windex so you can clean salt spray from prescription glasses, sunglasses, binoculars, the boat's windshield and electronics displays. I also store small Kleenex tissue packets in a Ziploc bag.

Handle Wraps: Here's another item from the Dollar Store. These 4x4-inch neoprene sheets have Velcro on each end and are sold as handle bag wraps for sports bags, luggage, and travel cases or other transportable items with handles.

You can use them to hold fly rods in the rocket launcher of the T-Top on the boat. When the rods are in the T-Top, you simply put a handle wrap around the fly rod, then around the blank of the rod above it so it holds it in place. If you need a larger one, use two together. They come in handy for holding all sorts of things in the boat and out of the way.

First Aid Kit: Everyone who fishes from shore or boat should have a good First Aid Kit handy. Whether from a boat or from the shore or beach a kit should be handy. I like the ones sold as survival packs since they come with just about everything you could ever need in an emergency. Be sure your kit has extra Band-Aids, Tylenol, some big gauze pads, a sports wrap, medicated cream or iodine, and some handy-wipes to clean small wounds.

Dremel Tool: I'm no Handy Andy, and have a hard time banging nails straight or cutting a straight piece of wood, but I can use a Dremel Tool when it comes to tinkering with fishing gear or anything to do with fishing. You can drill, grind, polish, cut, shape, and perform many other tasks. Suffice it to say it is one handy tool to have around.

Line Counters: Shakespeare and Rapala make a lightweight line counter that snaps or fastens onto the rod blank, and gives you precise depth control in trolling situations. Just run the line through the counter and the counter keeps track of the amount of line going out. Once you know that, you can mark that length and determine at what depth the fish are hitting.

Optronics Light: The submersible neon green light from Optronics is a fish-attracting light that can help increase your nighttime catch rate. It's a proven fact that a green neon light will attract both fresh and saltwater gamefish. The 12-volt fluorescent light attracts organisms, which in turn attract bait, which in turn attracts bigger gamefish to feed on the bait. It doesn't affect night vision and can be submerged or floated, whichever you prefer. We have used this light at night while chumming with clams and it really does draw bait to the boat. It's been used in freshwater now for striped bass fishing for quite a few years, and the success rate with this light is amazing.

Sunglasses: A very important piece of fishing gear, sunglasses should be with you at all times. Not only do they help you to see and

A top-quality pair of "shades" will help you spot fish and protect your eyes from harmful ultraviolet light rays.

spot fish in shallow water, they will protect your eyes from the sun's rays and from serious injury from hooks, lures and jigs being tossed around the boat. At least three or four times in the last 10 years, I have been hit in the glasses by a fly or a jighead. The lens saved my eyesight. UV rays are harmful to anyone's eyes and a pair of good glasses will help protect them from the sun's rays. Sunglasses come in both dark shades and light shades for different conditions. Having two pairs on board is a good idea—if only as a backup.

Choose the brown or amber for fishing during the day and spotting fish. The blue mirror finish is good for offshore fishing, as are the other types of mirror finishes. I like the mirror finish because they reflect the sun and glare so well. If you spend a lot of hours on the water, I have noticed that with the mirror finish, my eyes are not as tired and I get fewer headaches.

The other pair we use is yellow for early morning or late evening or very cloudy days. It makes everything brighter and easier to see in low-light conditions.

Choosing the right line and leader, and using the best knots will add to your success with plastic baits.

CHAPTER THREE

LINE, LEADERS & KNOTS

To achieve maximum success when fishing soft-plastic baits, you have to be rigged right. That means using the right type of line, the most suitable pound test, the most appropriate leader and the best choice for a snap or other terminal tackle.

Using the correct knot is also an important factor. A good knot will enhance your fishing capabilities, and won't weaken the line. The wrong knot, or a poorly tied knot, could cause the loss of a trophy fish due to a break-off. A bad knot can result in a high rate of line failure in an otherwise strong, high-quality fishing line. Even the best mono that money can buy will experience up to a 50-percent loss of strength with a bad knot.

Getting rigged-up is actually very simple. Many fishermen develop a system that they use for years and rigging up becomes virtually a habit. This is a good thing. Work out a system that is easy to use, simple to rig and very strong.

In the following pages of this chapter, we'll take a look at the many different types of fishing lines, the best leader choices, the strongest knots and the best way to "bring it all together." I'll show you what I use as a professional captain and guide, and provide some tips on how to select a rigging system from the many alternatives.

Line Choices

Most fishermen will use standard monofilament line, but there are many lines from which to select. Technically, some of them aren't even monofilament lines, but are blends of two or more nylon chemical formulations. These are known as copolymer lines and are blended to offer hard coatings for abrasion resistance and supple interior cross sections for good knot tying and casting abilities. Other blends of special multi-polymer lines utilize a mix of mono-filament and fluorocarbon characteristics.

Mono lines stretch. When fishing deep water, this stretch factor must be considered when setting the hook. A slow response time at the strike may cause you to lose a fish. The stretch, however, is an advantage when the fish gets near the boat or beach because it acts as a cushion when a fish makes a short, but powerful, lunge away from the net or gaff.

Clear or light-color monofilament lines are used by most of today's anglers on a daily basis. These lines have been around the longest and are the easiest to use. They are usually the least expensive, although some of the newer copolymer clear lines are at the top of the price ladder. Many clear monos have a built-in fluorescent quality added to them so they are easy to see above the water, but nearly invisible below it.

There are also multi-color monofilament and copolymer lines that some fishermen have great faith in because the line colors blend in, or disappear, in the water. Some are called camouflage line, while others are referred to as just multi-colored. There is even a new multi-colored fluorescent line with three or four different colors blended along the length of the line. I personally don't use them much, but some anglers rely on them for deep-water fishing.

What I have used frequently are the bright fluorescent green and yellow lines. These are just great after dark, or on dark, cloudy days. They are excellent when casting baits towards shore structure, or when fishing in the surf. You always know where your line, lure or bait is located, and can easily see if it is working in the area you believe it should be. Add 10 to 12 feet of mono or fluorocarbon leader material so the main line isn't visible to the fish. As long as there's a topshot of a short length of clear leader, I haven't noticed any difference in the number of strikes I get with high-visibility line. Actually, I believe that knowing where the lure and line are during the retrieve has allowed me to catch more fish.

Take your pick— today's fishermen are about evenly split on fishing with monofilament or high-tech braided lines—both have advantages.

Super braid lines are in great favor with many fishermen for casting and trolling. These lines are a space-age fiber manufactured from gel-spun formulations known as Spectra or Dyneema. There are several manufacturers that market super braid lines, including Power Pro, Berkley, Stren, Spiderwire, Western Filament and others.

Super braid lines tend to lay flat and lose their round shape unless treated with special additives. Manufacturers introduced waxes, Teflon or "secret" materials to make these lines retain their round shape so they wear better and cast better. Because of these additives, super braids work equally well on spinning and conventional tackle.

These lines offer a tremendous ratio of strength to line diameter so you can use a line of 10 or 12-pound test with the equivalent diameter of 4-pound test monofilament. This means more line on the reel spool when extra line capacity is needed. This is handy when fishing for long-running, fast fish such as false albacore (little tunny), bonefish or bluefish in shallow water.

Braided line is also good for trolling, casting and jigging soft-plastic baits. If you don't catch more fish with braided line when jigging, then something is definitely wrong or you are fishing where there are no fish. Over a four-year period, I conducted my own experiment with braided line. We used it on a Penn 930 Levelmatic for fluke fishing. I gave that rod to the most inexperienced angler onboard every time we went fluking. It didn't matter whether they were young, old, male or female, they got that rod and reel. On every day and in every circumstance, the person with that super braid outfit caught more fish, and sometimes, bigger fish, than those who used plain mono. They had a better feel, and with almost no stretch in the line, it was relatively easy to get a good hook set.

The one real drawback with braid is that if you get hung up on the bottom, you can't get your line free easily. If I'm fishing an area with lots of sticks, piers, pilings and rocks on the bottom, I will usually use mono line. If you do hang up when fishing with a super braid, don't try to break it with your hands. Its fine diameter and high strength will cut your hands. Instead, wrap the line around a boat cleat and let the boat break it as it drifts. What if your boat isn't that heavy? Then I suggest a good pair of scissors to cut the line.

Advantages Of A Leader System

Leaders are the vital link between the main fishing line and the fish. The main fishing line can be monofilament, copolymer or super braid, but they all work best when a leader is used at the end. A leader offers many fishing advantages. It acts as a shock absorber when a big fish strikes, and while casting. It resists abrasion. It also gives the angler something to grab and hold onto when landing the fish. With small fish, it serves as a handy way to haul a catch over the gunnel and into the boat.

One thing I learned standing on the poling platform of my flats skiff is that stripers (especially big ones) have a habit of heading for the nearest piece of structure when hooked, such as a rock, mussel bar, dock piling, reef or bridge abutment. They will try anything to dislodge that piece of steel in their mouth. In shallow-water situations, they turn on their sides and rub their face along the bottom to free the hook. In almost all circumstances when they are doing this, their bodies are parallel to your line. The line is now exposed to their fins, gill plates and scales that are sharp and can easily cut a light line.

When they do this, there are actually two things taking place. Not only is the fish rubbing its face against the bottom where sharp objects exist, but the line is running alongside its body and the bottom as well. Stripers are not the only fish that do this. Tarpon, snook, redfish, and many others will use the same tactic to free themselves.

Without a leader to absorb some of the shock, stress and most of the abrasion, chances are you will have a very difficult time landing anything much bigger than 10 pounds.

Leader Types

There are several basic leader materials: monofilament, fluorocarbon, single-strand wire and braided wire. Let's take a look at each one.

For most situations, mono is the favorite choice. It's inexpensive, ties good knots, is abrasion resistant, has controlled stretch and is readily available at any tackle shop. Mono is even available in colors, or in multi-colors, plus the traditional clear, the most popular. Mono is not highly visible in water, but it does not totally disappear.

Mono leaders are standard, but for extra invisibility and chafing resistance, many fishermen select fluorocarbon.

Fluorocarbon is a monofilament-like material, but it's a different chemical formulation. It feels somewhat like mono and the same knots can be used to attach snaps or to attach to the main fishing line. Fluorocarbon is slightly stiffer, and markedly more abrasion resistant. It is also less visible in water. Because it is much tougher and more abrasion resistant than mono, it's better suited for fishing rocky areas and places where there are numerous snags and other obstructions. Some fluorocarbon lines have a slick finish so you have to pay close attention when you tie your knots. If you hurry, they might slip under strain.

At different times of the year and in different areas of the country, there will be a time when those critters with teeth, such as bluefish, barracuda and sharks, will show up. When this happens we will no doubt have to go to a wire leader, often called a "trace".

I make up my single-strand wire leaders with a barrel swivel at the top end and Duolock snap at the other. This usually works well with most leadheads, but if the hook eye on the leadhead is too small, tie the wire directly to the leadhead. I tie a good supply ahead of time and store them in a PVC tube that is capped shut on one end and has a removable cap on the other. You could also just put them in a Ziploc bag.

Some of the new wire materials like Cobra, Tyger, Boa Wire, Cortland's Toothy Critter and American Fishing Wire are so flexible they can handle regular fishing knots. One of my favorites is the simple, but time-tested, figure eight knot. Make sure when you pull it tight to cinch it down, to pull the tag end first and not the main leader end. If you pull too hard in the main leader, the wire will kink and spiral (corkscrew) badly. Once this happens, the bait or jig will not work properly again.

Selecting A Shock Leader

Fishermen often call the leader at the end of the main fishing line a "shock" leader. Especially when fishing with light tackle and light line, the use of a shock leader can make all the difference between landing or losing the fish of a lifetime. Shock leaders also prevent excessive break-offs, which can get expensive if too many lures are lost. Shock leaders also give the angler something to grab hold of when attempting to land or boat a fish.

So what is a shock leader? A shock leader is nothing more than a length of stronger (heavier) pound-test line tied to the end of the main casting line to prevent breakage and wear-and-tear where your line is usually stressed and worn the most—inside the guides.

Each time you reel in to make another cast, the line returns to the same position inside the rod guides. Most fishermen pay little or no attention to this, but each cast causes friction from the guides and this slowly wears on the line. This constant casting will eventually cause a weak spot in the line unless you take the time to cut back on that portion which is always being worn. When the bite is hot, this is one thing no one wants to take time to check. When you switch from a light lure to a heavier one, it becomes easy to snap off the heavier lure after only a few casts. Most fishermen can recall this event happening more often than they'd like to admit.

Leader Length

Casting champion Ron Arra uses a ten-to-one formula when rigging his leaders. He multiplies the weight number by ten to determine the pound test of the leader. For instance, a 1-ounce casting lure would require a 10-pound test leader. He also uses a leader that is twice the length of the rod. A 7-foot rod would have a 14-foot leader.

Striped bass and snook have sharp gill plates, bluefish have razor sharp teeth. A heavy mono or wire leader will prevent cut-offs.

This leader formula is okay for distance and accuracy casting events, but not necessarily the best for actual fishing. The fisherman also has to balance several factors: too heavy a leader may reduce lure action, and too light a leader will not provide any protection. With extremely finicky fish, there may even be times when it's best to fish with no leader at all—just tie the main line directly to the lure. Other times, you may need a very heavy leader to avoid getting chopped off by toothy critters, or you may need a leader that is only slightly heavier than the main fishing line.

Most fishermen use a significantly heavier leader, and prefer a leader that is at least two or three times the strength of the line on the reel spool. For example, they use a 30-pound test leader when the main line tests at 10 to 15 pounds.

Having a long leader also guards against losing a big fish if it should turn sideways to your line or roll on it. This is a common problem in shallow water when a big fish is hooked. I've seen 20 to 30-pound stripers roll on the main line, or even the 20-pound leader and break it as if it were sewing thread. The gill plates and spines of stripers are very sharp and so are their scales, which resemble sandpaper.

When your lure is ready to cast, the leader should be long enough so it wraps on the spool at least twice. This will allow a smoother cast.

When strong gamefish lunge beneath the boat, push the rod at the fish to avoid breaking the line under the sudden pressure.

Connecting Line To Leader

Attaching the leader to the main fishing line can be accomplished with the angler's choice of four alternative knots: surgeon's knot, blood knot, Albright knot or nail knot. Which knot you choose will depend upon the difference between the diameter of the leader and the main fishing line. Lines of dramatically different diameters are best attached with the Albright or nail knot. Lines and leader of similar diameter can be linked with the surgeon's or blood knot.

The blood knot and surgeon's knot can be used to attach lines of dramatically different diameters, only if the main line side of the knot connection is first doubled-up by tying a Bimini twist or a spider hitch to the end of the main line. This effectively doubles the strength of the main line and allows it to be linked to the heavy leader via a blood or surgeon's knot.

When using a super braid main line, adding the shock leader requires a little more care. Power Pro suggests using the following knots (they work well with other super braids as well). To add a leader, use the reverse Albright, or a uni-knot. When using the uni-knot, double over the end of the super braid, but not the leader.

When tying any of these connections, don't forget to moisten the knot with saliva before drawing the knot tight. Snip the tag end close to the knot, and you are finished.

After tying a knot, if you aren't sure it is perfect, cut it off and try again. Be sure of your knots.

Important Knots

Several basic knots are easily mastered with a little practice and patience. Before tightening a knot, wet it with saliva for lubrication. This will allow the knot to tighten up evenly, preventing any binding. It's also important that the knot is tightened slowly, not jerked, by steadily and smoothly pulling the two ends in opposite directions. A pair of fisherman's pliers is good for this tightening task.

Clip the excess line protruding from the knot not longer or shorter than one-eighth inch.

Bimini Twist

This process creates a double line, most often used in offshore big game fishing, but also makes a shock leader for casting with light tackle in both fresh and saltwater fishing. The illustration shows making up a short double line about five feet long. If you want to make a long double line, you'll need help.

1. Measure off a little more than twice the length of double line desired and double back forming a very long loop. Hold the standing line and tag end and have your assistant rotate the end of the loop 20 times, putting twists into it.
2. Your helper can slip the loop over a stationary post, get inside the loop and force or "walk" the twists toward you until they are about 12 inches from the tag end. Sit in a chair, put your feet on the two lines and spread your legs slightly to put tension on the twists.
3. The twists will be vertical in front of you. Hold the standing line in one hand just slightly off the vertical angle. Hold the tag end at a right angle (90 degrees) to the twists. Keep tension on the loop with your knees. Gradually relax the tension on the tag end so it will roll over the column of twists, starting just below the upper twist.
4. Spread your legs slowly to maintain pressure on the loop. Guide the tag line into a series of tight spiral coils as it continues to roll over the twisted line.
5. When the spiral of the tag end line has completely rolled over the column of twists, maintain your knee pressure on the loop, release the standing line and place a finger of that hand in the V or "crotch" where the loop "legs" project from the knot to prevent slippage of the last turn. Take a half-hitch with the tag end around the nearest "leg" of the loop and pull it tight.
6. With the half-hitch holding the knot, relax some knee pressure but keep the loop stretched taut. Take the tag end and make a half-hitch around both legs of the loop, but do not pull it tight just yet.
7. Make two turns with the tag end around both loop legs, winding inside the bend of the line formed by the loose half-hitch and toward the main knot. Pull the tag end slowly, forcing the three loops to gather in a spiral.
8. When the loops are pulled nearly to the knot, tighten them to lock the knot in place. Clip the tag end.

2

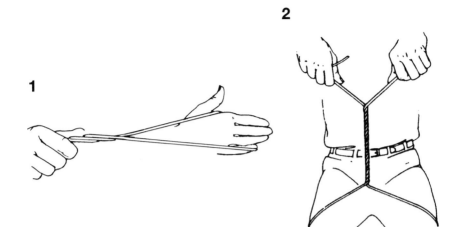

1

3

4

5

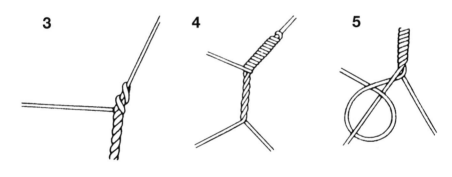

6

7

8

Spider Hitch Knot

This is a good knot to use when a double length of line is needed for jigging bucktails, and you don't want to spend the time tying a Bimini knot. The double line comes in handy when hooking a bluefish as opposed to a fluke. If one length of line breaks, you have the second length to land your fish and retrieve your lure.

1. Create the desired length of double line by folding the line back. Near the tag end, twist the strands into a small reverse loop.
2. Hold the small loop between your left thumb and forefinger, with the thumb extended well above the finger.
3. Wind the double line strands around your thumb and loop strands, taking five parallel turns. Pass the end of the original big loop through the small loop, pull the slack out, and pull the five turns off your thumb. Moisten with saliva, and slowly pull the tag end and standing line strands against the loop strands to tighten the knot. The coils should be even (if they wrap back over themselves then it's necessary to try the knot again). For final tightening, pull the standing line only against the loop.

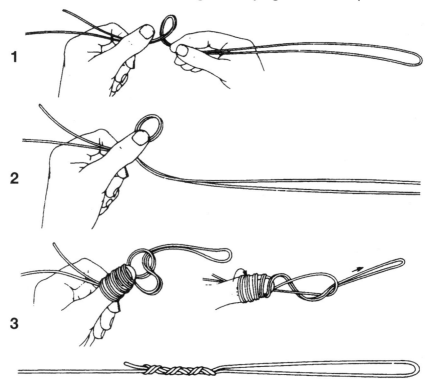

Improved Clinch Knot

An old standby, this is a basic knot for attaching hooks, lures and swivels. It works best with monofilament lines up to 20-pound test.

1. Pass the line through the eye of the hook, lure or swivel. Double and make five turns around the standing line. Hold the coils and pass the tag end through the loop formed at the eye of the hook.
2. Pass the tag end through the large loop as shown. This extra step makes this the "improved" clinch knot and brings the strength of the knot up to 98% of the main fishing line.
3. Hold the standing line and the free end, then pull the coils tight. Make sure they lie next to each other, not crisscrossed.

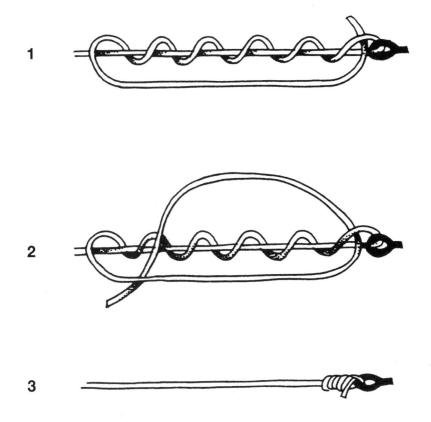

Surgeon's End Loop

Use this knot to tie a loop in the end of a line for attaching leaders, sinkers or other terminal gear quickly.

1. Double back a few inches of line and make an overhand knot.
2. Pass the end of the loop through the overhand knot a second time.
3. Hold the standing leg of the line and the tag end and pull the loop to draw the knot tight.

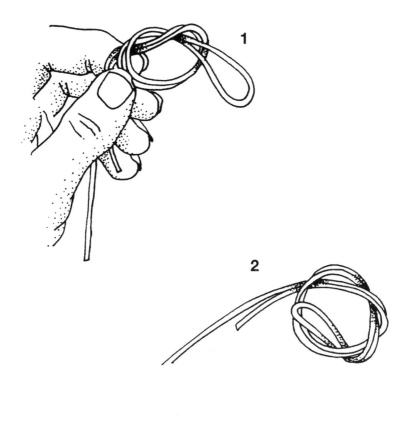

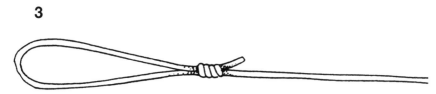

Snelling A Hook Knot

Years ago factory-snelled hooks were common. Today, fishermen prefer to buy loose hooks and leader material of their own choice and tie the snells themselves to suit a variety of bait-fishing needs.

1. Pass one end of the leader through the hook eye and past the bend. Pass the other end through the hook eye in the opposite direction. A large loop is now formed below the hook.
2. Hold both lines along the hook shank. Use the line of the eye side of the hook and make five tight coils around the shank and both legs of the leader.
3. Hold the coils and pull on the long end of the leader until the coils come tight, leaving no loop. Hold the tag end with pliers and pull against both lines to tighten the snell securely.

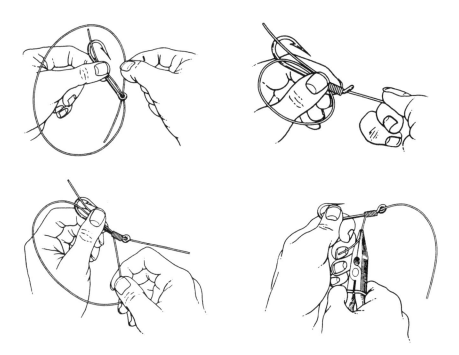

Surgeon's Knot

This is a handy knot, which can be used to join two lines of different diameters, such as when adding a leader to a reel filled with light line.

1. Lay the line and leader next to one another for about 12 inches.

2. Treat the two lines as if they were one line and make an overhand knot.

3. Pass the tag end of the line through the loop a second time.

4. Hold both sides of the lines and draw tight. Give a final pull by grasping the fishing line and the leader to set the knot.

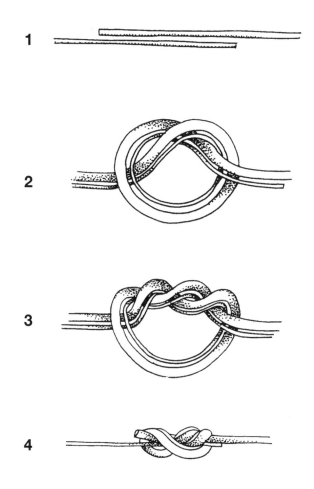

Uni-Knot

1. Run the tag end of the line through the eye at least 12 inches and fold it back against the standing line. Bring the tag end back as shown to form a loop.
2. Make six turns with the tag end around the two side-by-side lines and through the loop. Pull on the tag end and the standing line to snug up the coils.
3. Pull on the hook and the main line to draw the knot close to the hook eye.
4. Continue pulling until the knot is good and tight.

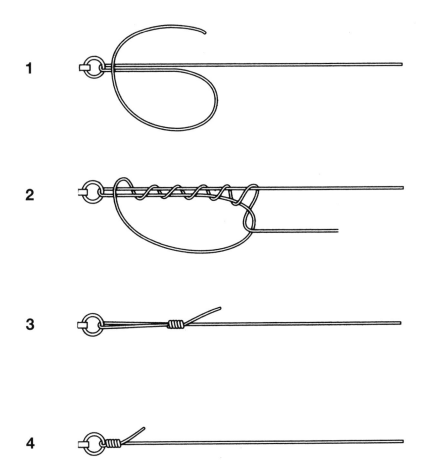

Palomar Knot

The Palomar knot is a favorite of light tackle anglers because it is easy to tie, yet is exceptionally strong and resistant to breaking under the rapid strain caused from sudden runs of hefty fish. Freshwater bass anglers depend on this knot for tournament winning fish so you know it is a strong knot capable of handling trophy fluke.

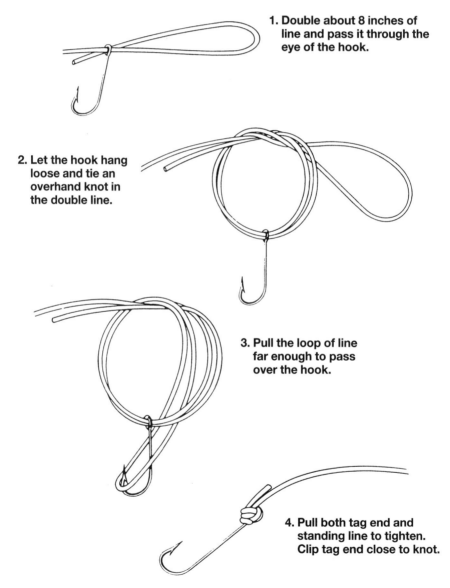

1. Double about 8 inches of line and pass it through the eye of the hook.

2. Let the hook hang loose and tie an overhand knot in the double line.

3. Pull the loop of line far enough to pass over the hook.

4. Pull both tag end and standing line to tighten. Clip tag end close to knot.

Albright Knot

This knot is used to add a heavier leader to a lighter line, such as attaching 30-pound or 50-pound test mono leader to the 12, 17 or 20-pound test mono on the reel. An Albright knot can also be used to tie a mono leader to the end of a super braided line. When connecting leader to line, an Albright knot provides a very significant advantage over a swivel. The Albright is a narrow-profile knot that will easily pass through the guides on most rods, and it will enable anglers to tie on long leaders and to reel down more closely to a hooked fish.

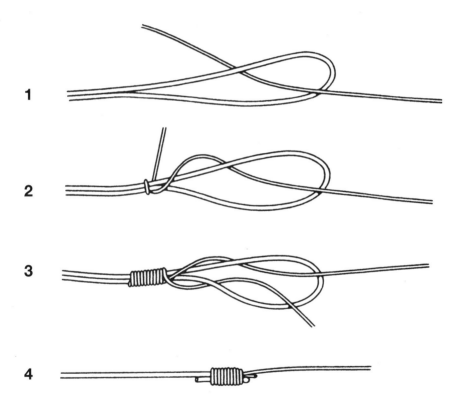

Tips For Tying Strong Knots

Knots fail for many reasons, but abrasion and slippage are the two most common. At knot connection points, the line is twisted, crisscrossed and pulled tight against the hard surfaces of hooks and lures, swivels and other terminal tackle. Even a good knot places a great deal of stress on the line. All these factors can reduce the effective test strength and durability of the knot and your fishing line. It's not unusual for a poorly tied knot in 15-pound test line to actually test out at only 8 pounds or less.

A good knot will test at nearly 100-percent of the unknotted strength of the line. First, choose the best knot for the application, and second, tie the knot properly. These tips will help.

WET THE KNOT—A little water or saliva helps lubricate the line, preventing abrasion and making it easier to gather and tighten the knot.

BE SURE THE KNOT IS TIGHT—A loosely gathered knot can come unraveled or slip under pressure. Slippage causes knot failure.

TRIM THE KNOT CAREFULLY—Be careful not to nick or scrape the fishing line when clipping off the tag end.

CHECK KNOTS FREQUENTLY—Inspect line and knots every time you land a fish. Re-tie if there is any damage or abrasion.

LEARN A FEW KNOTS WELL—You don't need to learn every fishing knot. Become proficient at a select few that you need for your style of fishing.

PRACTICE KNOT-TYING—Spend time practicing knot-tying skills until you can tie perfect knots every time.

The following tips will help you get the most from your fishing line:

STORE LINE PROPERLY—Store your line in a cool, dark, dry place. Avoid storing line where it can be exposed to any source of light or heat.

SPOOL LINE TIGHT—Spool monofilament line firmly onto the reel. This helps casting and keeps the line from digging into itself.

CHANGE LINE OFTEN—Re-spool at least every season or every month if you fish a lot. Old, weak line could cost you a big fish.

KEEP REEL SPOOL FULL—Reels that are low on line do not cast or retrieve as well as reels that are adequately filled with line.

Offshore or inshore, rigging soft-plastic baits correctly will enhance their action and fish-catching abilities.

CHAPTER FOUR

LURE RIGGING HOW-TO

Once you dive into the soft-plastic world and become a "rubber-bait" junkie, you will quickly learn there is a lot more to effectively rigging these lures than first meets the eye. After years of fishing and using soft plastics, I'm convinced there are probably a thousand ways, possibly more, to rig soft-plastic lures.

While reading fishing magazines and books, or watching videos or TV shows, I'm always checking out some new way to rig a soft bait. While researching this book, I came across nearly two-dozen rigging methods I'd never seen before. There is no doubt there are even more out there somewhere.

If I left out your favorite, or secret, soft-plastic rig, I apologize. Please don't send letters saying I'm lost in space or should be playing golf. I hate golf. I'd rather be fishing, even if I did miss a rig or two.

Keep in mind that rigging and fishing plastic baits is an ever-changing proposition. It's continually evolving as new products come on the market and innovative ideas are developed by tournament anglers, guides and savvy fishermen. Trying new ideas is another way to get more enjoyment out of your fishing. Don't hesitate to experiment. Who knows? Your secret way of rigging may become the hot new technique everyone will want to know about.

Getting Hooked

Let's start our journey through rigging techniques with a close look at hooks. Probably the first hook almost everyone thinks of is the "common" worm hook used for plastic worms. Well, the common worm hook ain't so common anymore, Ollie. Like everything else in the tackle industry it has evolved into a high-tech piece of fishing equipment while maintaining its traditional look and feel. In short, it's light years away from the hooks I used when I was 8 or 10 years old to catch bluegills, perch and horn pout.

Today's hooks are thinner, lighter and super-heated for strength. Their hook points are chemically sharpened for razor-like points, or they are designed with specially shaped points for quick penetration. Some hooks are even colored in special finishes of red, blue and green for enhanced fish-catching abilities.

All these attributes are important, but the secret to catching more fish is matching the proper size hook to the size of the bait. A hook that is too small will cause you to miss strikes. A hook that is too big will hinder the action of the bait.

The trick to deciding which hook is best is learned from the trial-and-error experiences that come from actual on-the-water fishing. No one picks the right hook size and shape each and every time. I don't, no one I know does, and if someone is telling you they are, they're yanking your chain. Once again, if we all made the correct choice each and every time, there would be nothing left to learn and maybe nothing left to catch.

For starters, consider what part of the water column you are going to target. If you are fishing on or near the surface with lures like Slug-Gos, Zoom Flukes, Bass Assassins, Fin-S Fish, Mann's Shadow or similar types of jerkbaits, a light-wire hook would be the probable choice. The lighter, thinner wire will allow the bait to stay close to the surface as you work the retrieve back towards the boat. A light-wire hook will allow the lure to ride high. When fishing deeper, you should choose a hook with a heavier gauge wire. The added weight of the larger diameter hook will help make the lure descend quickly and sink deeper in the water column.

Do not be fooled by the feel of today's light-wire hooks. They are super strong and capable of handling very big fish, provided you are using the proper tackle and not trying to drag the fish in like a crane hauling in an old junk car.

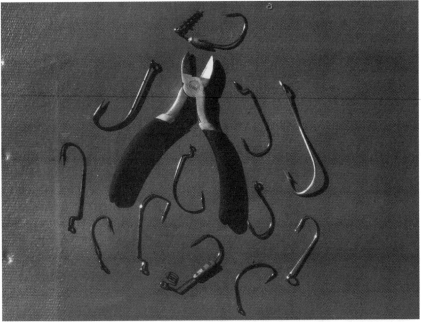

There is a wide variety of hook shapes, sizes and colors from several manufacturers specifically for rigging soft-plastic baits effectively.

Some anglers debate whether to use stainless steel hooks. I don't use stainless steel hooks anymore, not even when tying flies, because they don't rust. If a fish breaks off, the hook can't rust free and the fish will be stressed. Fish have enough problems without fishermen adding to them. I don't like leaving stainless steel hooks in a fish's mouth for the rest of eternity.

Most of the time I use black-chrome or cadmium-plated hooks. The most common hook is the Z-bend style worm hook, which has been around for decades and is used a lot in freshwater. Today's Z-bend hooks are stronger and sharper than their predecessors and have become popular in saltwater circles as well.

Another popular style is the Kahle hook, sometimes referred to as an English-style bait hook. It has a lot of practical fishing applications and most of today's wide-gap hook models came from the Kahle's original style. Wide-gapped, big-bite hooks are the rage these days. They offer a lot of hooking ability and can be used on dozens of soft-plastic imitations. The Eagle Claw Shaw Grigsby model comes with a hook clip to help hold the bait in place once it's attached. Hooks with some type of bait-holder attached to them are offered by Mustad, Mister Twister, Tru-Turn, Owner, Bass Pro and others. There really is a very huge selection to choose from.

As you build a hook collection, look for the new types of finishes that are offered by the industry. The black-chrome, platinum-coated, and traditional nickel-plated hooks are almost as good as any stainless steel hook in terms of corrosion or rust resistance. They are also extremely strong and very sharp. Minimal preventive maintenance will make these hooks last for many fishing trips. At the end of each trip, I wash all my tackle, including the hooks, with freshwater, and I have some hooks that are still in use after five years. There's no rust on them, because they were washed and put away dry. That's the key—dry.

Hooks with a Z-bend or L-bend are designed to hold the plastic lure in place while casting. Sometimes that works and sometimes it doesn't. As the puncture hole becomes enlarged from casting or setting the hook, the baits tend to move back along the hook shank. Lunker City Lures developed a hook they call the Tex-Pose. The Tex-Pose hook is similar to most other hooks except that it has a 90-degree angle between the top of the shank and the bend of the hook. When it's placed inside a soft-plastic jerkbait, the bait can't pull forward or backward as the angle of the hook's bend keeps it in place. At first glance, this design may seem weak, but it's not. I've used the Tex-Pose since they were introduced and I've never had one break or bend on me.

One thing the new hooks have in common is a very strong weight-to-size ratio when compared to hooks of similar size and shape from years ago. The hooks are tempered and undergo special treatments that make them so tough you can't bend them on a fish or even with a pair of pliers.

A good example is the Kahle style or English-style bait hook. It has a very wide bite opening on a relatively thin hook wire diameter. The wide opening offers the maximum amount of hooking potential at the strike, and the hook is very strong. Some of the manufacturers now offer this style hook with a screw-like wire device attached to the eye of the hook to which you can attach your plastic bait.

There are going to be times when you are going to need heavy-wire hooks. For instance, the hooks that come with the 9-inch Slug-Go and the 10-inch Fin-S Fish are very heavy duty and cadmium plated. These are 8/0 or 9/0 Z-bend worm hooks that probably weigh 1/4 ounce. Before you go fishing with one, or begin rigging it, put a razor-sharp point on it first. Yes, it will work right out of the package, but you'll catch more fish if it's razor sharp. Keep in mind this hook has to penetrate about an inch or more of soft plastic

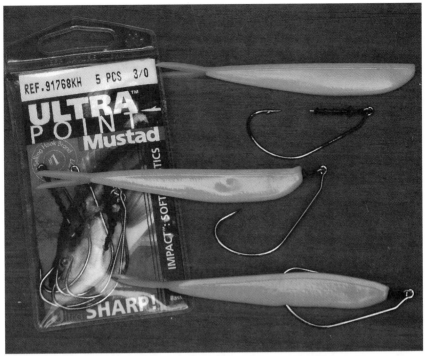

Special keeper-style hooks make rigging a soft bait quick and very easy. Several styles, sizes and shapes are available to choose from.

and also the jaw of the fish as well. Some fish have more bone in their jaws than others, so this has to happen in one quick, hook-setting motion. Any hesitation on your part or a delay in the hook going through all that plastic due to it being dull will most likely result in a missed opportunity. That miss could be the fish of a lifetime. It happened to me countless times before I smartened up and began to sharpen them to a needle point.

A good way to sharpen large hooks is with a slow-speed grinding wheel or Dremel tool with a grinding attachment. A file, like the Red Devil paint scraper file is also good. Once done, finish it off with a fine diamond file or stone to remove any burrs or excess metal filings.

Keeper-Type Hooks

Some hooks come equipped with what is referred to as special "keeper sticks". These can be a heavier piece of wire with ribs, barbs or serrations to grab and hold the plastic in place. Some newer models have clips or a spring wire attached to the top of the hook, (e.g. Shaw Grigsby Eagle Claw model). These hooks allow the soft plastic to move naturally and not be encumbered by the shank of the hook. Only the point of the hook needs to be inside the bait, which actually becomes a keel so the bait rides or swims properly.

Mustad offers a bigmouth tube hook with an extra-wide bite and a keeper-hook so you simply push the bait onto it. Mister Twister has a keeper-hook system that also comes with a weighted hook shank and so does the Gamakatsu Sure Grip Hook. Most of the companies like Mustad, Matzuo, Owner, Eagle Claw, and Tru-Turn offer some style of wide-bite, offset hooks for better hooking ability and penetration. Their biggest advantage is they can be used in a wide variety of fishing situations.

When you have to use a light-wire hook, good-size fish can be landed provided you follow a few simple rules. First, use a light action rod so it bends and flexes and absorbs the shock as a fish runs and fights to get free. That's one reason why anglers can and do land big fish on fly-fishing tackle—the rod acts as a shock absorber during the fight.

Second, use a light pound-test line on your reel. This will prevent you from trying to horse the fish to the boat once it's hooked, which is probably the biggest reason why light-wire hooks straighten out during a fight. Too much pressure applied too quickly to a "green" fish is a recipe for disaster.

Third, remain calm, pay attention, and allow your tackle to do its job. Remaining calm can be a challenge. It takes practice, practice and more practice. Anyone who has ever fished with me will tell you that I am the farthest thing from calm as you can get. I get so excited and pumped that I usually get my clients just as pumped. Some of them laugh themselves silly. It really does take practice to stay cool. The better you become at controlling your emotion, the more fish you are likely to catch.

Seeing Red

Colored hooks are the "in thing" in freshwater fishing today and many guides and pro fishermen claim their catches have gone up considerably since they started using red-colored hooks. The Tru-Turn Company now offers what they are calling the "Bleeding Gills" finishes. Tru-Turn, makers of their now famous 45-degree cam-action bait hooks, have been honored with being selected as the hook of choice in U.S. Navy and Army Ranger survival gear. Their new bright red finish has become the rage in freshwater and is quickly finding its way into the saltwater market as well.

From Daiichi comes the Bleeding Bait hook. After someone lowered some painted jigheads into a bait tank, the minnows in the tank ignored all the top colors but bumped and chewed on the blood-red color jig. Anglers were shown this and asked to try dark-red jigs. The anglers returned the next day to get more because they had used them up catching fish!

Years later, an angler pointed a laser light into a large aquarium. Every fish in the tank followed the little red dot all over like trained dogs. That's when it was decided that hooks needed to be red.

Underwater testing and testing under actual fishing conditions proved that the red color triggered a natural response feeding. The Bleeding Bait phenomenon works in two ways: first, fish are naturally attracted to blood or injury of other fish and second, the gill-flash phenomenon triggers the natural feeding response of the fish. They don't think about it, they respond to it as an opportunity to eat. A fisheries biologist explained it this way: "It works because the gills become engorged with blood as they flare to inhale food. This is known as gill flash. It's a signal from one fish to another that it is time to eat."

If your favorite hook doesn't come in a red finish and you would like to try that option, it's no problem. Get yourself a can of red Krylon spray paint and paint your own. You can also tie some hooks with red flash, or use a red Magic Marker.

We also carry a few weedless sproat-style hooks for fishing in or around heavy grass beds or in rocky areas. If you fish for redfish, seatrout and snook, then you're already aware they spend most of their time in these areas. Having a weedless hook available to get your bait into the cover as well as out of it again is almost a necessity. There are weedless weighted hooks for fishing tube baits, worms and jerkbaits.

When considering smaller hooks, one situation that comes to mind is using a smaller hook when you try tossing the 3-inch jerkbait during a cinder worm hatch. You need to match the hook to the smaller size bait so it maintains a lifelike action. I use a #1 or #2 bend-back style long shank hook as it fits this size bait perfectly and lies perfectly straight when rigged. To my knowledge, the bend-back hooks are not available anymore, but they are easily made by bending a hook in a vise at your workbench.

Circle Hooks

I've experimented with circle hooks and personally I've had mixed results. To be honest, I'm not a big circle hook fan because I still want to strike and set the hook as I have since I've been old enough to walk. I guess you could call it more of a habit than anything else. I just can't get used to just standing there and reeling in the line tight. It just doesn't seem like fishing to me for some reason. Call me stupid.

This is not to say that circle hooks don't, or won't, work on soft-plastic lures. I'm sure that someone will find a use for them if they haven't already. I'm too old, too spoiled and still get too excited when I get a strike. I like to set the hook, and to stop what has become a natural reaction at this stage of the game is just not possible.

I prefer to "cross his eyes" as the old fishing tackle ad said. To just let my clients stand there and reel in—well, duh!—it's not very exciting. The strike, in my opinion, is the essence of fishing. Give me the excitement!

I tried it with my grandson last season while taking him scup fishing. I broke down and tied on a couple of small circle hooks and said to him, "Now listen DJ, just reel in when you feel the line going tight." He stood there and stood there, lost in his young world trying to figure out what I wanted him to do. I finally said, "Reel up, we are going to change those hooks." I quickly tied on my usual scup hooks, baited them up and sent them back to the bottom. Immediately his rod tip began bouncing as the scup picked at the bait. I showed him by using my rod the proper way to set a hook. His young eyes focused on me with all the intensity a youngster has for his grandfather. When the fish hit again, he turned, swept his rod upward with all the strength a 4-year-old could muster. The rod flew over his head and into the water. Now THAT is how you set a hook!

Beak/Octopus Style

Beak hooks, and the similar Octopus-style hooks, work great when employing the new drop-shot technique that is so popular on the professional bass circuit. These hooks are also effective in saltwater situations as well. Even though the hooks are somewhat smaller than you would usually use, you can still hook and land some

Circle hooks always catch the corner of the mouth which minimizes harm to the fish and affords a quick, healthy release.

big fish with them. We'll talk some more about these hooks later in the book when we talk about the drop-shotting technique.

Extra Pounds—Selecting Weights

Not all plastic fishing is done with jigheads or hooks alone. There are many fishing opportunities that will require a good assortment of different weights. The ability to add, change or subtract weight makes fishing with soft-plastic lures much more effective.

Adding weight makes it possible to cast farther, dive deeper, alter the lure's usual action or movement, and sometimes improve upon the lure's presentation. You can easily add weight for distance, depth and action change on large baits, such as the 9-inch Slug-Go and the 10-inch Fin-S Fish, the huge shad bodies or tube bodies like Lindy's Tora tube.

There are several ways to add weights. Let's take a look at the most popular weight systems.

NAIL WEIGHTS: Lunker City Lure specialists developed a unique weighting system that can best be described as a "fancy finishing nail." This is a truly unique idea that uses lead sticks or nails that have built-in ribs along their entire length so the bait won't slide free from the soft plastic. Where the weight is placed in the bait—head, middle, tail, top or bottom—results in a change of action as the lure moves through the water.

For example, inserting a nail weight in the bait's tail section causes the lure to sink tail first as it falls. By inserting one or more weights in the head section, the bait will sink headfirst as if it's dying. By placing two or more in the center of the lure, you can have it sink slowly and evenly down towards the bottom, slightly bent in half. Just be careful not to overweight the lure and kill its action entirely. Be sure you have done it correctly after rigging it by dropping it in the water to visually check the action.

The nail weights come in three or four different sizes, and are made of a soft lead-like material that can easily be trimmed or cut with cutters or pliers after they have been inserted into the body. This makes a neat looking appearance when finished. The weights stack nicely inside plastic film canisters and the tops can be marked for quick reference as to what size each contains.

The smaller size inserts work in the small 6-inch Slug-Go, Zoom Fluke, Power Shads, Bass Assassins, Lindy's Shadlyn, and grub tails and twister tails.

BULLET WEIGHTS: Another crossover from the freshwater bass scene is the traditional worm fishing bullet weight. Bullet weights today are available for use with soft plastics in an amazing variety of styles and compounds, including brass, tungsten, lead and new high-tech alloys. Some of these weights have a Mylar, nylon or synthetic core to them so the line doesn't get cut or frayed from the constant casting and retrieving motion of a long day on the water.

Others have a ribbed neck extension so they grab and hold the bait securely. Still others have a twist-on wire corkscrew built in, so the bait is twisted to the weight. Still others have built-in rattle chambers that emit a high-pitched clicking sound. All these weights are sold in a wide variety of colors.

The bullet weights that slide up and down the line are used in the Carolina rigging and Texas rigging methods. Both these techniques can be highly effective when fishing beaches or shallow sand flats. The bullet weight can be pegged with toothpicks or rubber bands to hold it in place when casting and fishing the bottom. Rubber bands can be pushed inside the head of the weight and won't fray or cut the line. They also allow for quick adjustments from one point on the line to another.

SHAFT WEIGHTS: Lunker City Lures and D.O.A. Lures offer weights that are squeezed onto the hook shank. The Lunker City weight has a molded-in hole that accepts the hook point and shaft. On the opposite end is a small neck with a rubber stopper attached to it. This secures the weight in place so it doesn't move around when casting. The weight doesn't interfere with the casting motion, hooking, playing or landing of fish. The system is true simplicity. These weights work best on the newer style of wide-gap hooks.

The D.O.A. Lures shank weights are pinched directly onto the hook shank and are segmented so the angler can break off a small piece to add just a small amount of weight or as much as is needed.

STICKY WEIGHTS: This product is available from Lead Masters and is 99-percent lead-free in keeping with state laws banning the use of any lead, (as in the state of California, where Sticky Weights are manufactured). If lost in the water, Sticky Weights will totally

Choosing the right sinker or weight allows the fisherman to get plastic baits to run shallow or deep. There is a wide assortment to choose from.

dissolve within 18 to 24 months, so they are environmentally friendly.

This paste-like substance is very similar to Silly Putty. It can be molded on either the hook shank, onto the line, to the lure itself or inside the hollow body cavity of a tube bait. It is made from tungsten and is very handy to use, especially when you need just a small amount of weight. The tungsten compound is 30-percent heavier than lead. It's snagless when going through obstructions and is easily re-useable. It comes in 1-ounce plastic tubs with snap-on lids.

To use it, simply apply the sticky substance to a clean, dry, surface. Roll it between your fingers and apply pressure to mold it to the line, lure or jighead. Since it's soft, you can remove it from the line, lure or jighead and place it in a small Ziploc bag to re-use it later.

RUBBER-CORE and EGG SINKERS: When you need to get down deep, say 20 to 25 feet or more, rubber-core or egg sinkers are the best choice. I like the rubber-core sinker because it's so easy to place on the line, and can be removed without nicking the line. Once I figure out how much weight I need for a particular fishing situation, I switch to the egg sinker.

Rubber-core sinkers won't damage your line or leader as long as you attach them properly. Simply grab one end of the rubber insert; pull on it while sliding your line inside, then simply twist both ends at the same time. They come in sizes from 1/4 ounce to 3 ounces. Use them when trying to get a big shad body or that giant tube bait down to deep structure. Rubber-core sinkers work well with any type of plastic lure that you would use to fish deep-water rock piles, reefs, wrecks, channels or deep water points. It's a good idea to always carry at least a few rubber-core or egg sinkers in your tackle bag.

SPLIT SHOTS: Split shots are useful for making slight weight adjustments to your lure while fishing. They can be added to the line or pinched directly to a hook shank. Placing it on the line ahead of a 4 to 6-inch soft plastic will cause the plastic to rise above the split shot as it sinks to the bottom giving a very slow-falling presentation. This is excellent for fishing flats, around rocks or beaches, or when you want your lure to be off the bottom, but you don't need a lot of weight to get it down. For the slowest possible fall sink rate, try a large soft-plastic bait with a small spit shot.

SNAGLESS WEIGHTS: Here's another freshwater sinker easily adaptable to the salt. While researching this book, I was amazed to find so many different magazine articles that made reference to this technique. Snagless weights usually have an elongated shape and usually are made of lead with a slight bend in the center. Sometimes a snagless weight is encased in a rubber or plastic tubing material like the Lindy Snagless System; other times it is left bare or coated with a painted finish. Snagless weights glide over, through and in between bottom obstructions like rocks, grass, trees, branches, stumps, clam beds and gravel areas.

The new Rattlin' No-Snag slip sinker is virtually snag-free. This weight pivots and shakes itself loose from rocks, weeds and brush. The inside of the weight has built-in brass rattle chambers. This is great for drifting tubes, plastic squids, grubs tails, big plastic worms and mid-size shad bodies.

LEAD SOLDER: Soldering wire can be used to add weight to a hook shank, and has the advantage of being inexpensive and pack-aged in convenient spools at every hardware store in America. Be sure to get resin-free solder, and if you want to be environmentally friendly, get the solder that plumbers use for drinking-water piping, which is 95-percent lead free.

WEIGHTED HOOKS: There is a wide variety of pre-weighted hooks now on tackle dealer displays. Not only does this provide necessary weight for casting a very light soft plastic farther; it also gives the lure a keel to ride on to keep the bait in an upright position.

Companies like Tru-Turn with their Bleeding Bait series, Eagle Claw, Mister Twister, Mustad, Owner, Gamakatsu, Bass Pro Shops and others, all offer an excellent line of weighted hooks. Some are made so the weight becomes imbedded inside the plastic (as with a tube bait), which makes the weighted bait almost snag-free.

DROP-SHOT WEIGHTS: These specialty weights were designed for what is now referred to as "finesse fishing" in freshwater circles. The technique is sweeping the country's freshwater tournament circuit in a big way. Originally brought to this country from Japan, it only took a few big tournament wins before everyone started to jump on the bandwagon. For saltwater purposes, the weights can be obtained from sizes ranging from 1/8 ounce to 1/2-ounce. Drop-shot-ting works for summer flounder, weakfish and striped bass.

The weights come in a wide array of styles and shapes to fit specific fishing conditions. Anglers use diamond shape, teardrop, elongated, bell style, round and a pyramid version to fish different bottom structure. There is also a weedless version available from the Mojo Lure Company of California. This weight has a wire that sticks out the bottom to help the sinker move over and around snags as you reel in the line.

MORE WEIGHTS: There is no doubt there are many more sinkers available on the market for use with soft-plastic lures. There are egg-style river sinkers, bead chain trolling sinkers, keel sinkers, and probably a few more I couldn't find, but which might be popular locally in some parts of the coast.

All of these sinkers and weights are useful at different times and under different conditions. Many have probably never been used before in saltwater for any particular purpose. We'll leave those for all of you who dream of coming up with a new hot rig. That opportunity always exists when you begin fishing with soft plastics.

The Eyes Have It

Experience has taught me if you show a fish a lure that catches its interest with an extra dip, dart or dive, contrasting color, or an eye to focus on, you'll trigger a strike from that fish. As a professional guide, I depend on this theory, and it has worked for me for many years.

It has long been an accepted fact that predatory fish key in on their prey by focusing on the eyes of the target. When you look at most baitfish in the ocean, you will notice a large, prominent eye in almost all species from the smallest to the largest. Some species even have fake eyes or "deception eyes" as I call them. Menhaden or bunker are ones that have an extra spot or dot just in back of their gill and towards the top of the body. It is believed that when predators focus on this, they tend to miss or be off target. It's nature's way of providing baitfish species with a little bit of protection.

Fly fishers have known this for a long time, and the most productive flies have a bold eye tied in, or glued, to the pattern. Some of the plastic-bait manufacturers now offer their lures with eyes that are glued on or molded right into the bait itself. Just a few are the Striper Magnet by Bill Hurley, the Button Eye Minnow from Creme Lures, and the Livin' Shad from Storm.

There are some lures that do not have eyes, but you can add them. There are many different types and styles of eyes available today for use on plastic baits. They range from the simple stick-on type eyes used in fly tying to more elaborate 3-D models. They come in many shapes, styles, and color combinations to fit a wide variety of fishing conditions.

Stick-on eyes are sold on sheets of glued or sticky paper. Peel off the backing and stick them on. It's that simple. However, on plastic lures, you should hit the back of most of them with a shot of Super Glue to hold better. A good source for stick-on eyes is Jann's Netcraft, out of Maumee, Ohio. For a catalog call 1-800-NETCRAFT. They carry eyes that are reasonable in price and offered in three or four different sizes and colors. They stick on well right off the sheet.

Today, plastic eyes are available in 3-D, holographic finish and Doll Eye types, some of which also have a built-in rattle. Large eyes help make the head of the bait stand out as a target for stripers, bluefish or other gamefish. Doll Eyes are best applied to baits of 6 inches or more. They should be glued on, and are available in bulk at most craft shops and at some fly-fishing shops.

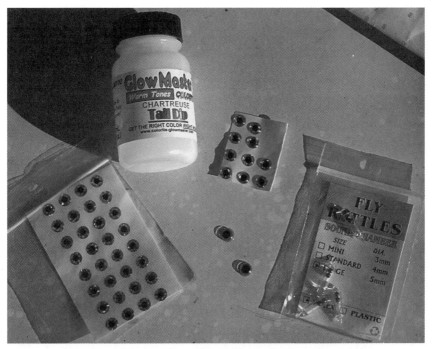

Adding eyes to the plastic bait can increase its fish-catching ability. Many styles and colors are available. A dab of Super Glue will keep them in place.

The 3-D and holographic eyes are good for small to medium-size soft plastics. The best time to add eyes to your lures is when you are at home and have the time to do it right. Over the winter, I get as many soft-plastic baits ready as I can for the coming season. It saves time and aggravation on the water.

Other types of eyes are the screw-in type available from Cabela's and Bass Pro Shops. These are usually a plastic doll-type eye ranging from 3 to 10-millimeter, and come in red, yellow and orange. A wire has been attached to the back. All you do is twist the eye in and it stays in place. These are great on a 9-inch Slug-Go, Fin-S Fish and large shad bodies. The advantage to these eyes is they can be used over and over again, even after the soft plastic is ripped or torn. The eyes just screw out and pop back into another bait.

Bead chain is an overlooked item for eyes. It's available in most hardware stores, home improvement stores and most fly shops. It is usually sold in lengths of 2 to 3 feet, in silver or gold finish, but you can make it any color you prefer by dipping it in jig paint or spraying it with Krylon rust preventative paint that dries immediately. Now you can have eyes of any color.

These bead chain eyes work best on the small-size baits such as 6-inch stick baits, 3 to 5-inch shad bodies, tube baits and even some worms. All you do is purchase a length of chain, paint it or use it as is and cut off two to three eyes at a time so it looks like the following: "o-o-o" or "o-o." Whether to use three or two beads depends upon the thickness of the soft-plastic bait. I like to cut as many as possible with three beads so the middle beads hold the eye in place when casting.

To place them in the lure, use a rigging needle or a long, thin piece of wire. Punch a hole in the plastic bait so the bead chain will fit inside. Push the beads into the hole and pull until it's centered in the bait. It's that easy.

Lead or brass eyes, like the type used by fly tiers to make Clouser minnows, serve as both an eye and a weight. Tie the eye on the hook shank with fly tying or jig thread to hold it in place. Once the eyes are in place, you can add red flash to resemble a throat. Tie the throat in back of the hook's eye and in front of the lead eye. Use the largest size eyes, which weigh in at around 1/8 ounce. They are available unpainted or in red, white and yellow with black pupils. Most fly shops sell them. These eyes are great for fishing 7 to 10-inch rubber worms in shallow water. There is just enough weight to get the worm to the bottom, and you still have the ability to jig the worm with the weight of the dumbbell eyes.

You can add stick-on eyes to these as well, but you will have to file down the outside edge of the dumbbell. File it flat, then add a bit of Super Glue and stick on the eyes.

Marking Pens

Waterproof marking pens are a handy way to add gills to the sides of shad bodies, eyes to the head, and stripes and two-tone color schemes to the body and more. All you need is some imagination.

Select colors that will add contrast to the plastic bait that you are using. I keep red, black, olive green and yellow on the boat at all times, and there have been many occasions when they come in handy. Sometimes, adding that one extra touch means more fish.

Noise And Sound

Noise and sound is one thing that few fishermen pay much attention to when fishing. You'll hear guys yelling back and forth to

Sound travels quickly, and far, in water. Adding a small rattle to the plastic body increases the lure's effectiveness.

101

one another, tackle and bait containers banging the deck, sinkers falling on the deck and lures plunking down on the deck. All this is unnoticed—except by the fish. They've been listening to everything. When you are talking, yelling, singing, dropping things, stomping and so forth, the fish are hearing it all. In fact, hearing plays an essential role in both the fish's survival and feeding habits.

The better you understand how fish relate to this external force, the more successful you will be. The ears of a fish are found inside its head on either side beneath the skin and bone. Sound passes right through to the ear itself. Some fish increase this sounding effect by using their swim bladder to amplify sound. Besides their ears, known as otoliths, fish have a lateral line capable of picking up low-frequency sounds to help them pinpoint the source. This is why a striper or bluefish can find an eel in total darkness and swallow it in one bite even on the blackest of nights. There aren't many fish that won't scoot off to safety and as far away as possible from strange and foreign sounds.

How easily, quickly and loudly it travels became even more evident to me after filming one day with my good friend Captain Joe Pagano of the charter boat "Stuff-It". On this particular day, we were coming in from fishing off the Narragansett shoreline when we ran into a massive school of baby bunker in the channel entrance to the harbor. We figured we would get some good baitfish shots, so we lowered our waterproof camera down about 2 or 3 feet below the surface and began to film. As we went along, I kept the camera as far beneath the surface as possible. Just then, while shooting, a second boat approached our position about 60 to 70 feet off our stern. The boat's captain yelled over to us, "Hey, what kind of fish are these below?" Joe answered, "Baby bunker", and I continued to film the massive school beneath us.

When we got home and replayed the tape to see how much useable footage we got, we were amazed to learn that we could hear every word on the tape as clear as a bell from the guy in the other boat who was over 75 feet away. Now remember, that's 75 feet away and 2 or 3 feet below the water surface. Just imagine how that sounded to a 20-pound striped bass feeding in that same water.

The day we filmed, the water was over 20-feet deep in the channel and there was a very swift current running into the harbor. It doesn't take a lot to figure out how far and how fast noise of any type is going to travel in shallow water. Keep in mind that sound travels through water five times faster than it does through air. This translates into about one mile per second.

When I'm standing on my poling platform all day, it affords me one of the best teaching mechanisms I've ever had. Observing how fish react to my talking clients, sudden movements, baitfish swimming by, current, boat sounds and noise from nearby boats has been a tremendous learning experience, and has caused me to change the way I fish in all water depths. I use to maneuver very slowly using the main engine, but not any longer. I'll use my electric trolling motor or push pole, or anchor up, depending on the prevailing conditions.

When conditions are right, I'll pole. I can move silently and quickly, making as little noise as possible. I can even get close to finicky fish when I take my time. If the wind blows too hard and poling becomes a problem, I'll turn on the electric motor. That doesn't mean you have total stealth by any means. I've turned on the electric motor and seen fish scatter so quickly your head would spin. The fish hear that low electric pulse and hum, and they respond by moving quickly out of the area.

Fish can also be inquisitive about sounds. Ever notice when you have one fish on, other fish are attracted by the thrashing and they instinctively react to feed and investigate? That's why many fishermen like to add some sound to their lures.

Plastic worm rattles add sound to the lure and in many instances, this can be critical to catching fish, especially those that have been hammered by boat traffic and angling pressure. I add rattles to many saltwater fly patterns, so it was only natural that I also began adding rattles to plastic baits. I believe they give me an extra edge in my fishing, and I am firmly convinced they do make a difference. Rattles have been used in freshwater B.A.S.S. tournaments for decades and have won millions of dollars for pro anglers. Saltwater anglers need to start paying attention to what is happening in other fisheries and cash in on their success.

Rattles have been refined to amazing levels. They now come in bullet weights with the rattle built-in. They come as clip-ons, trailers and harnesses. By adding rattles to your baits, especially when the water is dirty, roiled, silted, muddy or rough, you increase the effectiveness of that bait significantly. Fish use all their senses to find food in the wild: smell, sight, taste and their ability to pick up vibrations through their lateral line.

Plastic Extractor

An added perk from doing this book is all the additional "stuff" I discovered. The plastic extractor is one such item. It was a problem to get plastic worm rattles inside large plastic baits, such as a 10-inch shad body. A company out west devised the simplest tool I have ever seen to overcome this problem, and it works like magic. Available in small and large sizes, the extractor is a piece of copper tubing with a red plastic top. To use it, simply insert the tube into the soft-plastic bait that you are going to use and then pull it back out. Voila! Out comes a small plastic piece, leaving a small, perfect hole for a rattle to slide into.

Before you say, "Hey, I can easily make one of those tools myself," keep in mind that the extractor costs less than two bucks. By the time you buy the tubing, cut it, and make the top (not counting your time) you've more than surpassed the price of the gadget in the first place. They are available from Bass Pro Shops.

Waterproof Dye

Special dyes can add color and scent to plastic baits. Having a selection of dyes onboard your boat or buggy allows you to fine-tune a lure to the conditions on any given fishing day. For example, a 6 to 9-inch white shad body can have a chartreuse, green or pink tail in a matter of seconds with a quick dip into the dye jar. When the water is muddy or roiled after a storm, that extra bit of color contrast can make all the difference in the world.

Not only do the dyes change the color of the bait instantly; they dry faster than you can blink an eye, unlike older dyes that took about a minute to dry. The new generation dyes dry in less than two seconds and don't drip at all, so you needn't worry about staining your boat or vehicle.

Plastic Glue

For a long time, there really wasn't much you could do after your soft-plastic bait got ripped or torn. About the only choice you had was to toss it away and hook up a new one. Today, there is a whole generation of new glues that help mend torn plastic.

There are several glues favored by guides, captains and local pro fishermen. They include Pro's Soft-Bait Glue, Zap-A-Gap, Fishin' Glue, Thick CA Built-It, Miracle Glue, Bait Stick Glue and Pro CA Glue. They are in the cyanoacrylic glue family and will repair old-plastic baits to like-new fishing condition. One word of caution, do not get this on your fingers—you can literally glue yourself together! Acetone will remove any access glue or "unglue" stuck fingers.

Glue also aids in making rigs, keeping large baits on hooks, holding lures in place, and a wide range of fix-up projects. It is a very handy item to have and will save you money in the long run. If you catch even one more fish on a torn piece of plastic, you are ahead of the game. Obviously, it's not going to be of much use when fishing for bluefish, barracuda or other gamefish with sharp teeth, but it will help with most others.

Try Toothpicks

Simple, inexpensive, yet very useful, toothpicks have been used by bass anglers to peg slip sinkers when rigging. Toothpicks are useful to saltwater anglers as well. You just need to look for their niche.

Very large baits tend to slide down the hook shank once the head of the bait gets torn or ripped. A toothpick will help anchor the bait so it doesn't slide. Push the plastic bait toward the hook eye (the hook is already attached to the fishing line) insert the toothpick through the plastic and through the eye of the hook. Use a pair of cutters to snip off both ends of the toothpick. The plastic bait will stay in place for a few more casts, and hopefully another fish or two.

You can also use a toothpick to peg a Carolina rig, Texas rig or other rig you are going to find in the upcoming pages of this book. Only lack of imagination will prevent you from finding further uses for these small pieces of wood. And if the fish aren't biting that day, you can always use them to clean your teeth after lunch.

The Popper Option

One of the things I enjoy about guiding is that you are always learn-ing something new and different, either on your own by fishing every day, or from customers who are really into their sport. A client from Virginia introduced this next add-on to me. He learned it from a guide in Tennessee while fishing for landlocked stripers.

At our first fishing location he asked me if I minded if he started with a rig he'd had a lot of success with. Naturally I answered, "Not at all, I don't mind a bit." He proceeded to tie on a white foam popper with a 5-1/2-inch Fin-S Fish behind it. As you can guess, I asked him what in the world was that rig? He said he called it his "Pop-Fish" and said, "Just watch." He tossed it out up against the grass line and started popping it back towards the boat. After 6 feet or so, the water exploded, and a 14-pound striper engulfed the rig in no time. Since that day, I have similar rigs tied and ready to go on my boat on each charter.

You can turn a Zoom Fluke, Bass Assassin, Slug-Go, Fin-S Fish, Power Bait, or tube lure (to name a few) into a floating, popping, teasing, dancing, top-water bait just by placing a piece of foam or cork in front of the bait. It's that simple.

By adding a fly-rod popper or wine-bottle cork or piece of foam from a lobster buoy in front of the soft plastic, you can create a bait with an entirely new dimension to it. You really have to witness firsthand how one of these soft plastics reacts when it's popped across the water surface. Once you toss one out and retrieve it, you immediately notice how it flips, flops, twists and jumps like no other popper you have ever seen. It has an action that no hard-bait popper I've ever seen can duplicate.

Fly-rod popper heads come in many different sizes and shapes, and are very buoyant. Most of these foam poppers already have a hole down the center to accept a hook or your line. If they don't, just use a long rigging needle or something with a sharp point to penetrate the foam and make a hole.

When purchasing fly-rod poppers, make sure you don't buy the ones with the slit on the bottom of the body where a hook usually goes. I found that once they are drilled, they don't float very straight and tend to turn over and not ride correctly.

After threading the popper head onto your line or leader, you may notice that it slips too much or moves a lot. Eliminate this by using a heavier leader with a larger diameter, or peg it with a toothpick.

If you choose to use wine corks or corks purchased from the hardware store you can spray paint them or use a stick-on tape material sold at fly shops for making fly rod poppers. Just cut the tape to size and stick it on. Sand the cork first to make it smooth so

If you aren't using soft baits as top-water lures, you're missing out. Simply slide a popper head, or a D.O.A. Chug Head in place and you're ready for topwater action.

the tape sticks better. A Dremel tool can be used to scoop out the face so it pops more.

Most of the soft plastics described above (or something similar), have hooks hidden in the body of the bait, making them weedless. Once you add the popper head, you have a popper that can be tossed into rocks, grass beds, inside pilings, close to docks, piers, next to bridge abutments and almost anyplace you can think of, without fear of hanging up. Since your hook is totally hidden inside the bait, the chances of hang-ups are very slim.

Poppers work best on calm days when there is little or no wind or just a slight chop on the surface of the water. Early morning or late evening as the sun goes down are excellent times on flats, at the mouths of rivers and creeks and inside estuaries. The strikes are explosive like nothing you have ever seen. Popping plastic will work for you as well. All you need to do is try it.

Trolling Rigs

Most soft-plastic baits can be draped onto a spoon for added flash and action while trolling, and casting, too. Trolling a small Tony Accetta Pet Spoon, Drone or Clark Squid Spoon with a plastic bait creates an astounding lure action. Lots of flash can also be delivered with a willow leaf trolling spinner rigged ahead of the plastic. I've also removed the treble hooks from 1-ounce Fiord Spoons and Little Cleo's, added a short length of wire and a 3/0 Salmon Siwash hook, and then placed a twister tale, shad or worm in place and have taken striped bass, bluefish, weakfish, fluke, sea bass, scup (porgy) bonito, albacore and several southern species as well. All the rigs work and are relatively simple to use with a bit of practice.

Making Scents

Striper anglers are right up at the top when it comes to innovation and imagination. No doubt, it is the same down south with anglers who pursue tarpon, bonefish, redfish and snook. The one thing everyone is looking for is an edge in getting the fish to bite.

When I first started guiding, I just grabbed a bag of plastic baits, ripped it open, put the lure on a jighead or hook, and started fishing. In this guide business you need to keep your wits about you. You must constantly be focused on what is going on, and why or why not the fish are cooperating.

Watching the plastic baits in the water, it didn't take long to notice that we'd have a lot of close follows right up to the boat, followed by fish refusing to eat the artificial. We then began to question the reasons why. The first thing we noticed was it happened more with new baits right out of the package than it did with baits that had been on the boat awhile. Why? One very calm evening, I was getting some brand-new baits ready, but as I tore the package open, I immediately noticed a very powerful smell of plastic. I wondered, "If I could smell these things, how much of a smell are the fish picking up?"

For years it has been an accepted fact that scents make a difference when added to almost any lure. One thing's for sure. It can't hurt. Scents not only mask unwanted odors but will also hide our own body scent as well. And, of course, they also can attract fish.

Some lures come with their own scents already built-in, like the Berkley Power Bait series. When you open one of those bags, you can be sure the fish isn't going to smell too much of anything else. It stinks—and that's why they catch fish! Today, every new lure that I take from the package gets rubbed, dipped, sprayed or wiped with some sort of scent to make it more fishable. I've tested the theory with clients and the results to date have been very impressive indeed. The scent-covered soft plastics usually out-fish the non-scent baits by a very wide margin.

The scents I use frequently are from Smelly Jelly, Jack's Juice and Atlas Mike's, but there are many more scent companies on the market. They produce scents in herring, menhaden, squid, shrimp, eel and crab in liquid form. There are also some in paste form like Uncle Josh, Berkley and Smelly Jelly.

The best scents are those that usually match the local bait. If the predominate bait forage in a particular area is brine shrimp, then using a shrimp scent is better than using a crab or herring scent. When I'm fishing at night, I like the eel scent which helps the fish locate the plastic (with the exception of the Power Eel that is already scented) and zoom in on it in total darkness.

A shrimp scent works great on tube lures, plastic shrimp and the small stick-type baits that are 3 or so inches in length. Weakfish like these lures and will feed heavily on shrimp, especially during the early part of the spring and early summer.

Remember that, at the very least, using some sort of scent to mask any unwanted plastic odor or human odor can only help. You will also

Adding color is only a quick dip away. Customizing soft baits with colors can add a few extra fish to the day's catch.

find yourself fishing these lures with more confidence than ever before, and that translates into more fish in the boat or on the beach.

Spin-N-Glow And Lil-Corkers

These flashy items have their roots in the salmon and steelhead fisheries of the Great Lakes and Pacific Northwest. In recent years, they have found their way into saltwater angling situations from New England to the mid-Atlantic and into Florida. In my local area, they have become popular for attracting fluke. Many fluke fishermen place one in front of a plastic squid used as a dropper above the jig. The motion of the boat while drifting causes the foam ball to spin around, thus the name Spin-N-Glow.

Luhr-Jensen manufactures the Spin-N-Glow with small wing-like propellers which send out flashes and vibrations that fish key-in on. The Lil-Corker has shorter wings that are built right into its body, and does not spin as violently in the water. Both items are excellent attractors in front of plastic squid when fluking or in front of a jig and plastic bait when fishing for seatrout or weakfish.

Silicone Skirts

Small silicone or nylon skirts add a lot of extra motion and color when draped over a jighead. This technique is especially productive when fishing a jig-and-worm combination. The skirts come in many different solid colors and color combinations, but I stick with white, pearl, yellow, black, watermelon and pink. When added to the collar of a jig dressed with a long plastic worm, the combo can't be beat. In the water, those skirts come to life like nothing you have ever seen.

Plastic Beads And Cotton Balls

Plastic beads are often used when tying bottom rigs such as the Carolina and Texas worm rigs. These keep the bullet weight from wearing at the knot to the hook, preventing line failure. They come in many sizes and colors, but size #6 in red or yellow is all that you will need. Plastic beads can also be used as a spacing tool to keep hooks and weights away from one another, or to lengthen the area between a hook and the bait.

Cotton balls soaked in fish scent can be used to place the scent inside a hollow plastic lure such as tube rigs. They come in very small sizes, on up to 6 and 8-inch jumbo sizes, and they simulate a squid very realistically.

Split Rings

These small items can add a new dimension to your lures by attaching them to the heads of swivels or the eyes of jigs and hooks. It gives you a good place to attach your line and will allow barrel swivels to work properly. They have many different uses. To get them on and to take them off, you will need a good pair of split-ring pliers. These are specialty pliers with a hooknose on one end and another from below. There are different size pliers for different size rings, so either buy two or make sure you purchase the one size that you will use the most.

A purple worm and a white bucktail fooled this hefty weakfish. Worms and leadheads are a traditional soft-plastic bait that continue to catch big fish.

CHAPTER FIVE

RUBBER WORM REVOLUTION

Rubber worms have probably accounted for more freshwater largemouth bass than almost any other lure ever invented. The book *Bait Tail Fishing*, by the late Al Reinfelder of Alou Eel fame, discusses freshwater plastic worms in 1969 and how well they work for striped bass, weakfish and many other saltwater species. Reinfelder was a pioneer in the early use of plastic baits in saltwater, and developed many techniques that are still in use today.

For many years, former editor of the New England edition of *The Fisherman* magazine, Tim Coleman, wrote article after article detailing the effectiveness of soft-plastic worms to catch striped bass along the beaches and the rocky coast of New England. Even after he displayed some very impressive catches he and his friends had made on their outings, it was still a rarity to see many anglers using rubber worms to tempt stripers. Whether you fish from a boat or from the beach, you just don't find many anglers tossing 9, 10 or 12-inch rubber worms up against the shoreline for stripers.

This is unfortunate because soft-plastic rubber worms are just as effective in saltwater as they are in freshwater. Although they can be effective during daylight hours, worms really come into their own right after the sun goes down and things get quiet.

The best places to fool fish will be found around rocks, ledges, drop-offs, and channels. Worms will even take fish on shallow-water sand flats, especially when a ribbon worm hatch is occurring. These worms are anywhere from 8 to 18 or 20 inches, and come out of the mud for short periods of time in the late spring and early summer, though few anglers pay any attention to it or even see it happening. When it does, using 10 or 12-inch rubber worms is a deadly way to catch a lot of

113

fish. No self-respecting striper is going to let an opaque white worm float around near the surface for too long without striking.

When you are fishing a worm during the night, the belief is that you are probably imitating the small eels, lobsters, crabs and other baitfish that come out of hiding under the cover of darkness. I'd have to guess that it most likely appears as a small eel to most bass.

There are so many types, styles and colors of plastic worms available, you really need to pick just a few and try them. That is another nice thing about plastic lures. They are inexpensive to buy and use so you can change from one to another and not go broke. When you find a good size and color, you can stock up and still put some money back in your pocket.

Many Shapes, Many Colors

Worms are molded with straight tails, curly tails, ribbon tails, split tails and flat tails. The ribbon tail and Mister Twister-type tail give off the most vibration and the most action in the water, but sometimes just a plain old flat-tail worm will out-produce all other types combined. Besides tail shapes, worms also come in several body designs from smooth to rippled, to jointed, to sandworm-like shapes with tiny "legs" along the sides.

Color selecting is an important question when choosing a lure. The "problem" with plastic worms is they are manufactured in such a huge array of many different colors and combinations that it's sometimes mind-boggling deciding which one to use.

When selecting worm color we've found that the most productive colors over the long haul have been black, red shad, June bug, watermelon and green. If you have a few of these colors with you, chances are you will find some fish that will eat them.

I would suggest the choice be kept as simple and easy as possible. I probably have over 200 different colors of worms in my basement, but I still only use five or six primary worm colors on a regular basis. If I were just beginning to build a worm collection I'd stick with the basics and then add other colors one or two at a time. That way I can weed out what does and does not work for the areas I fish. The most effective colors will actually be "chosen" by the fish because they will either hit the worm frequently or ignore it. Not all colors work in all areas, on all species, at all times.

A fat striped bass that fell for a well-rigged "rubber worm". Freshwater rigging works just as well in the salt chuck.

Let's start with basic black because it works almost anywhere at any time. Black is a universal color that will work at night as well as during the day. On the opposite color spectrum, white is also an excellent color, but hard to find in worms in many areas. Among the most popular is the Senko white/pearl worms made by Gary Yamamoto, which are extremely effective for striped bass.

Red Shad is a red and black, two-tone color that is a favorite up and down the coast. Green watermelon is good in many situations, especially when fishing shallow water of 15 feet or less. Strawberry red and grape purple Jelly Worms have been working on striped bass and weakfish for over 30 years and still continue to produce fish. Strawberry Jelly Worms are good trailers in off-colored water on the backs of tube lures if you run out of real worms to use as trailers.

Bubblegum (pink) worms work great during the worm hatch in the Northeast in small sizes, and in the larger sizes when the squid are running in the early spring and again in the fall. Weakfish or squeteague also place bubblegum-colored worms and other plastics high on their choice of food. With those basic colors, you will not have any trouble catching almost anything that swims from north to south.

115

In North Carolina, the root beer color is a favorite for seatrout, while metal-flake red with a white tail is a good choice for redfish.

Fluorescent colors such as chartreuse will also work. No one knows exactly why, as there isn't anything in saltwater that is fluorescent in coloration, but they do work. Fluorescent green (lime or chartreuse) is a great color in stained or off-color water. Summer flounder seem to like the hot pinks and greens a lot, probably because they are so visible in deep water where other colors tend to wash out as they get deeper in the water column. These colors are also popular for codfish, pollock, haddock and hake. Worms in these colors are used as teasers above a heavy jig or bait rig and many times account for more fish than the bait does.

Other colors should be added to your collection as needed and depending upon where you fish and what you target. There are so many choices you could spend an entire season testing them out— but half the fun of fishing is finding new and different lures to use.

Leadhead Jig

One of the simplest ways to rig a worm is to slip it onto a leadhead or a bucktail. A bucktail will have built-on color to the head and added action because of the bucktail hair, nylon hair or feathers, depending on how it's manufactured. Many fishermen today use a simple leadhead, painted or unpainted, with a collar molded around the hook shank so it will grab hold of the worm to avoid slippage. The leadhead can be shaped like a bullet or ball or have any of several shapes that help it to dance seductively. The head shape will help the lure sink quickly, or run shallow over a sand flat. The Kalin jig, Rip Tide, Cotee and Lunker City jigs are fine examples of head shapes that work well.

In the early 1970s, the white bucktail/purple worm combination was the hot item for Delaware Bay weakfish. This was a time when vertically jigging a worm and bucktail lure so it bounced along the bottom was a sure bet to catch fish in excess of 10 pounds. Tackle shops displayed bucktails by the hundreds and worms were sold by the bagful from jars where you reached in your hand and grabbed a big fistful of plastic baits. Some tackle shops sold worms in small cardboard deli salad containers.

Wherever you fish bucktail and worm combos, the depth of the water you fish will determine the weight and the size of the jighead you need. Once you choose the size of the jig, it's a good idea to add a few drops of Krazy Glue, Super Glue or Lunker City plastic glue

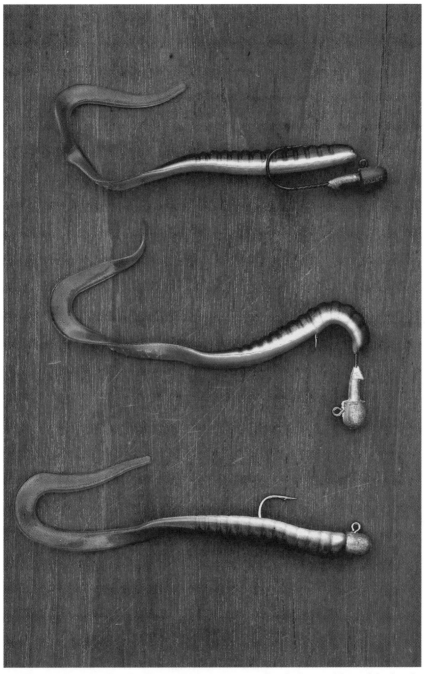

Lay the leadhead or bucktail next to the worm to check the position of the hook. Insert the hook into the tip of the worm and push along the hook shank, bending the worm around the hook bend until the point exits. The worm should lay straight on the hook with no unusual bends or twists.

117

so the worm stays up on the shank of the jig. On some jigheads, the collar around the jig's hook shank is too thick for some worms and it will cause them to tear or rip when pushed up over the collar. You can also take a pair of pliers and squish down any barbs on the jig and crush the collar a bit so the worm goes on easier.

When fishing really heavy, thick cover, put the worm on a weedless jighead such as the Rip Tide weedless jig with a "J" hook bend. The eye of this jig is in the front of the head and not on the top like most jigs. Behind the eye is the jighead that is shaped like a cone and designed to go over and ride through and around rocks, weeds, and other types of bottom structure.

In front of the jig and worm, tie a 3 to 5-foot leader of 30 to 50-pound test fluorocarbon leader material. Tie a Bimini twist between the main fishing line and the leader. This will provide an invisible line connection that fish can't see, and will protect the jig and worm as it comes across any underwater obstructions.

Now before you say I think it's better to use live eels than rubber worms, consider this; live eels cost nearly $20 a dozen. Do you know how many 10 to 12-inch worms you can buy for twenty bucks?

Do not forget the weedless freshwater jighead models. A jighead of 1/4, 1/2 or 1 ounce with a molded-in weed guard is capable of hooking and holding most saltwater stripers you will encounter. Just remove the rubber skirt collar and thread on a rubber worm. These jigs come with a wide bite hook that is very sharp, strong and almost unbendable. In the jig's head are thick fibers that come back to cover the hook of the jig to make it weedless. A lot of these jigs are manufactured to go in heavy standing submerged timber, fallen logs covered with limbs, rocks, rocky walls, and all types of bottom structure. There is no reason they can't be used to take stripers, bluefish, snook, redfish, weakfish and other gamefish as well.

Carolina Rig

The Carolina rig has been around since the early 1950s, and was borrowed from an old southern catfishing method. Since then, it has been used in freshwater to catch largemouth and smallmouth bass with deadly effect. It is also a method that is effective in a lot of saltwater situations and more anglers who fish the brine should be using it, or at least become familiar with, to call upon in those tough situations we are often presented with.

As a professional captain/guide, I have to use as many tricks and

Using a Z-style hook, insert the hook point about 1/8 inch into the nose of the worm, then exit out the side. Slide the worm from the hook point toward the eye, then turn the hook and push the nose of the worm to the hook eye. Lay the hook alongside the worm to verify the position of the hook bend, then insert into the worm. For a weedless rig, do not expose the hook point.

119

ideas as I can possibly find to get my clients into fish. There are many days when even the best of guides can have a hard time getting the fish to bite. The Carolina rig is a method that has worked for me on many occasions and it will work in saltwater for you too, regardless of where you fish or what you fish for. From Maine to Florida the Carolina rig is effective on many saltwater gamefish.

It's a simple rig that works in water from 2 to over 30 feet in depth. Its best attribute is that it gives you the ability to make a very natural presentation to fish that may be in a negative mood and off the feed. The plastic bait has a lot of freedom of movement. The leader for the Carolina rig can be from 6 inches on upwards to 5 feet or more.

Probably the biggest thing anglers have to get used to is learning the "feel" of the rig. It takes patience and practice, and concentration to know when a fish picks up the bait and begins to move with it. Stripers will take a worm on a Carolina rig almost exactly like a large-mouth bass will.

Where this rig shines is in deeper water where you want to fish bottom structure such as rockpiles, channel edges, ledges, drop-offs and the end of sand or mussel bars. Use a 1/2 to 3-ounce lead weight, preferably an egg sinker or a trolling sinker, and you can work almost all types of bottom effectively. Place a plastic bead between the sinker and the knot tied to the swivel so the sinker doesn't cut away at the knot as you work the rig.

The lead weight and the beads will also cause the rig to produce sound as they bang together. In freshwater it is believed this sound duplicates the sound made by crawfish using their pincers to fight or move from place to place. In saltwater, the same effect is achieved as lobsters do the same thing with their pincers. That sound may help to attract fish to your plastic offering.

Worms are the logical choice when fishing a Carolina rig, but several other soft-plastic baits can also be rigged Carolina-style. Some of the more effective plastic lures for this style fishing are 7 to 12-inch plastic worms that float, tube baits, jerkbaits and small eel-type baits. If you don't have a floating worm, you can make it float by adding a small fly-rod popper body in front of the hook on the leader.

Keep in mind the shallower the water you are fishing, the shorter your leader will be. The reverse is true for deeper water, as the leader needs to be lengthened to 3 to 5 feet.

It's a good idea to pre-tie your rigs and store them in Ziploc bags so they are ready for fishing. At one end, tie on a 4/0 to 6/0 worm or wide gap hook using a Palomar knot. Next, decide on how long your leader is going to be. I like to use Triple-Fish Fluorocarbon leader for all my rigs since it is more difficult for the fish to see. At the end of the leader, tie on a good swivel. Ball-bearing type swivels are the best. Before tying on the swivel, thread on an egg sinker and a plastic bead or two between the swivel and the knot. I experiment with different colors of beads also. I find that red is the best all around color but the bright chartreuse or yellow colors are very good in murky or roiled water and just may give you that needed edge. In either case, the Carolina rig belongs in every saltwater angler's arsenal.

Texas Rig

The Texas rig is another basic freshwater worm rig that can also be used in saltwater for many fishing situations from shallow water flats to deep rocky areas. The rig consists of a hook and a bullet weight. You simply place the sinker on the line above the hook, tie on the hook and then thread on the worm. Simple. But that was then and this is now.Today you have bullet-head weights that are made of different kinds of material such as brass, steel, tungsten and more. Some even have built-in rattle chambers. Texas-rigged worms can be "pegged", that is, using a toothpick or rubber band to hold the weight in place.

The sliding bullet weight or small egg sinker makes the Texas rig effective. Some fishermen prefer to use a toothpick to prevent the weight from sliding.

Mojo Rig

The Mojo rig is similar to the Carolina rig, but without the leader. The rig is tied directly to your line in this case. The weight is unique and made in California under the Mojo brand name.

The weight itself is a long, slender piece of lead, which has a round and blunted head. You need to peg the weight with toothpicks or a piece of rubber skirt material using a special tool that is called (what else?) the Mojo Tool. A dental-floss threader that is used for cleaning dentures will also work.

The weights come in sizes from 1/4 ounce which is perfect for flats fishing on up to 1 ounce which will cover deeper water. The biggest weight is around 2 ounces.

The rig is very effective in fishing heavy cover or structure like the ends of points, rocky areas, drop-offs, river channels, bridge abutments, reefs, underwater humps, and flats so it doesn't ride up the line when being cast or worked below the surface.

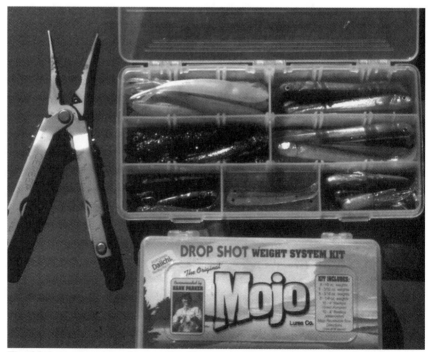

The Mojo system can be used with every shape and size of soft-plastic lure body.

The Hitchhiker Spring

Want to turn your plastic shad, grub or tube bait into a Motion Minnow such as the one advertised on television? Well, it is simple to do, and there are two ways of doing it.

The first option is to buy a small piece of corkscrew wire known as the Hitchhiker rig made by Tru-Turn Hooks and available from Bass Pro Shops. It was originally developed for the redfish fishery down south, so here is another example of how a rig from southern waters has made its way not only up north but into the freshwater world as well. Its use will no doubt be just as effective in New England on striped bass, weakfish, seatrout, bottom fish and more.

Tru-Turn makes another rig called the Stoopid rig, made with circle hooks. The first thing you need to remember is that when you get a strike, you cannot set the hook with the rod like you do with other lures. You simply reel until the line comes tight and the fish hooks itself. The hook will almost always get the fish in the upper or lower part of the jaw when it's set. The hooks that the rig comes on are painted red and known as the Bleeding Bait series and come in 2/0 and 3/0 sizes.

The second method is to make your own by utilizing the spring from an old ballpoint pen, and cutting it in half. Take a pair of pliers and form or bend a loop at one end, and then leave the corkscrew end alone. You simply take the soft plastic and twist it onto the wire until it meets the hook shank. This allows the bait to move without any restrictions in the water and no interference from the weight of the hook.

If you don't like using circle hooks, as many anglers don't, you can substitute with an Octopus style hook and if you are really into it, paint it red.

Split-Shot Rig

Split shot can also be used to get the worm down to where the fish are with a bit more finesse than other types of sinkers. With split shot, you can add weight as needed or as the current dictates. You can also remove them just as easily when going from deeper water to shallow water. Just place one, two or three on the line or the leader ahead of your worm and you are ready to fish. The best part is you spend more time fishing and less time re-rigging. One thing I've learned over the years is the guy with his lure, bait or fly in the water the longest is the winner no matter what.

Stinger Rigs

Stinger rigs seem to be having somewhat of resurgence in salt-water angling over the last few years. Some of the larger hook manufacturers are now making and marketing their own variations of a stinger rig, which saves the angler the trouble of rigging his own.

Stingers are widely used when fishing live bait, such as large size menhaden, herring and squid. They have also been used for a long time in the Pacific Northwest salmon fishery on their rigs for both live baits and artificial lures. In the Northeast, the double-hook stinger rig or harness has been used for bluefishing when pogies (bunker) are the bait and even when rigging bluefish for shark fishing offshore. So they really have been around for quite some time.

The new type of single-hook stinger that is being marketed is very useful on jigs and big soft-plastic baits when the fish are either striking short or when the fish, such as striped bass, tend to strike at the head first when feeding. So it is probably a good idea to have some of these stinger rigs on hand. Take several minutes and tie some up to keep in your tackle box.

Any time you are on the water, fishing conditions are constantly changing and you have to change and adapt to in order to stay on top of things. You never know when the fish will turn on or turn off or become picky and just slap or nip at the tail of your plastic bait. Being ready for those times—and there are many of them in the course of a season—will allow you to catch more fish.

For those of you who prefer to do things yourself, you can easily tie up your own stinger rigs and have a number of different size hooks and lengths available for different species and conditions. To begin with, get yourself a few Octopus style hooks in sizes No. 1, 1/0 and 2/0. They will cover most situations you will run into. Buy quality hooks like Tru-Turn, Eagle Claw, Mustad or Gamakatsu. These hooks are super strong and extremely sharp.

Select the Octopus style because of its unique bend in the hook's shank. Once you snell it on its rigging loop, you'll get a good hook set when a fish hits. The bend in the hook's eye and the shank follow a direct path or plane when you have to strike, so the hook goes in straight and true. These hooks are used quite a bit in the live-eel fishery, so they have a good track record of catching fish.

To make the stinger, snell the hook with braided line such as Power Pro or Western Filament, so the end of the line sits in a direct or straight line with the bend of the hook's shank and the hook eye. Snelling the hook properly will increase its hooking ability.

Now double the line over to form a loop above the eye long enough to pass the entire shank of the hook back through it when it is attached to a jig hook or an eye of a plain hook. It is a good idea to make these rigs of various lengths like 3, 4, 5 and 6 inches for baits of various lengths.

Take the tag end and tie it around the shank with some fly tying thread and use a rod-winding wrap so the line comes underneath the wraps and back out again, then cover it with some five-minute epoxy. This should more than protect the wrappings of the hook while you are fishing.

You could also order the hooks in the new Bleeding Red color for additional attraction, or tie in some red fly tying flash next to the hook's eye. Then you can shrink-wrap the top with electrical heat tubing in red, blue, black or yellow. Just cut a piece of shrink tubing to the size of the hook shank, heat it so it conforms to the wrappings and the hook, and you are done and have a professional looking stinger rig ready to go.

Stinger hooks can be added in a jiffy with special hooks made by Gamakatsu and Owner. They are made in several hook sizes.

Drop-Shotting

Drop-shotting was introduced to America from Japan where it was developed and used on reservoirs with high fishing pressure. It proved to be so effective that an American Pro Bass angler decided to try it here in the States. In saltwater, drop-shotting works best where there is short grass growing off the bottom or in areas where there is patchy cover of weed and rock as found on the edge of many saltwater flats up and down the East Coast.

The drop-shot rig and the technique of drop-shotting are very simple. At the business end of the rig, in this case the leader or line from your rod, is a specialized weight that takes the rig to the bottom. These weights come in many different sizes and shapes to cover an assortment of fishing situations and bottom make-up. There are weights for sand, gravel, rocks, and grass, to name a few.

After attaching the weight, you add the hook. The placement of the hook is going to depend on water depth and how far off the bottom you want the plastic bait to be. The hook is attached via a dropper loop right off the main line. Hook size will depend on the size of the plastic you are going to be using. I usually use a 2/0 to 4/0 Matzuo or Gamakatsu hook. Sometimes, I use a worm or wide gap hook, and other times, an Octopus-style hook. In any case, just make sure the hook is very sharp so it comes out of the plastic when you set the hook.

Once the hook is in place and the depth is determined, you now add the bait you are going to be fishing with. I like 4-inch tube baits that resemble squid, or 6-inch red shad or black worms. My next choice would be a Fin-S Fish or Bass Assassin-type bait that offers good tail motion. When weakfish are the target or seatrout farther south are present, a good shrimp imitation will often produce gun-shy fish.

When fishing in very shallow water, a sand or mud flat, you can just cast the rig out and let the sinker take it to the bottom. Then slowly reel it in with short jerks and twitches of the rod tip to make the plastic bait jump and wiggle. You really want very little movement as you work the bait. The longer it stays in one place, the better your chance of aggravating a fish into striking. You want it to appear that the lure is not trying to escape or get away from any predators in the area. In theory, a bait in a fixed position will aggravate the fish so much that it will strike out of frustration, instinct or just plain anger.

A similar method has been used in the big rivers out on the West

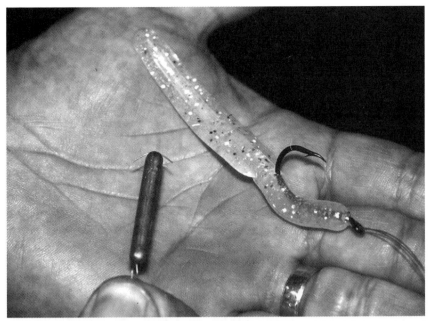

The drop-shot rig is very effective for school stripers, weakfish, snook and sea trout. Even bottom huggers like summer flounder can be taken by drop shotting.

Coast and in the Great Lakes for years. Out there, it is known as "Hot Shotting." You place your lure in what looks like a productive area and just let it sit there and wiggle on a tight line. You then let out line a little at a time so you cover the entire pool area. Our East Coast method is similar, except that you are casting and retrieving the rig back, rather than drifting to.

I tried this rig on one of the flats inside Narragansett Bay that once held hundreds of stripers. Now, the ones that show up are bigger, very spooky, and extremely cautious when feeding. Tossing out a white or yellow tube bait, or a five-inch Fin-S Fish and working it ever so slowly has proven to be extremely effective in enticing these wary stripers.

In deeper water, it is better to drop the rig to the bottom and fish it in a vertical presentation. A good fishfinder will even show the rig below the boat. If the fish suspend off the bottom like many southern species do, you can then adjust your bait's position on the line relative to the sinker to put it in the strike zone.

Whatever depth you work, always fish the rig on a tight line. If you allow too much slack in your line with this rig, you will miss a lot of strikes in the course of a day's fishing.

127

When fishing over rocky areas, or on flats where there are rocks and boulders present, you will no doubt lose a few weights and rigs in the process. But as the old saying goes, "if you aren't losing tackle, then you aren't fishing where the fish are."

For beach fanatics, this rig really shines for stripers, bluefish, weakfish, and fluke. Further south, you'll pick-up seatrout, redfish, drum, croakers and other beach dwellers. All these fish will strike at a well-placed plastic bait.

When fishing is tough and the fish seem to have lockjaw, try not moving the rig at all once it's settled to the bottom. The longer you let it stay put in one spot, the better it works. If you do reel it back to the boat or shore, be sure you have long pauses in between the taking up of line.

The Mojo System

The Mojo Lure System consists of several rigging systems to present soft-plastic lures to finicky fish. The systems include the Rig Saver, Rock Hopper, Pineapple Down Shot, Carolina Slider and Slip Shot.

The Rig Saver has a weight that hangs on your line in a vertical, straight-up position, by using a stainless steel wire loop. A number 10 to 30-pound swivel is used to stop the sinker. This allows the sinker to pivot and swivel on the line in any direction with a lot less resistance and drag. The design eliminates any damage to the line from abrasion because the line doesn't slide through the entire length of the weight, just the wire eyelet.

The biggest advantage to this rigging method is that the wire can be attached to the line in a matter of seconds without cutting the line or re-rigging. The weight can be inserted onto the wire loop, which is now attached to your line. Slide the wire legs of the Rig Saver wire through the weight bore, bending both sides up the entire length of the weight at the same time, using your thumb.

Now cut the bent wire legs flush with the outside of the weight. Be sure the wire doesn't extend beyond the end of the weight, as this will cause it to foul. Because of its unique design, if the sinker does happen to snag, it will release from the wire at approximately 4 pounds of resistance, allowing you to get the rig back minus the weight. Instructions are included in each weight and rig kit.

The Rock Hopper System allows the angler to be almost entirely snag-free in most situations. The Rock Hopper weight is computer

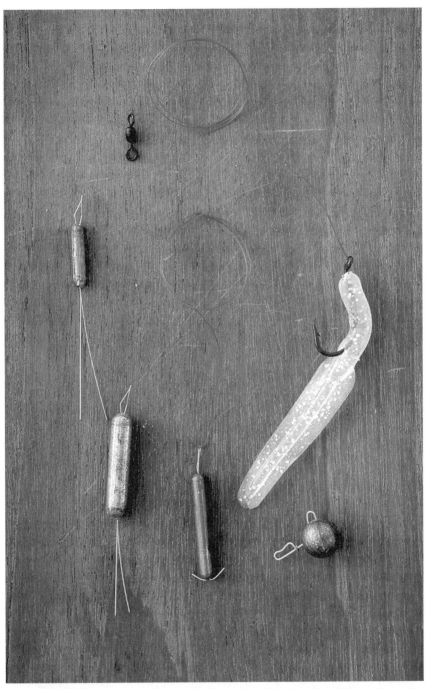

The Mojo rigging system utilizes a variety of weight shapes, which allows the angler to present the plastic bait in the most fish-catching way for virtually any fishing situation.

designed with a cross-cast line bore on one end of a long cylindrical weight, which has a small angle incorporated into the bore. The line bore is also strategically placed in a position at the cone end of the weight. The Rock Hopper glides over bottom debris with little problem. The Rock Hopper can be pegged on the line with rubber or you can use a small swivel as a weight stopper.

The Slip-Shot rig uses the same diameter the entire length of the weight; its unique design allows it to come through the heaviest cover without hang-ups. This rig allows you to feel the fish bite—not the weight—as it glides smoothly over structure and cover. To begin fishing, you simply insert the line into the sinker cavity. This allows you to slide the weight up and down the line to adjust your leader to the length you need without damaging your line. You then insert rubber strips into the sinker core, with a special tool provided with rigs.

Since this rig is referred to as a finesse fishing method, it is normally used with lines of 4 to 10-pound test in freshwater. In

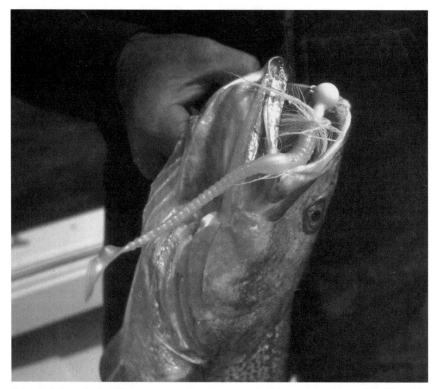

A bucktail and plastic worm combo is a sure bet for many gamefish, like this nice weakfish that couldn't resist a pearl worm on a white bucktail.

saltwater, you can go from 8 to 15-pound-test or so and still be finesse fishing. The leader length from the weight to the bait (lure) varies from 8 inches to as much as five feet. Note that the longer leader will normally produce more fish and strikes in tough conditions. This rig is great with smaller size baits in water that is very clear, where fish are finicky and only respond to subtle presentations.

The Pineapple Down Shot gives fishermen the same advantages of the long and small diameter cylindrical Slip Shot Sinker. The line clasp swivels will not prematurely cut into your line. This swivel with line clasp is perfect for a vertical presentation known as Down Shottin'. The method of rigging is very productive when targeting fish that are suspended over or relating to structure or bottom cover. The line can be easily attached to the weight by inserting the line through the wire line clasp where desired and gently pulling up with minimal force. If the weight snags, the line will weaken and the sinker will release before breaking the main line. The swivel eliminates all possible line twists, especially with spinning reels.

The Carolina Slider gives an angler all the advantages of the Slip-Shot Sinker system, plus the added weight for long casts. The weights come through heavy cover and over structure better than any other type of sinker on the market today. They come in sizes ranging from 3/8 to 1-ounce.

The author nabbed this striper on a plastic bait fished on a jighead. With so many lures shapes and colors to choose from, jigheads are extremely versatile.

CHAPTER SIX

FISHING WITH JIGHEADS

In Al Reinfelder's classic book *Bait Tail Fishing*, he describes the universal appeal of jigs in this simple statement, "Actually, jig lures have left us a legacy of angling success that can never be matched." That was 1969, and to this day, the statement is still true. Nothing matches the effectiveness of a well-fished jig.

From the ancient times of the Egyptians, Africans, Polynesians and Native Americans, the jig has been an extremely effective lure in producing fish on a consistent basis. In modern times, when the U.S. Navy went looking for that one particular item to place in a fighter pilot's survival kit, they choose the jig.

One of the best things about fishing a jig is the great satisfaction achieved once you learn its unique fish-catching capabilities. No other lure I know of is so satisfying to use. Once the technique of bucktailing is mastered, you can literally fish anywhere in the world and be successful at catching all species of fish.

With an endless array of soft-plastic tails available to dress up those jigs, another fish-catching dimension is added to an already superb lure. Soft plastics open up a nearly limitless inventory of possibilities with a wide variety of body shapes, actions, color combinations and tail shapes.

A thousand years ago, jigs were made from all types of material such as wood, bone, rock, bronze, tin, steel, and lead. Jigs are effective on everything from small trout in a hidden brook to giant bluefin tuna a hundred miles offshore.

The Jigging Action

In the dictionary the name or word "jig" comes to us from the German word "geige", which actually means "to fiddle". The movement of the fiddle's bow back and forth across the strings of the fiddle is called "gigan". Over time, as the word was used in many different dialects, it evolved to the current meaning of "jigging", meaning any rapid, erratic movement. Even folk dances that were lively became known as "jigs".

It is important to understand there are numerous ways to fish a jig besides using an erratic retrieve. Its effectiveness is also determined by its size, shape, weight, color, the position of the jig's eye and the type of tackle selected to fish the jig.

The three most popular hook-eye positions are offset where the eye of the hook comes out of the head at a slight angle; straight out the front of the head's nose; and at a 90-degree angle, pointing straight up. Nose-eye jigs are excellent for bottom jigging and offset eyes are effective when you want to troll or cast and would like the jig to ride parallel to the bottom as you move along.

A little known angling fact is that most species of fish hooked when using a jig, be it a bucktail or a dressing of soft plastic are almost always hooked in the upper jaw. This happens because the hook point rides upward on the jighead. The jig rides through the water with the hook up.

To learn more about jig fishing, I highly recommend you get a copy of Reinfelder's *Bait Tail Fishing,* published in 1969 by A. S. Barnes & Company, Inc. of Cranbury, New Jersey (ISBN #498-07356-4). Yes, it is a very old book but worth the trouble trying to find as it contains some of the best and most detailed work I have ever read on how to fish jigs effectively and successfully. To locate a copy, try looking through fishing flea markets, or contact the following collectible fishing book dealers: Judith Bowman, Pound Ridge Road, Bedford, NY 10506 914-234-7543. Or try David E. Foley, 76 Bonny View Road, West Hartford, CT 06107 860-561-0783.

Back in 1969, the Bait Tail was one of the few plastic baits or lures that was actually designed and manufactured for saltwater fishing applications. Its streamlined design, with its thick body shape and virtually no action of its own, is what no doubt made it less appealing to the general angling public. I recall Bob Pond of Atom plug fame telling me how difficult it was to get the public to read the instructions on the back of the package of his lures. He believed that anglers would have saved themselves hours of frustration had they only read the instructions that came with each lure. Imagine trying to communicate to an inexperienced angler, the many ways to fish a jig—a lure with no action.

Jigheads

Today there are an infinite number of jighead styles to choose from, and many can be used in conjunction with soft-plastic bait creations. In simple terms, the jig takes the soft plastic to the bottom where most fish live, and especially where most of the bigger fish are usually found. The key here is in selecting the proper size, shape, weight and plastic tail to get the job done.

It pays to be prepared with a variety of head shapes in several weight sizes and colors to cover all the possibilities.

Let's say you are fishing a sand flat that is only 3 or 4 feet deep at high tide. You don't want to use a heavy jighead that weighs an ounce or more. A better choice is a light jighead that is 1/8 to 1/4 ounce so it sinks slowly and allows time for the fish to spot it as it falls. By the same token, if you are fishing a deep channel of 20 feet or so in depth, you'd likely go for a 1 to 2-ounce jighead to get your bait down to the bottom quicker and keep it there. Although this may seem very basic, I can tell you first-hand from my charter business that the majority of the angling public does not think in simple terms, like the more experienced angler does. What seems simple and basic to us is a total and complete revelation to most.

The modern jig comes in all manner of sizes and shapes and the type or style you select will in many instances effect how your plastic bait reacts. There are many plastic lures that only work on certain styles of jigheads. The only way to be certain is to fish your favorite soft plastic on different jighead styles, and see how they perform. We'll give you a quick overview of some basic jigheads and what techniques work best for each, but in the end, it's up to you, the angler, to determine what works best for you. Where you fish, how you fish and what you are fishing for, will all come into the equation when it comes to your selections.

Ball-style jigheads are great for fishing with plastic rubber worms of 6 to 12 or more inches. They are also effective with Mister Twister tails and grub bodies. For shad bodies, go with an arrowhead or shad-head jig made specifically for those lures, such as the D.O.A. heads. If you want to cut through the water, consider an arrowhead-shape jig, which is especially effective in fast-moving water. There's also the semi-arrowhead shape, like the Cotee jig, which is a compromise between two jig styles. The jig is not completely an arrow shape, but it isn't purely round either. It will cover many different fishing situations and its weight-to-size ratio is excellent.

There are swimming or stand-up style jigheads that are only recently being taken seriously by more saltwater anglers. In these models, there aren't a lot of jigs available with a hook strong enough to hold saltwater gamefish. Eventually, I believe that will change, as the demand for what those jigs can do will no doubt increase as time goes on.

I've been using freshwater-style swimming jigheads to catch bonito and albies by placing a soft-tail lure such as a Mister Twister tail, Fin-S Fish, small shad body or short worm onto it. They are super effective on these small tunas. You only need light line and a long rod of 7-1/2 feet with light action. The lighter line accounts for an amazing number of hook-ups and the rod helps to keep the light-wire hooks from bending or straightening out.

The swimming jig and stand-up jigheads are also effective in shallow water. My son and I use these jigs on flats and in shallow bays and they work great. The stand-up jig is effective with a soft-plastic crab that looks like it's in a fighting position. Some even swim with an erratic motion. Yes, hook strength does become a factor, especially if you encounter bigger fish, but isn't that half the fun, trying to land big fish on light tackle?

Even the standard largemouth bass jigs will and do work in salt-water applications. There's an amazing selection of bass jigs available for saltwater fishermen to choose from. The ones with rattles built-in are particularly effective. In rocky areas, try fishing the jigs with crawfish trailers that will simulate crabs or small baby lobsters trying to escape. Just be sure you wash these jigs at the end of the day as their hooks will rust out in a hurry if you don't.

In most instances, you only want a jig large enough to get the job done and to take the plastic where you want it to go. Too heavy a jig interferes with the plastic bait's action. Too light a jig, and you probably won't get deep enough. In many cases it's a matter of matching the proper size plastic bait to the proper size jighead in the correct weight, shape and form.

Some of the more interesting jigheads to come onto the market in recent years are two designs from Cotee Industries. Their new Crankin' JigNLip is a revolutionary design of a standard jighead with the lip of a common hard-plastic crankbait. It employs the same corkscrew fall as their original Liv'Eye Action jig, and with its realistic wounded baitfish action is something to behold. You rig it like a normal jig, but you can fish it like a crankbait. The jig has 3-D lensmatic eyes and is made of Alloy-82 that is corrosion resistant in both fresh and saltwater. The second new addition is the Buttoneye Jerk for soft-plastic jerkbaits. The eyes and the head are built to slide into the jerkbait, making it virtually weedless, a huge benefit when fishing for redfish, snook and other snag-hiding gamefish.

Some jigheads now come with built-in rattle chambers so you can now add sound, as well as weight and action, to your bait. As soft-plastic fishing grows in popularity, I predict that we will see even more innovations in the years ahead.

As you can see in the accompanying side bar, there are approximately 25 different jighead shapes. The information was provided by Do-It Mold Company and if you can't find a particular jighead in your area or from our extensive listing in the reference index, you can certainly try making your own.

Fish-Catching Jigheads

Arrowhead: A flat-tapered head resembles a stone arrowhead. This streamlined shape helps the jig to pierce strong currents. Its sleek, flat-sided jighead shape enhances the action of paddle tail grubs and shad bodies.

Banana Head: Bent-body head shape allows this jig to be pulled over branches, rocks and other debris. The forward center weight of the jig gives it a unique nosedive action. This jig is popular in both fresh and saltwater.

Bullet Head: A center-balanced jighead with a tapered, bullet shape. It smoothly shoots through water, attracting most gamefish species. The Darter Style jighead is similar, but with larger hooks.

Bullet Nose: A true saltwater jighead using an Eagle Claw 413 jig hook. The double-barb collar on the shank is excellent for holding shrimp bodies and other thick-bodied plastics. The larger size jigs are outfitted with Mustad style 34184, 8/0 hooks.

Chub Jig: A tapered head swims through the water with a baitfish-shaped, swollen-belly profile. A great choice in shallow water situations.

Egg-Head Jig: Known for its versatility, the tapered egg shape cuts the current, resists snags and hang-ups in rocks. It slides into tube baits much better than the round-head jighead style. A great tube jig 1/4 to 5/8 ounces and a 4/0 hook.

Erie Jig: The Erie Jig lure, which is a weighted-forward spinner popular in the Lake Erie walleye fishery, spawned this jighead. The jig is designed for center and stand-up balance. It has a ball collar or a barbed collar for holding plastic. Comes in 1/4 to 1-ounce sizes.

Flat-Head Jig: One of the most popular saltwater jigheads of all time, with its coin-shaped head. Commonly known as the "Upperman" jighead, it can overcome the upswells in strong currents and still ride straight. Great for fishing rivers, rips and taking plastic tails to great depths. Usually, the eye placement comes in standard balance (slightly offset) and center balanced pointing up straight. Available from 1/4 to 4 ounces.

Flat-Grub Jig: Flat sides means that more water flows along the sides of the head to give a wiggle action for paddle-type grubs and shrimp tails, also shad bodies. This jig can come with recessed eyes to accommodate 5/32" stick-on lure eyes for added attraction. Usually 1/4 to 3/4 ounces, with hooks ranging from 1/0 to 5/0 in size.

Football Jig: A freshwater jig with saltwater applications when probing deep. Its wide head shape prevents the jig from turning over on its side. Instead, it stands up along the bottom with the hook remaining upright ready to strike. The broad head face helps to transmit signals up the line about changes in bottom features. Available in 1/8 to 1 ounce, size 1 to 4/0 hooks.

Hot Lips Jig: Commonly known to saltwater anglers as the "Smilin' Bill" jig. The bullet style head with its wide mouth open is usually painted red to mimic an injured baitfish. The jig has protruding eyes and a flair collar for tying on bucktail. However, if you crush down the end of the collar, smooth it out with a Dremel tool, it will accept plastic shads, worms and eels easily. Great in currents for a swimming action and great for fluke, sea bass, weakfish and other bottom feeders. In 1/8 to 5-ounce weights, 1 to 9/0 hooks.

Ultra-Minnow Jig: A new design, the Ultra-Minnow jig has a center balance, H-design and a collar for holding soft plastics. Also has molded-in gill plates, fins, lips, scales and recessed eyes. It's one of the most detailed jigheads on the market today. Comes 1/8 to 1-1/2 ounces, 1/0 to 5/0 hooks.

Style H Jig: A very versatile jighead style with a swollen, pregnant-looking belly that helps to stabilize the jig as it cuts through the water. Recessed eye sockets accommodate stick-on eyes. Comes with either a ball collar for tying on bucktail or a barbed collar for attaching plastic tails, worms, grubs or shad bodies. From 3/8 to 4 ounces, 2/0 to 8/0 hooks.

Minnow-Head Jig: A tapered-head design for smaller plastics and shad bodies. Has a barbed collar and standard balance, in 1/8 to 3/8 ounces, 1 to 2/0 hooks.

Round-Head Jig: One of the most popular jigheads. New versions with a Gamakatsu hook have double collar on the hook shank to better hold soft-plastic tails. Weights of 1/8 to 2 ounces, 1 to 6/0 hooks.

Shad-Dart Jig: This jig's tapered and slanted face causes the jig to rise and fall, especially in a river or where there is a good current. A darting action is achieved by raising and lowering the rod tip. Some big fish have hit very small shad darts so you must always be ready. From 1/32 to 3/4 ounces, 6 to 3/0 hooks.

Shad-Jighead: A streamlined head slices through water with little resistance even when fishing in strong currents. This jig is made for soft plastics to be well secured to with its ring and barbed collar. Sizes 1/4 to 4 ounces with 1/0 to 9/0 hooks are most popular. The Style 9 shad jig has a triangular shape to its head and is even better in strong currents. It has a staggered collar barb with one pointing forward and one backward to hold large plastics and thick bodies very well.

Sparkie Jig: The special forward balance design allows the Sparkie jig to be pulled over snags and through weeds. The wide head shape keeps the jig from tipping on its side as it rests on the bottom. This lets you fish with a slider method, as well as a regular jigging motion. Good for redfish, snook, seatrout, bonefish and more, in 1/8 to 5/8 ounces and 2 to 4/0 hooks.

Spearhead Jig: Often called the Turbo Water jig, its sleek dynamic shape gives it minimal water resistance so it's excellent in turbulent currents, rivers or offshore rips. Available in 1 to 4 ounces, 1 to 7/0 hooks.

Spire-Point Jig: Looks like a rifle bullet, and delivers the same impact. Designed for trolling and jigging with sizes ranging up to 8 ounces with a flared collar and big-game hooks, recessed eye sockets. Wide variety of sizes from 1/8 to 12 ounces, 2 to 12/0 hooks.

Popeye Jig: An East Coast favorite with protruding eyes, hence its name, for a very lifelike appearance. Usually tied with bucktail but can be outfitted with plastic as well. Sizes from 1/4 to 2-1/2 ounces with 2/0 to 7/0 hooks.

Stand-Up Jig: A jig from the walleye pro-fishing circuit. When it drops to the bottom, the jig stands up with its hook poised for a strike. The wide, flat foot decreases the jig's rate of fall, suspending it longer for fish to see. Good for finicky fish all along the coast. Falls slowly enough when cast next to bonito or albies to entice strikes. Try 1/8 to 3/4 ounces, 1/0 to 3/0 hooks. There is a heavy-duty saltwater version available as well with hooks up to 5/0.

Swimmin' Jig: The Swimmin' jig is a longer, wide-bodied jig that actually wobbles when falling, retrieved or trolled. It's a very versatile jig for saltwater anglers, especially in southern fisheries. Light weights of 1/8 to 3/8 ounces and 4 to 2/0 hooks.

Tear-Drop Jig: A weight-forward design with good tracking and a swimming action when retrieved. Has a nose-first falling action when jigged. The collar is excellent for plastics, in 1/8 to 1-ounce sizes, 1 to 5/0 hooks.

Tube & Tail Jig: A versatile gamefish jig with a special design for rigging it into tube baits, or a plastic tail can be added. Both tails can be used at the same time for a very unique look. Its holding collar will accept rubber skirts as well. Available in 1/8 to 3/4 ounces, and 1/0 to 4/0 hooks.

Old Bayside Jighead: These round and blunt heads have a strong Mustad jig hook and are available in 12 different colors. Has a triple ribbed collar for holding soft plastics that is unique to jigheads and a wide-gap hook in 1/8 to 1/2 ounces.

These jig styles are described in the Do-It Mold Company catalog. They've been in business for over 40 years, and manufacture high-quality molds for the do-it-yourself angler. If you can't find a particular jig at your favorite bait shop, consider pouring your own.

When selecting the jighead, take a moment to check out the collar on the hook shank. These are usually molded as part of the head shape and cover the hook shank closest to the jighead. They are designed to hold the soft-plastic tail in place while casting and retrieving. Big tails can fit over most every collar ever made, but small, slim-profile tails may tear easily when slid over a large collar. Be sure to match the tail size to the collar size.

Jig Hooks

Any discussion on jig hooks is usually open to some hot debate. For many years, the hooks used on many production jigs simply didn't hold up under tough fishing conditions. They were either too easily bent, not sharp, rusted very quickly or were just plain junk, in my opinion. Manufacturers tried to keep costs down to make jigs affordable, but at the same time, a growing number of anglers were willing to pay extra for the best quality available. In recent years, companies like Gamakatsu and Owner have spawned an entire new market of high-quality jigheads and hooks. These new hooks sport special hook points and finishes that grab hold of saltwater fish, and won't rust in the saltwater environment.

Even with the more costly hooks, jigheads are a bargain. With prices rising for hard-plastic baits and wooden lures, the jig has become quite an attractive, low-cost substitute. When you add in its fish-catching abilities and its easy adaptation to inexpensive soft plastics, you can quickly see how it has driven jig makers and sellers to ask their suppliers for better, stronger, higher-quality hooks on the jigs they manufacture.

Some jigs have a light-wire construction. Light-wire hooks have their place in the saltwater fishing arena, but they aren't for everyone. Let me relate the following fishing experience to prove my point: some years ago, I was using the Lunker City jigs, which have very light-wire hooks that are easily straightened by a good-size fish. My problem was that many of their baits, like the Slug-Go and Fin-S Fish, worked so much better on the lighter wire hook that it was difficult for me to consider changing to another jighead with a beefier hook. The light-wire hook in the jighead allowed the lure greater freedom of movement and action than a heavier hook would.

Some anglers felt, mistakenly I have to add, that the jigs were cheap and not good for catching stripers or bluefish, because on heavy tackle, the hooks straightened out too easily after a fish was hooked. Well, the answer to this dilemma is two-fold. Yes, the hooks did straighten easily when a big fish took the lure, but it was a case of the angler using the wrong tackle to begin with and probably not fighting the fish properly. Catching these big fish required lighter tackle, proper equipment, skilled fighting techniques and taking just a little extra time and care when landing the fish. If the fish wasn't "horsed" in, the catch was made easily, and hooks never straightened.

In the guide business my son and I operate, we have landed fish up to 31 pounds on very light-wire jigheads. We fished in the right areas, at the right time, with the proper tackle and experienced little or no bending of the hook. What is needed is premium line, a sensitive rod with a light action that has its strength in the butt section and a reel with a good drag. Couple that with something called "PATIENCE" and you can whip most—not all, but most—of the fish you will encounter. In my 35 years of on-the-water experience, the one factor most anglers fail to control or account for is patience.

The position of the hook eye on the leadhead will influence how the lure will dance or hop on the retrieve.

There are some companies utilizing very strong stainless steel hooks in their jigs. Check out the jigs from Cotee, Gamakatsu, Owner, Daiichi, Matzuo, Tsunami and others. Whatever your head-shape preference, take the time to look around and find a jighead that will fit your needs. Lunker City now has the Pro Model jighead that has light-wire hooks that are super strong and sharp. The Kalin Company manufactures a jig that has superior strength in relation to its size, and D.O.A., Cotee and Rip Tide jigs are made to the highest standards and have never failed us.

Jigs, overall, are not that expensive, so having a bunch available for different uses is not out of the question. About the only time I'll go to what I consider a less expensive jig is when fishing for bluefish. I look for a mid-priced jig that will get the job done and won't cost a fortune when the bluefish bites it off. The Hurricane brand sold in tackle shops and chain stores works just fine, as do the several styles of Sea Striker jigs. The hooks are relatively good quality, they don't bend all that easily, and most of all, they are inexpensive to purchase in large quantities. I save the high-end jigs for stripers, weakfish, fluke, bonito and albies, or if I take a trip south and fish for redfish, snook, cobia or tarpon.

Colors

The importance of jighead color is dependent on water conditions and atmospheric conditions at the time and in the area you are fishing. The amount of sunlight, cloud cover or the darkness of night will all effect how colors are viewed beneath the water's surface.

Today there is a growing trend back towards the color red, which is believed to attract fish because it gives the appearance of a bleeding bait, hence the popularity of red hooks. Freshwater tournament anglers report much higher catch rates while using red-plated hooks in tournaments.

After going through my own tackle box of jigs at the end of the season, it always seems there are fewer heads of red color left over from the season. I've tried to keep it simple when stocking jighead colors in my tackle inventory, preferring white, red, chartreuse, yellow and black. If I don't, or can't catch fish with those five basic colors, then the fish can just go and bite someone else's line!

I will use a darker color on dark days and lighter colors on bright sunny days or in very clear water. However, one of the worst things you can do is to get locked into color choices. Sometimes I think anglers overlook the obvious need to change colors. You don't have to be so inflexible and choose colors by a magic chart, a local opinion or from some mystical Druid ceremony of the 13th century. I can find in my logs literally hundreds of times where it paid off big time to try colors that were the opposite of what was considered "true" for a given area or time. The key is to be flexible and experiment all the time.

As with any topic, various differences of opinion exist as to how or why you should do something when it comes to fishing. In my view, if everyone was correct all the time and each opinion was correct and valid, there wouldn't be any fish left for the rest of us. There is a strong belief that natural baitfish colors that blend with black, blue and green are the best for clear water. In stained, muddy or water that is roiled, yellow, gold, orange, and chartreuse are thought to be good choices. When the sun is shining brightly and you're fishing shallow water, fluorescent yellow and chartreuse are great choices. Do you want to know what I think the best color is? It's the color the fish are going to bite or hit most often in any kind

Plastic tails are inexpensive and can be used to catch toothy gamefish like this bluefish for a few pennies a fish.

of water. What color is that? It's the color you discover after trying several different colors on that fishing day.

Speaking of color, someone recently told me he read purple was the most visible daytime color. Soon afterwards, someone else told me purple was the best color at night and in low light situations. Confused yet? I am. The point is, I had already written an extensive article for a nationally published magazine on this very topic. I found documented, detailed, scientific studies that said all of the above is a pile of old fish chum. If you are not catching fish, then experiment, change, adapt and overcome. It sounds like a plug for army commandos, but being flexible and creative will pay off in more fish strikes. Pay attention to what is going on and what is working and remember it for future reference. The best idea and the best technique to follow is to keep an open mind—period.

Tails

Here's another wide-open subject loaded with controversy and old wives' tales. Tail selection—what to use when and why—doesn't have to be difficult, so let's make it simple. You use what is going to catch fish and forget everything else. How's that? Simple right?

Selecting what tail to use usually is governed by the type of forage or baitfish the targeted species are feeding upon. If the predominant bait happens to be alewives, you certainly wouldn't rig up with a 10-inch rubber worm or a 3-inch grub tail. But then again, you might. Let me explain.

When we choose a soft-plastic tail to fish, or at least begin the day with, we usually go with something that has a lot of action or life to it. A Fin-S Fish for instance, or a Slug-Go—something with good tail action or lots of movement. I usually try to see how aggressive the fish are on any given day, then, let them tell me what they want and how they want it.

Sometimes we start with a 5-inch Fin-S Fish. If we notice some-thing good-sized following it to the boat, we immediately switch over to the 7-inch version, which usually gets the attention of the fish in a hurry. By scaling up or scaling down, you can usually find which size lure they prefer or like best.

When fishing with a buddy or a couple of friends, everyone onboard, or in the surf (if we are beach fishing), should be using a different size, color, shape and weight. That gives you two, three or four times the searching power, eliminating that many more possi-

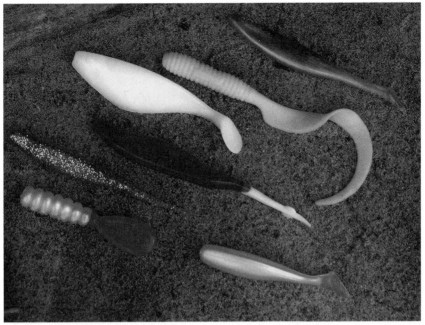

Long or short, fat or skinny, plastic tails of all shapes and sizes can be dressed to a bucktail or leadhead.

bilities as you begin to fish. All that planning should be complete prior to actually fishing, so everyone knows his assignment. On our light tackle charters with two to four fishermen, no one is ever using the same bait, jighead, size or color until one is producing consistently. Don't become too anxious and let one fish landed or a few strikes rush you to change prematurely. Give it time to establish a definite pattern then switch over.

In shallow-water situations, un-weighted jerkbaits like the Slug-Go, Bass Assassin, Zoom Fluke, Fin-S Fish, Shad Dart and others are best fished with only a hook tied directly to the line. Their erratic darting, diving motion drives fish crazy in shallow water.

For shad bodies, I let the prevalent bait situation dictate what size shad I should use. If I know there are alewives or menhaden around, I'll use a 6 to 10-inch swimming shad fitted to the proper size jighead. The shad body should fit the head snuggly and lie straight free of kinks in the body so it swims naturally. The larger soft-plastic shads make excellent trolling lures and imitations when large size bait is present. Sometimes I even use them instead of live bait and it works just as good. To be honest, I didn't come up with that one on my own, I learned it from Captain Fred Bowman, skipper of the

Bottom Line, who enjoys a good reputation for his ability to put big bass in the boat for his clients on a regular basis. It was his tip that started me using the 6, 9 and 10-inch shad bodies on 2 or 3-ounce jigheads.

Shrimp bodies work great in backwater situations and on sand flats up and down the coast. There are usually lots of grass shrimp present in the back bays, rivers, coves and estuaries as they have made a tremendous comeback in recent years. Shrimp are a staple diet to most gamefish from Maine to Florida on over to the Gulf Coast. The soft-plastic shrimps available today are so realistic it is scary when you look at one. D.O.A. shrimp bodies look like they're ready for a fine barbecue, and Creme produces one that is almost an exact replica of a living bay shrimp. These can be fished on jig-heads with a single hook or on a popping cork that is very popular down south, but used little in the Northeast. More on the popping cork in another chapter.

Many have laughed at the new soft-plastic crabs that have hit the market, but let me tell you right now, if you're one of those who are laughing, the joke may be on you. Companies don't tool up to produce lures that aren't going to work and spend millions doing it because they have nothing better to do. Before it hits the market it has been tested on fish by guides and pro anglers to make sure it works. Let me ask you this: have you opened the stomach of a striped bass in recent years to see what was inside? If you have, you should have noticed that a lot of bass are full of half digested crab parts, which to me indicates they are eating a lot of crabs. I believe that it hasn't become more popular and probably its major drawback is that it takes a lot of patience to fish a plastic crab correctly, just as it does a crab fly. If you don't have the patience, then it probably won't work for you.

You need to fish this bait very slowly, and I do mean s-l-o-w-l-y. These new soft plastics are causing quite a stir for those who can master and control their nervous systems. I have clients who have done extremely well with these baits fishing on the flats, and others who would like to toss me overboard after I've told them to slow down around sixty or seventy times.

The one unique thing about the jig is its ability to do so many different things at the same time. It can be jigged, swimmed, hopped, glided, twitched, crawled, bounced or raced at just about any speed from just below the water's surface to the depths of the ocean bottom.

Swim Baits

In recent years, a new soft-plastic lure came on the scene with an internal leadhead. First introduced by Storm Lures as the WildEye Shad, it was soon followed by Bimini Bay's Tsunami Real-Shad Lures, then Calcutta Lures and now there are several companies with a selection of lures commonly referred to as swim shads or swim baits. The original shad-body shapes have been augmented by an expanding array of tail shapes and actions. These new lures have taken the striper coast by storm (pun intended), and are now catching snook, seatrout and weakfish, redfish and tarpon. Tsunami's "limetreuse" tailed Trout Mauler is a deadly lure on weakfish and seatrout, while its Paddle Tail Minnow is noted for fooling big fluke (summer flounder). D.O.A. pioneered the idea of replaceable tails on swim baits with their TerrorEyze, and MegaBaits has followed with its version of replaceable tails on their L.A. Slider. There's a lot more to come in swim bait advances in the next several years.

The new creations go beyond the typical leadhead and plastic tail. They have an amazing lifelike finish enhanced with an internal holographic foil molded inside the body of the lure to reflect light. Hold one in your hand and it looks ready to flip off your palm and swim away! They look exactly like a live peanut bunker or mullet. In fact, they imitate all the common baits. Manufacturers offer both chubby and slender profile swim baits so it's easy for the angler to choose a bait that resembles an alewive, blue back herring, mackerel, gizzard shad, threadfin shad, sand eel, spearing or killie, and just about any other bait fish.

The success of swim baits is attributed to a realistic finish and an action that previous shad baits didn't have. With the leadhead molded inside the lure, several unique actions can be achieved. Swim baits can be cast, trolled, or jigged with equal effectiveness on a wide variety of species.

You can fish these shad bodies by simply casting out and reeling in. The built-in action will do the rest of the job on most days, but on others, it is much more effective to jig the lure in a stop-and-go retrieve or a retrieve that has a quick burst of speed followed by a slower retrieve and another fast burst. They can also be bounced over the bottom rocky structure and in fast moving water or currents. These baits make excellent lures for fishing from bridges during the nighttime hours.

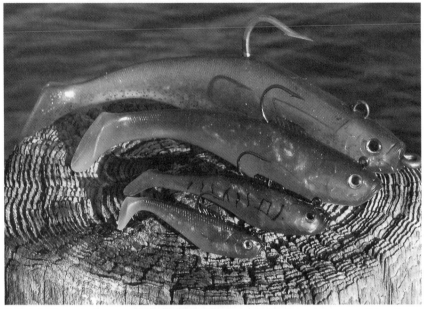

Swim baits run the range from tiny to huge and can catch everything from pan-size seatrout to yellowfin tuna.

What action do you need? Swim baits sport a variety of tail shapes for many different actions.

Swim baits range in sizes from 2 to 10 inches, and lure weights range from 1/4 ounce to heavy-duty jumbo swim baits of several ounces. Some have single hooks and some are armed with trebles. All are very effective and should be included in the lure selection of every coastal fisherman.

With the weights of these baits molded inside the body, these plastics stay correctly positioned on the hook. The hook and weight prevent the plastic body from moving or sliding on the shank of the hook. This is a big improvement over standard soft-plastic baits where the tail can be moved along the hook shank from short-striking fish. Because the plastic is molded around the hook and jighead, swim baits can often withstand several bites from toothy gamefish such as Spanish mackerel, kingfish and bluefish.

When a swim bait gets chewed up, try this great tip from Jerry Gomber of Tsunami Lures. Once the shad body has been torn or ripped and is no longer useable, Jerry saves the weighted leadhead and hook and re-uses it with tube lures, worm bodies and other soft plastics. They don't have to be discarded. Instead of tossing them out, recycle them and tie some with bucktail and feathers for fluke, weakfish and other species.

Casting & Jigging

One of the biggest mistakes I constantly see on a daily basis aboard the White Ghost, is the way clients will make a cast, turn the handle on the reel and begin retrieving the jig back to the boat. As they are doing this, they are looking at the sky, the birds, the water, their shoes, their watch. When a fish hits, I hear them say, "Oops!" I just missed one, Cap." Sometimes, it's rare when they yell, "Hey, fish on!"

When fishing a jig you can either cast it out and retrieve it back, or jig it off the bottom or at some pre-determined depth. When casting, the rod tip is what imparts life to the jig. What you do with the rod tip controls what the jig does and how it does it. If you aren't concentrating on what you are doing, how you are moving the rod tip, chances are, you aren't going to catch many fish.

Sometimes an angler will get frustrated by my requests to "concentrate," and finally say to me, "Here, you try it for awhile." Often I make just a few casts before getting a strike and a hook-up. They then ask how did I do that so quickly? My answer is always the same—"Concentration." It usually has nothing to do with being better than anyone else. It has everything to do with total and complete concentration on what you are doing. I'm flippin', hoppin' and shakin' that jig, and can visualize it inside my head. I know what it is doing, and how I want it to appear to the fish. It's not magic—it's concentration.

I believe if the jig is working in a realistic, proper manner then the fish will respond and eat it. Sounds silly and simple. To fish a jig properly and correctly, your head has to be in the game as well as your body, the rod, the reel and the line. If it's not, the game is over—no extra innings, no overtime, no sudden death. Go to the showers.

When bouncing the bottom for fluke, sea bass, cod, grouper or snappers, it's important that the jig is hitting and touching the bottom. If it rides too high, chances are you aren't going to catch too many fish either. It takes concentration to do that consistently and effectively. Bottom species are every bit as challenging as the more prized species such as striped bass. They all attack their prey with the intention of killing and eating it. That is what makes the fish world go round. If it looks like it just fell out of a Rollie-Pollie-Ollie show, the chances are they will look for something else to eat.

The ability to make the jig and soft plastic come alive is what separates the men from the boys. It starts with concentration while retrieving the lure, but it takes something else to learn all the secrets. Those secrets only come from doing something akin to a very dirty word—WORK! Heavens to Betsy, did I really say that word? Many fishermen rely on luck, but hard work is what makes the best fishermen.

Bridge Fishing Techniques

Striped bass, bluefish, weakfish, tarpon, snook and many other exciting gamefish feed around bridges. Bridges seem to attract lots of bait, and that's probably why gamefish like to hang around. Bridges also provide comfortable hiding cover, shadow lines, eddies and feeding stations that gamefish rely upon for safety and a steady supply of food.

Two pioneers who popularized bridge fishing in modern times, especially with plastic baits, were Lou Palma and Al Reinfelder, inventors of the famous Bait Tail Lure and the Alou Eel. The Bait Tail was among the early soft-plastic lures invented in the northeast and was used exclusively for saltwater angling, and specifically for fishing from a bridge.

Plastic baits and jigs, especially the shad-type bodies, are a very effective lure when fished from bridges. They can be cast from a boat towards the bridge pilings, or fished when standing on the bridge by simply dropping the jig into the water. Either way, a jig and piece of plastic will attract fish with excellent results. Anglers all along the coast are usually familiar with fishing bridges from a boat, but the technique of fishing from the bridge is practiced primarily by saltwater bridge-fishing specialists in Long Island, New Jersey and Florida. These hardy anglers usually fish the night shift and have made bridge fishing with jigs and plastic into a science.

Bridge fishing can be successful during the day, but many of the popular species, such as snook and striped bass, are usually caught under the cover of darkness. Besides the diminished boat traffic, gamefish will line up along the shadow line formed by the lights on top of the bridge during the night hours. They take up feeding stations along the shadow line and wait for the water-born buffet served up by the tidal currents. On full-moon nights, the light of the moon will cast sufficient light to create a shadow line beneath bridges that have no lights at all. A shadow line is even formed in the early light of dawn and dusk. In particular, during the morning as the sun is rising, a distinct shadow line will form on the water depending upon the angle of the sun and the bridge.

Tackle Tips

Most bridge fishing is accomplished with conventional tackle, as the angler has a much greater degree of control over his line and lure than with spinning gear. Conventional gear has more muscle and power to apply pressure that keeps a hard-running fish away from the barnacle-encrusted pilings. Spinning tackle doesn't have the same leverage as conventional, although some fishermen who fish bridges from a boat will use spin gear just because it's easier to use. Conventional tackle, in the hands of a skilled angler, will allow more accurate casts to be made directly to the bridge pilings. A lure cast within a few feet of the piling will usually get the attention of the fish, but a lure that lands too far away will be ignored.

How heavy your gear must be depends greatly on how strong the currents are where you are fishing, the height of the bridge, the number of local obstructions and the size of the fish you hope to catch. I've used line as heavy as 50-pound test while bridge fishing and still had the fish break off. Most bridge fishing is not for the light-tackle enthusiast. Big fish will almost always head for the nearest piling or bottom obstruction. The angler must stop and turn the fish as quickly as possible, or risk losing the battle.

When attaching a lure to the line, use a good-quality snap that won't open or fail under extreme stress. Many bridge specialists prefer to tie directly to the lure with a 60, 80 or 100-pound test hard mono shock leader. Use a loop knot so the jig swings freely on the end of the line. The more freely it moves and swings, the more strikes you will get. The heavy shock leader will guard against a cut-off if the fish rubs the line against a sharp barnacle, rough concrete or rusty piece of iron.

Bridge Leadheads

Early in their careers, Al Reinfelder and Lou Palma discovered the best lures for bridge fishing were those that would swim parallel to the surface of the water. The eye of the leadhead that attaches to the snap at the end of the line was positioned somewhat on the top of the bait. Many other leadheads of that time had attachment eyes near the front face of the lure. Although the Bait Tail and its leadhead have been out of production for many years, there are fortunately

When fishing from on top of a bridge, most fishermen prefer a soft bait with the hook eye positioned on the top of the head rather than right off the nose. The lure can then be worked with more action and appears more natural.

many modern jigheads that are made with the attachment eye on top of the leadhead.

Choose a leadhead that when attached to the line will balance so the lure is parallel to the surface of the water. Attach the snap and check the balance of the lure by holding the line a few inches above the snap. If the leadhead and the soft-plastic tail angle downward at the rear, or hook side, of the leadhead, it's not the best bridge-fishing jig. The head and the tail of the lure should be level with one another. This allows the caster to work the lure in a lifelike manner when fishing from on top of the bridge.

Boat fishermen will do better with a leadhead that has a hopping action, and a leadhead with the eye in a forward position. The lure can be made to dance in an erratic manner by working the rod tip up and down, or by holding the rod tip low and retrieving the lure in short sweeps.

There are many jigheads that meet this criteria, and virtually any type of tail can be fished on them—shads with paddle tails, curly tailed Mister Twister types and crazy acting Fin-S tails. In particular, many swim baits have attachment eyes positioned perfectly for bridge-fishing action.

Locating The Fish

Fish will be positioned close to the pilings, and along the shadow line. They will always be facing away from the bridge and into the current. Rarely will they be found directly beneath the bridge itself. They may be found high in the water column just inches below the surface, or they may be hugging the bottom. How high or low they may be is often determined by the bait as it flows past the bridge. At night, most bait will be located from the mid-water depths to near the surface.

Bridges are also best fished on the changes of the tide. The period from the end of the high tide through the slack and into the start of down tide, and again on the end of the falling tide, through the slack and at the start of the incoming are the best times to fish. At mid-tide stages, the water is often flowing so quickly beneath the bridge it's often impossible to fish successfully.

Even at peak currents, however, some bridges are still fishable. Look for the slower water near the backside of the pilings, or areas at each end of the bridge where the water is shallower. Both areas offer gamefish a place to rest and to feed without over exertion.

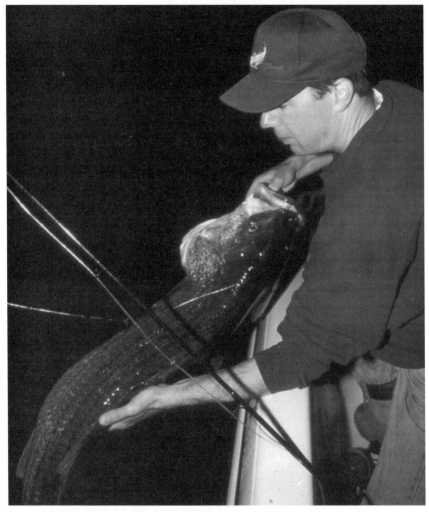

Some of the best bridge fishing occurs at night when lights from the bridge cast a shadow line onto the water where bait and gamefish congregate.

From The Bridge

Casting from a bridge is best done in short accurate lob casts and not with the traditional long tosses as in beach fishing. Much of this is best accomplished by tossing the bait or lure in an underhand cast, kind of a flip cast. Keep the rod tip pointed downward toward the water at all times, since this position offers the best lure control and also makes setting the hook easier.

This casting technique allows the angler to toss the lure underneath the bridge and also lets the weighted lure enter the water quietly with little or no splash. This is very important on calm evenings when there is little noise going on around you.

The simplest tactic is to cast the jig out so it can be worked in the current near the edge of the shadow line where it meets the clear water. Gamefish will usually strike the jig and plastic as it nears or crosses into the shadow line. Many times you will even be able to see or pick out individual fish or pairs of fish feeding and patrolling the shadow line for an easy meal.

Another method is to cast and allow your line to play out in the current and let it sink to the bottom. Now you can either bounce it back, jig it back or reel it in slowly back towards the bridge and the shadow line. Usually, any fish that are feeding around or near the structure of a bridge will be found closer to the surface, within a couple of feet and close to the pilings that break the current. Some will hug the bottom where rocks, holes and the current help them ambush their prey.

From The Boat

Although many bridges can be fished by boat while drifting, the engine noise created every time the boat is moved back up into the current to begin a new drift may cause the fish to spook. For this reason, most boaters will prefer to anchor, or stake out, near the bridge on the up-current side. To avoid excess noise, slip the anchor into the water gently, not with a hefty toss like you are trying out for the Olympics. Let the current ease the boat toward the bridge and snub off the anchor line when the boat is about 50 to 75 feet from the pilings and bridge. While individual bridges may require a closer position, this is about right for most casting.

The leadhead is cast towards the bridge, allowed to sink momentarily and then retrieved in short hops. It can also be cast to the side at 90 degrees to the boat and the lure allowed to swing in an arc with the current until it reaches the bridge. The same hopping action is then employed to retrieve the leadhead and plastic tail back to the boat. Many fish will hit the lure just as the line begins to straighten at the end of the swing. Be ready to set the hook because this is the prime strike zone.

Stripers of all sizes will eagerly take a Fin-S or Slug-Go type plastic bait in the surf or from a boat.

CHAPTER SEVEN

FIN-S AND SLUG-GO BAITS

Prior to Herb Reed's introduction of the Slug-Go in the mid 1980s, no such soft-plastic bait had existed. The Slug-Go was a groundbreaking simple shape—just a long, thin, piece of plastic that is thicker in its center like a worm, then tapering to be narrower at both ends.

When rigged properly, the bait darts, dives and hops in an erratic motion on the retrieve. Stop reeling and it sinks slowly. The retrieve technique and natural action of the lure changed the way plastic baits were fished, and spawned a new line of lures. This erratic, unpredictable movement is what made the bait so successful with anglers.

Today, there are many different versions of the original Slug-Go. Some are fatter and some are thinner, but they all catch fish with remarkable success. The Bass Assassin, Power Slugs, Cabela's Livin' Eye, Mister Twister Exude RT Slug, Mad Man Shad, Tsunami, Strike King Zulu Shad, Yum Houdini Shad and others all utilize the same action and concept as the original. In total, these baits made a big impact not only in freshwater, but in saltwater as well, and they are still making inroads as more anglers discover their fish-catching potential.

The Fin-S Fish, another Herb Reed invention introduced shortly after the Slug-Go, has a fish-like appearance, thin body and forked tail, which make it hop and jump when the bait is worked properly. In particular, the Arkansas Shiner color is the closest thing to a real live silverside that I have ever seen. The photo with this section shows just how real the two look together. Ledge Runner Baits has a similar lure that has thicker plastic, is very hard to tear and works in the same manner. The Zoom Fluke has a thinner, less dramatic split in its tail, and there are several others available on tackle dealer's shelves.

Where To Fish 'Em

The shortest models of Slug-Go and Fin-S Fish baits are best fished in shallow water to water that is maybe 15 to 20 feet deep. In deeper water, there are other lures and baits that will be more effective. I would classify both these lures as "search baits". They run from a small 3-inch size up to 7 inches or even the giant 9 and 10-inch models. The 7-inch model is really considered to be a bigger fish bait and falls in the middle of the standard sizes and the large size. The most popular sizes for daily fishing are the 3 to 5-inch lures, which are capable of catching fish such as striped bass up to, and over, the 15-pound mark. Weakfish, snook, jacks and redfish also can't resist them.

When fishing thick grassy areas, heavy cover or sections of water where pilings or docks once stood, rig the baits so they are weedless and you won't get hung up on every cast. The Fin-S type bait has a hidden pocket in its belly, as do many of the other similar lures, for the hook to hide in after rigging. The Slug-Go types need to have the hook point stuck just beneath the surface of the plastic much as a plastic worm would be rigged. Most of the time, these are being fished on sand flats, mud flats, in rivers, along grass beds, along rocky shallow shorelines, or visible rocks, in estuaries, over mussel bars or oyster bars, and around and over points and sandbars.

Early in the morning or early evening, we like to fish them with no weight other than the hook itself. In shallow water, you get the best action with no weight attached to the bait most of the time. Once you have to go deeper, you need to pick a good jighead or add weight to the line (like a bullet weight, or some other type of weight) to get the lure down into the strike zone.

When choosing a jighead for the smaller size baits, be sure you pick a jig that fits the bait properly. The Slug-Go really doesn't lend itself to being rigged on a jighead because of its thin head design. The head tends to tear when trying to get it on a jighead. The Slug-Go type lures are better off being rigged with a weight in the front of the lure or on the line itself. Slip sinkers, bullet weights, egg sinkers, and such, or even adding weight to the hook's shank is a good technique. Sticky Weight, split shots, keel weights and the specialty weights made by Lunker City Lures for the hook's shank work fine. Even the small, nail-type weight or lead soldering wrap will work on the hook shank.

For Fin-S Fish type lures, be sure the soft bait fits the jighead properly. The arrowhead type of jigs seems to work the best because of their flat aft, or hook, side. Before threading a Fin-S-style lure on the leadhead, take a moment to cut off the nose of the bait. You want the front of the plastic bait to match in size, the back of the leadhead. When slid up onto the hook shank, the plastic body and leadhead should have about the same profile. Believe it or not, this makes a big difference on how the bait will act in the water, as well as how effective it will be.

Tackle Tips

When selecting tackle to fish these lures, you actually need three different outfits—a light-action, a medium to medium-heavy action and a heavy-action rod. This range of tackle will cover lures from the smallest and lightest to the heaviest. Obviously, a 3-1/2-inch bait with a 3/8-ounce leadhead is best cast and retrieved on a rod and reel combo capable of handling 6 to 10-pound test line. The heavyweight heads of 1-1/2 ounces need a more powerful rod and reel capable of handling 15 to 20-pound test.

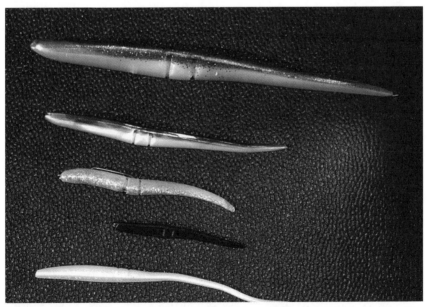

The Slug-Go revolutionized soft-bait fishing, followed soon after by the Fin-S Fish. From tiny to jumbo sizes, both lures are famous for impressive catches of gamefish.

When selecting the rod, remember you need enough power to set the hook. A wimpy rod just won't do it, especially with the larger lures. You can't punch a hook through the 9-inch Slug-Go and the fish's jaw with a light action rod. Chances are you will miss or lose fish 98-percent of the time. There is no rod that is going to be a do-all rod when it comes to fishing soft plastics of this type. It just isn't going to happen.

One of the necessary drawbacks to fishing with these lures is that they have a tendency to twist your line after a while, sometimes quite a bit if you aren't careful. To eliminate much of this problem, or at least cut down on it considerably, try using a narrow spool baitcasting outfit like freshwater anglers do. It eliminates almost all of the line twist immediately. If you prefer spinning tackle, then use a leader with a good swivel on the top end. The better the quality of the swivel, the less line twist you will experience.

Many Color Choices

A wide range of colors are available, and they all have their peanut galley cheering for them, depending on what part of the coast you're fishing. Bright colors, such as pinks and chartreuse are popular in the northeast and mid-Atlantic region, while the Carolinas like reds and browns, such as root beer for seatrout, and in Florida the whites and pearl colors are often in favor. The funny thing is that all these colors work at some time, everywhere. The best color is often more dependent upon the amount of daylight, or darkness, rather than the ability of one color to do a better fish-catching job in any one geographic region.

Color choices can be quite complex, or quite simple. Manufacturers go to great lengths to develop lifelike colors that resemble actual bait-fish, and many of them are remarkable in their exact imitation. Even simple colors like pink, also called bubblegum, can be modified to have silver flecks added, a white belly, white body with pink tail, dark body with pink tail, or pink body with a darker tail. The combinations are mind-boggling, but essential for many fishermen who swear that a particular color or color combo is the "perfect" color for their region. Having many colors from which to choose is a good thing.

I like to keep my color choices simple: white, yellow, black, chartreuse, pearl and bubblegum are pretty much all you need to be consistently successful. If you can't catch on those six colors, almost anywhere along the coast, then you're in the wrong tackle shop! Virtually everyone carries them—by the pegboard full, and often in several sizes.

Fishing Techniques

The basic retrieve will catch fish almost anywhere along the Atlantic Coast. After making the cast, let the lure settle a few seconds, depending on how deep you are fishing, and then give the rod tip a few quick twitches. Pause to let the bait sink slowly, then repeat the process over again. The more erratic the movement and retrieve, the more strikes you will probably get.

Sometimes a "do-nothing" retrieve is very effective. This tactic is useful when you are fishing in a good current and trying to dead-drift or dead-stick the bait in the flow of the water so it appears natural. Usually, however, some type of action needs to be applied.

The smaller size lures from 3 to 5 inches work well in water that is clear or relatively decent, and not much debris is obstructing visibility. However, when rain, storm runoff, and storms cloud the water at sea, it is best to go to a larger size lure. Once the water becomes murky or dirty, go to larger bait that produces more vibration and also adds some rattles to them for sound.

A good tip to remember is that once you have located a decent number of fish with the smaller lures, come right back with a larger one before leaving. Immediately toss a bait of 7 to 10 inches before you depart. Keep this lure rigged and ready to go on another rod just for this purpose. You may even see a good size fish following the smaller bait in on occasion; that is the time to pick up the other rod with the bigger bait and come back with a meal that will seem more appealing. Chances are he will strike the larger lure. We have taken many nice fish using that technique. The opposite also works as well. When tossing a big bait and fish are following, but not eating, immediately come back with a smaller version and they just might eat it.

Small baits will attract strikes from big fish. I recall one morning when I had a client tossing his bait onto a shallow water flat near a steep drop-off. This area was inside a cove we had fished for a few days with some good success. He had already taken a few decent fish when suddenly his line stopped dead in the water. He instinctively struck back at what appeared to both of us as a hit. Nothing happened. He struck twice more and started to say that he was probably hooked on the bottom and began to ask what I wanted him to do when his line suddenly screamed off his spool. The 7-foot light-action spinning rod he was using was bent over like a buggy whip as the surging fish did pretty much what it felt like.

Ten minutes or so later he got it close enough to the boat so I could Boga Grip the fish. It measured an amazing 43 inches that pulled the scale down to just a bit over the 30-pound mark. The guy was using 10-pound test mono, with a white 5-1/2-inch Fin-S Fish, on a 3/8-ounce Pro Jighead—proof that if you take your time, have good equipment, and fight the fish correctly and intelligently, you can land some nice fish on the smaller soft plastics and light tackle.

Vertical Jigging

Vertical jigging is an excellent method to use when the fish are holding tight to deep structure and the boat is anchored, or when the fish are scattered, but still holding in tight packs over a wide area and the boat is on the drift. Good bottom for jigging is usually found over rocky areas, shoals, deep drop-offs, ridges, reefs and wrecks. These areas will hold a variety of fish that will eagerly take a soft-plastic bait and include such favorite gamefish as blackfish and sea bass, weakfish, stripers, bluefish and croaker. Vertical jigging also works in shallow water for gamefish such as summer flounder (fluke), southern flounder, weakfish, sea bass, snook and seatrout.

When jigging vertically in deep water, it's best to keep the line nearly vertical, with the line entering the water as close to 90 degrees as possible, straight down from the tip of the rod. This gives the fisherman the best feel and ability to work the bait properly. Once it begins to get out and away from the boat at an angle, reel in your line and begin again. If the drift speed is very fast, add more weight or tie off a drift sock or sea anchor. Even a 5-gallon bucket on a short line tied to a cleat will slow the drift speed to make fishing more effective.

In shallow water, the angle of the line can be increased slightly to about 30 degrees, but should not exceed 45 degrees roughly. The rod tip is worked up and down, and the angler should feel the lure "bump" the bottom each time the rod tip is lowered toward the water. If you can't feel bottom, the lure may be ineffective and will not catch fish as well as if the lure was bumped along the bottom.

School bass tend to hold tight to rocky bottom formations, and can be jigged easily with shad bodies, tube baits, plastic worms, and

This teen-size striper whacked a big Slug-Go fished near the surface. Surf, bay or inshore, Slug-Go type baits catch fish.

big twister tail bodies. Fluke (summer flounder) also respond to vertical jigging, one of the "sportiest" ways to catch this gamefish. When fluking, it's a matter of lifting and lowering the rod tip so the jig rises about 3 to 6 inches off the bottom. Many of the pros like to do very short and fast snaps of the rod tip using their wrist so the jig dances up and down quickly and violently like a frightened baitfish. This lifting and lowering triggers the fish into hitting the jig aggressively. On some days, a slower presentation is required, and the rod tip is worked so the lure is just hopping along a few inches above the bottom. On other days, a faster jigging motion is best. Experiment with different actions until you find the one the fish are keying in on.

Rod selection for this type of fishing is usually one with a soft tip, but not too soft. It should have plenty of backbone in the lower portion to get a good hook-set and still be able to lift the fish up off the bottom. Using braided line such as Power Pro or Fire Line also helps in getting a good hook set, since there is no stretch in this material. It also cuts the water better with its thinner diameter and makes getting to, and holding, the bottom easier and faster.

When deep-jigging bluefish you usually want a fast retrieve. Back in the 1980s, this was called speed jigging, and anglers fished large diamond jigs to reach bottom. Once the bottom was felt, the jig was reeled back up as fast as the reel would allow. This technique will still work today with soft baits substituted for the hard metal jig. Although bluefish make short work of the soft tails, the catch ratio can be much higher on soft baits than on standard metal jigs. This is especially important on slow days when every extra fish counts.

A slower retrieve works well for striped bass, weakfish and croaker. Since these fish are usually bottom huggers, it pays to drop the leadhead to the bottom and then reel in only a few cranks, then free-spool the lure back to the bottom. If the fish are on the bottom, it makes no sense to retrieve the lure all the way to the surface and then drop it again. You've wasted three-quarters of the retrieve in the zone where no fish are located. Some party boat striper fans don't even retrieve, they just work the rod tip up and down to make a large Fin-S Fish, a shad body or swim bait dance just a few feet off the bottom. This short up-and-down jigging action can be deadly on fall stripers from Long Island to Virginia Beach.

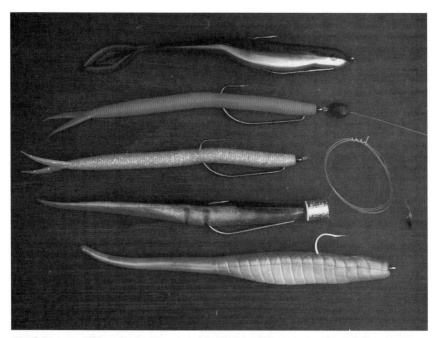

Fin-S Fish and Slug-Go baits can be fished on jigheads, or rigged Carolina and Texas style, or on the surface.

Rigging Tips

These lure types can be Carolina-rigged when fishing shallow sand or mud flats, and shallow, sandy beaches. The Texas rig is the better choice for rocky areas, and over oyster bars and mussel bars.

Here's a trick to make them fishable on the surface: use a fly-rod popper head or a small cork float ahead of the plastic lure, and you quickly have one of the most effective poppers you'll ever fish. A hard-plastic popper does not have this kind of action, nor can it duplicate the jumping and hopping of the soft baits. When using a cork, drill a hole just large enough through the middle of the cork to thread your leader through. Refer to the rigging diagram on how to make this and the other types of poppers with soft plastics.

Most striped bass trollers who use soft-plastic tails on their umbrella rigs usually employ the shad tails. In fact, in many areas, umbrella rigs are now more commonly known as shad rigs. There's no doubt that shads work very well to imitate a peanut bunker or a fat little herring, but how about sand eels? When slim baits are in residence, a Fin-S Fish is a much better imitation, and many savvy skippers are making the switch from shads to slim plastics when they need to imitate skinny baits.

With the HitchHiker rigging system from Tru-Turn hooks, your lure can now be rigged in tandem fashion or have a smaller bait in front with a larger bait behind or even two different types of baits all together. Both the Slug-Go and the Fin-S Fish type of baits can be cut in two and put back together with the HitchHiker rig for a broken-back lure effect.

Rigging Jumbo Slug-Go And Fin-S Fish

I'm sure there was more than one angler who raised his eyebrows when Herb Reed, owner of Lunker City Lures, introduced his first jumbo 9-inch Slug-Go and 10-inch Fin-S Fish. These baits were said to be as effective as a live eel at night, but most saltwater jocks quickly turned their noses up and totally ignored this new, fantastic lure. The guys along the coast were a hard sell when it came to trying new ideas, items and techniques for stripers, bluefish and other sport fish.

Freshwater anglers were already well versed in the importance of trying new baits. In their world, being in front on new ideas can mean the difference between a big tournament win and finishing last. Bass pros are eager to embrace new lures and techniques, and they immediately saw the great advantage to having a large piece of plastic to mimic a big threadfin shad.

The huge 9-inch Slug-Go comes complete with an 8/0 worm-style hook of heavy cadmium plated wire in every package. The first thing you need to do is sharpen that hook before you rig the bait. Be sure you use a good hook hone or file and get the point razor sharp, as it needs to be able to penetrate both the plastic and the striper's bony jaw (or for southern anglers, tarpon, cobia, redfish and other gamefish).

One of the better methods when rigging the large 9-inch Slug-Go stick bait for casting is to use a 7/0 to 9/0 Mustad Limerick offset tube hook. It's the same type hook used in rigging tube baits that are used on umbrella rigs. This rig came to us from River's End Tackle Shop, in Old Saybrook, Connecticut, whose owner Pat Abate has been fishing for years for striped bass and is one of the most inventive anglers I know. The hook has a bend in the shank that you can remove (somewhat) by taking two pairs of pliers to straighten it a bit. You will also need to close the open eye at the top of the hook with a good pair of strong pliers. You don't want to remove all the bend because this is what gives the bait its great action.

To provide a good, non-slip base so the Slug-Go won't slip down the hook shank, wrap the shank with some Dacron fishing line. I use 20 to 50-pound test, whichever is handy. Since this hook is not a welded-eye configuration, add a few extra wraps just behind the eye of the hook so there is no space for the leader to escape if the hook gets twisted while fighting a fish.

When threading the Slug-Go onto the hook, make sure the hook point comes out of the belly of the bait, the round side, not the flat side of the top. Rigging it in this fashion will cause the Slug-Go to jump, hop and flip all over the surface as you retrieve it back in. Work the tip of your rod in short fast twitches so the Slug-Go stays near the surface. The surface strikes when doing this are violent and fierce to put it bluntly.

After adopting this rigging technique, my hook-up rate rose sharply to almost 85-percent. If you rig it with a stinger hook in the tail section you will catch more fish, but most of them will be on the small side.

After you catch a number of fish on the bait, you can then glue the Slug-Go to the Dacron line, so you get extra mileage from each

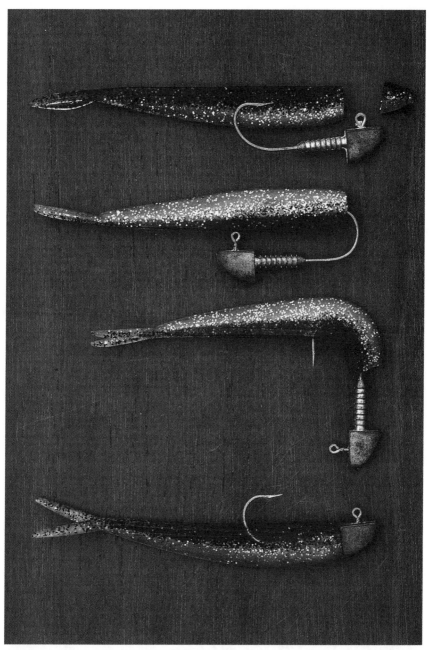

Place the jighead alongside the bait to determine the hook placement. Snip the nose of the bait so it matches the size of the leadhead. Insert the hook point into the bait, then thread the bait around the hook shank until the hook pushes through the top of the bait. Slide the Fin-S forward until it meets the back of the jighead. For a little extra holding power, some fishermen add a drop of Super Glue to the hook shank before sliding the tail into place.

bait. My son and I have taken up to a dozen or more good-size fish on one Slug-Go without having it rip or tear apart. It's the way it's rigged that allows you to do this. If the bait isn't constantly sliding or slipping down the shank of the hook, it tends to tear very easily. This rigging method corrects that problem.

It's important to have the lure rigged straight as an arrow. The hook actually acts as a keel and stabilizer to the lure when it's being fished. I've tried many other types and styles of hooks and haven't found any that work as well for this set-up. In a double hook rig, however, you can use other style hooks.

Slug-Go lures got a bad rap over the years because they could cause line twist. This is true, but there are several things you can do to lessen the impact of line twist or eliminate it totally. First, switch to conventional casting gear. Because of the way the line comes off the spool (over the top and not from side to side in a circular motion like a spinning reel) it lessons the twisting considerably. Second, adding a simple split ring to the eye of the hook and then a quality ball-bearing swivel, will cut down significantly on line twist as you flip and flop the lure back towards you. Using a leader with two swivels will also help in controlling line twist. In any case, to not use this bait because of any line twisting is simply ridiculous. It is far too effective to be tossed aside and forgotten.

When rigging on a leadhead, be sure to get the hook of the jig to come up and out the top of the bait on the flat side of the Slug-Go so it rides in the water properly. The huge 10-inch Fin-S Fish have the same problems and the same solutions as the Slug-Go does.

Fin-S Fish, Bass Assassins and Mister Twister RT Slugs and others of this style have a molded-in groove, or slot, in the underside of the body. This cavity is designed to help hide and embed the shank of the hook to make the lure weedless. This thin-walled cavity is suppose to collapse when a fish strikes the lure and then to expose the hook so the fish can be caught. I don't particularly trust that scenario since there is already a lot of plastic in the way to begin with. I rig mine to have the hook point outside and exposed so it's ready to strike anything that grabs it.

Adding A Stinger Hook

An inherent problem when striper or snook fishing, especially for big fish, is that many fish will strike the bait in the head portion of the lure. The hook point is actually located about 2 to 3 inches away from the head area. This means the hook is not in contact with the fish's mouth at the moment of the initial strike. This causes a lot of missed strikes unless the lure is totally engulfed in the fish's mouth.

A method of adding a stinger treble hook to the head of a big Slug-Go or Fin-S Fish comes from our freshwater cousins who pioneered this technique. First, use fly-tying or rod-wrapping thread to wrap a hump of thread to the shank of the leadhead hook just about at the bend of the hook. Next, slip the treble hook onto the shank, then tie another hump of thread near the forward part of the hook leadhead hook shank. The treble should now be on the hook shank between the two humps of thread and can move freely. The humps of thread will keep the treble in place yet still allow it to be able to swing freely on the hook shank. This makes an excellent stinger type set-up as most stripers will hit a bait headfirst to begin with. If the fish missed the main hook, the treble hanging from the shaft of the hook beneath will usually catch it. This will increase your hook-ups dramatically.

Another stinger-hook method adds the treble hook to the top of the head area of the bait. The treble can be mounted on a swivel just ahead of the hook eye, or to the eye of the hook itself. In either case,

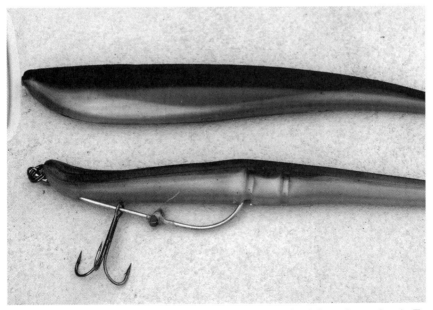

A treble hook can be added as a stinger to the shank of the primary hook. To keep it from sliding free, tie in a set of fly-tying bead eyes to the hook shank.

one of the hooks on the treble is pushed into the head of the plastic bait to keep the treble hook securely in place and ready.

Both methods worked very well, but an old-time saltwater eel-rigging method also works. The rigging material consists of two hooks, a rigging needle, some braided 50-pound test line, a spool of fly-tying thread and some Super Glue. Get two wide-gap hooks of 7/0 or 8/0 in size. I like the Matzuo brand since they are light in weight, strong, won't break and are extremely sharp. Thread the braided line to the eye of the rigging needle and push it into the bottom third of the Slug-Go. Begin to work it up and through the plastic as shown in the accompanying diagram. When you reach the end, attach the first hook and pull it inside the bait so only the bend of the hook and the point are showing. Come out the top of the head with the braided line. Now thread on the second hook as if you were going to rig the bait Texas style. Push the shank and the eye out of the top so the eye is exposed. Bring the braided line around the hook shank and through the eye of the hook. Hit the wrap with some Super Glue and make sure the whole thing is hanging straight. If it isn't, start over again.

Proof of the Slug-Go's fish-catching ability is in the catching. Author's daughter, Ashley, caught this nice striper on a Slug-Go bait.

Selecting the right rod to fish these behemoth lures is critical. You really need a rod with a lot of backbone and strong enough to drive that huge hook home through a half-inch of plastic and then into a big cow's jaw. When a big fish hits right at the end of a long cast (don't they always?) you better hope you have enough backbone in your rod to bury that hook. That is one reason we opt for baitcasting gear over spinning. I believe it lends itself to more control over the bait and the fish. Muskie-style rods are ideal for this type of fishing.

Once rigged, place both of these lures in a Ziploc bag and add some scent to it to eliminate any odor of plastic. We covered this already in the section on scents. Letting them sit overnight is of major importance.

Both of these large baits can be tweaked further by adding eyes, color from a marking pen, dye to change the tail section or the head (and many other things that haven't been thought of yet). On some hooks, we tie on red flashabou as a red throat on the shank of the hook and even color or paint the hooks red. Along with the addition of plastic eyes, you now have two of the most effective and consistent plastic lures ever invented.

Keep a tube of Super Glue or Zap-A-Gap with you so you can make quick repairs to the lure if it is torn or ripped. After a few hits the heads of these large lures tend to split open. Gluing them on the shank and back together again will get you a few more fish before you need to toss it into the dead lure pile.

These jumbo sizes of their smaller brothers can also be loaded with lead weights to fish them deeper and to change their action completely. By adding weight to the head, the belly or the tail end, you can control how fast or how slowly the lure sinks, and how it moves in the water when retrieved. By adding weight to the head of the lure, it will dive headfirst. When you jerk it, it will rise up and flop over like it's dying. When adding weight to the tail, the bait will sink tail-first and spiral downward. When jerked, the bait will hop forward and almost turn over. By adding weight to the middle of the lure, you can achieve almost neutral buoyancy, and adjust its rate of descent.

Jim White fooled this big striped bass on a large Tora tube fished deep at night. Tube baits are becoming a favorite soft bait for striper fanatics.

CHAPTER EIGHT

TUBE BAITS

Tube baits have been popular for quite some time in freshwater. Their use along the coast in the southern part of the country on snook, redfish and seatrout has also seen a sharp rise among anglers who target these salty gamefish. Up north, however, they haven't yet gained the same following as in other areas and other fisheries (with the exception of some fluke (summer flounder) sharpies). Despite their somewhat limited appeal to saltwater anglers, they are an excellent soft-plastic bait.

Originally designed to be used as a drop bait fished in a vertical up-and-down motion, tube baits are popular as a mid-water swim bait or a bottom bait, and anglers are discovering it can be fished virtually anywhere other soft baits will work. Tube lures are generally credited to being invented by freshwater bass pro Bobby Garland sometime in the early 1970s. The first were very small, measuring only about 1-1/2 inches. They were mainly used in challenging clear-water fishing situations. They grew to 3-1/2 inches by the late 1970s, and caught some pretty impressive stringers of fish for many of the pros.

Today, these same tubes are being used in both fresh and salt-water, as a growing legion of anglers begins to experiment with them for the first time. They now come in mega sizes of up to 8 inches and nearly 1-1/2 inches in diameter. Many saltwater anglers feel it is a superb representation of a live, natural squid. They weigh almost nothing, yet the big ones can be cast on spinning gear with only a hook imbedded in the bait for some amazing surface action. At the end of the cast, and because of their design and great buoyancy, soft-plastic tube lures will corkscrew their way to the bottom as they fall to the depths. This action is credited with its huge success in freshwater, which now is being experienced by saltwater anglers.

As with all plastic lures, no matter what size or shape, picking the proper size hook or jighead to rig this bait can make a significant difference in the lure's ability to catch fish. Just as with plastic-worm rigging or jerkbait rigging, the tube needs to be hanging in a straight line without any bumps, kinks or twists when on a jighead or a hook.

Try using a quality wide-gap hook with a "Z" or "J" bend to its head, the hook preferred by pros. The tube needs to sit evenly on the hook shank to work properly.

The standard measuring trick used by many of the bass pros including Triton's Pro, Shaw Grigsby, is to select a hook size that lets the hook point sit approximately 1/4-inch in front of the tail skirt. Grigsby then suggests marking that spot with a felt tip marker because that is where you want the point and the bend of the shank to enter. Using too small a hook will cause the tube to kink; use a hook too large and it won't swim the way it was designed to. It's really that simple.

Fishing Techniques

For saltwater fishing we are going to use the larger tubes from 4 to 8 inches. Therefore you are going to need tackle with a bit more power to it than most tube fishermen would normally use. My preference is a 6-1/2 to 7-foot casting or spinning rod with a braided line that has the same diameter as 10 to 14-pound test mono.

The jigs usually weigh in from 1/4 to 1/2 ounce for most inshore fishing situations. This may vary depending upon the area of the country you are fishing. For some species, you may need to go lighter, with smaller jigs and bodies than we need up north.

Grigsby likes tube baits because of their versatility. You can fish them from the surface on down to the bottom and everywhere in-between. When we fished together in Narragansett Bay, he showed me how he rigged and fished the bait in both fresh and saltwater. Surprisingly there really wasn't any big difference in the way he rigs his baits as compared to how mine were rigged. Using the tube in saltwater is no different than fishing in freshwater. You are going to cast the bait to some type of known structure, a rock, a weed line, a drop-off, a boulder field, sod bank, piling, bridge abutments or sandbar.

After making the cast, pull off 2 or 3 feet of line before you engage the spool on a conventional reel or close the bail on a spinning reel. This extra slack will allow the tube to sink freely and spiral as it sinks towards the bottom. Once it hits bottom, jig it back slowly. Gently raising and lowering the rod tip as you reel in is usually the most effective retrieve method.

When fish are feeding on silversides, mummies, shrimp, baby bunker or small sea herring close to the surface, you can skip it across

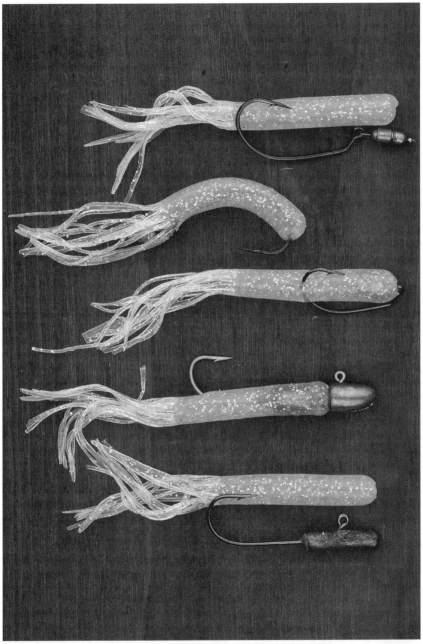

This method of rigging a tube bait uses an Owner Phantom Tube Hook. Insert the hook point into the hollow tube bait from the tail end until the hook point exits just slightly off center of the nose of the bait. Pull the hook through until the hook eye is outside the bait and the lead weight is seated inside the nose. Insert the hook into the bait as shown. Bottom two rigging options use leadheads to add weight and lure action.

the surface as you would a flat rock skipping and hopping and diving. This effect is deadly on surface-feeding fish. If they don't strike at the bait right away, just let it sink again and reel it back slowly.

In mid to late June when the large sand shrimp emerge from their burrows to spawn on the sand flats in our bay system, these tube baits work great. Sand shrimp are dark gray in color and average from 2 to 4 inches. The fish will normally just swirl and slurp them down like a trout does feeding on some bug hatch. When this is happening, the fishing can get pretty tough as they are so focused on the shrimp they tend to ignore most other types of food. Using these tube baits in the 4-inch size can make all the difference in the world.

Having the opportunity to fish with such a fine pro as Shaw Grigsby and learn his tricks firsthand was an amazing experience for me. He showed me how he rigs his tube to spiral downward by using the proper size jighead or by placing a weight on his patented Eagle Claw Quick Clip hook, which he helped to develop. The weight actually goes inside the tube's body cavity.

Twitching the lure across the surface and then letting it sink can draw impressive strikes from striped bass, weakfish and bluefish, as well as many other species. Use the bait with just a hook and let it free-fall after hopping it across the surface a few feet.

Tube baits are visually appealing to gamefish when jigged to make the skirts dance and pulsate. They are a very close imitation of a natural squid, which is a favorite meal for most gamefish.

Fish Scents

A relatively new technique is to stuff the tube cavity with cotton or foam inserts and load it up with some type of scent. Cotton balls or foam inserts can be pre-soaked in plastic Ziploc bags with menhaden, squid, crab, or shrimp scent and then placed inside the tube baits. This will leave a scent trail as the tube is being fished. Alka-Seltzer tablets have also been used and are sometimes broken into pieces and inserted inside in order to help create bubbles and that fizzing effect once cast out. It has been extremely effective in freshwater and works in saltwater as well. Other anglers looking for that big edge have actually stuffed the tube with pieces of shrimp, crab, menhaden, herring, and squid and used that as a scent trail.

Pure Fishing's scientists have done a lot of research on fish scents and have used this data to develop some excellent scents in their Berkley Power Tube line of soft lures. The built-in scent is popular among deep-water bottom fishermen who seek cod, pollock, haddock and many other bottom feeding fish. Tubes will catch stripers, bluefish, fluke, seatrout, weakfish, snook, redfish, jacks, and just about anything that swims.

Colors

Weakfish just love the bubblegum-colored tubes and watermelon tubes with fire tails, red sparkle, and white with yellow sparkle. Fished slowly close to the bottom or near the surface in the late evening or early mornings, weakfish will devour these baits.

Tubes are good on their own in water from 15 to 25 feet deep. Let it spiral down to the bottom so it acts like a dying baitfish as it is falling. The lure has to fall on a totally slack line for it to work properly. Lift the bait one to three times while it is on the bottom. If there isn't a hit, reel in and cast again.

For extra weights there are many options available. The Florida weights that have a corkscrew in the tail end can be twisted into the tube to hold it in place. There are weights with rattles built-in as well as a spot for the hook to go through when rigging so the weight isn't lost while fishing. You can pinch on split shots to the hook shank, rig it Texas or Carolina style, using the shaft weight weighting systems and many more options.

Rig A Spoon Tube

Tubes can be rigged on jigging spoons and casting spoons such as Acme Kastmaster, Fiord Spoons and Hopkins type lures. Push the tube over the spoon's body and make sure you have a swivel at the head. You now have a tube lure that can be throw a great distance and still have that soft feel to it. If the tube is one solid color you can use Spike-It dye to change the tail section for more visibility and appeal to the lure.

Tips And Tricks

To slow the tube's decent as it falls, place the jighead back further from the head in the body. A jig eye at the head of the tube will cause it to fall faster with much less spiral effect. You can also rig it backwards. Bring the hook point out of the head about 1/4 inch. This will depend on the size of the hook that is being used.

To get the tube to last longer and stay on the hook better, break off some old rubber or plastic worms no longer of any use and stuff the tube with them. You can now screw in the new type of hook holder that now comes on many of the finer hooks. This allows the holders to keep the bait in its proper rigging position for a longer period of time.

When you place the jighead inside and push it inside the tube's body, push it until it stops at the head. Now just push down where the jig eye is sticking up and it should pop right out so you can tie to it. Be sure no legs or arms of the tube get caught in the line or inside on the jig's head. Once a hole begins to get too big, usually after catching a few fish, simply rotate the tube slightly and do the same thing all over again and you are ready to fish again.

By inserting a piece of foam you can keep the bait off the bottom, especially on sand flats or mussel or oyster bars. Make a Carolina rig with a 6 to 7-foot leader. The extra long leader lets the bait stay in the strike zone longer. Tie on a 3/4 to 1-ounce egg sinker with two or three red plastic beads in the front of it for that "clicking" effect and to protect the knot. Move the rod from 10 o'clock to 2 o'clock position while reeling in any slack in the line making sure you are watching your line all the time. You need to learn to become a line watcher when fishing a tube and many of the other soft plastics. The rig is also effective on sandy beaches. Try using the newer Spider

Tubes that not only have tube tails on the rear of the baits but legs on the head as well. They are great for summer flounder and even striped bass when fishing a beach.

You can turn a tube into a small but effective surface popper by taking a pair of needle nose pliers or a pen or pencil and pushing the head of the tube inside of itself making a small cup or bowl. Now use a 4/0 to 6/0 wide gap worm hook making sure that you go through both the top and the bottom of the indentation of the cup. Now continue to rig the hook in a normal fashion as you would with any other type of tube or hook system. This will create small popping sounds and splashes on the surface.

Another type of popper can be made by simply cutting the head of the tube off the bait itself with a knife or razor blade. Push the tube body up onto a foam popper head or piece of cork. The tapered fly rod popper heads of hard foam work great for this. Now drill a small hole with a Dremel tool or hand drill down the center of the cork or foam body so you can get your leader through it. At the rear end where the tube tails are, stack red beads to form a separation between the popper body and the hook you will attach. Make sure the hook winds up extending between the legs of the tube. Tie on the hook, make a surgeon's loop in the top, and add a small swivel to attach to the main line. You now have a tube popper.

You can get fancy and add doll eyes that rattle or use stick-on 3-D eyes to give the tube, especially a big one, a more lifelike appearance. There is really no end to what can be done when rigging tubes.

School tuna are suckers for a well-rigged soft bait. Squids, eels, giant twister tails and ballyhoo imitations are favorites.

CHAPTER NINE

PLASTIC SQUIDS

Natural squid are one of the most important food sources for gamefish of all sizes and species. Clean the stomach of a fresh-caught striped bass, bluefish, weakfish or seatrout, and you'll stand a good chance of finding a squid. When it comes to squid, fish aren't much different than fishermen, and don't mind chewing on some fresh calamari.

In the northeast, there's a squid migration during May and June and then another smaller one sometime in September. Squid can be found offshore throughout the entire year. To the south, squid can be found year-round along the ocean-facing shoreline.

The use of soft-plastic squids has long been associated with both the inshore and the offshore fishery. The large plastic squids used for tuna and marlin trolling have been part of the offshore fishing scene a lot longer than they have been on the inshore scene. The inshore fishing really didn't see any serious use of plastic squids until about 25 years ago. I suppose there were a few enterprising fishermen experimenting with new ideas, but broad acceptance of inshore squids wasn't popular with the majority of the angling fraternity. The one exception to this was in the Pacific Northwest, California and Alaska, where soft-plastic squids have been in use for many years. They have been used extensively for king salmon, as well as rock bass, halibut, and a variety of other gamefish.

My first recollection of a fake squid being used was back in the late 1960s or early 1970s when they became popular in the inshore fluke fishery. Most of these squids were lifelike 4-inch plastic imitations, usually amber or white in color, but some were available in two-tone colors, which at the time was a pretty new concept.

In today's world, there are some pretty sophisticated plastic squids on the market that are available for anglers to use either inshore or offshore. Some are so realistic it's hard to tell them from the real thing at times, especially once they are in the water. Tsunami,

Luhr Jensen, Boone, JT Tackle, Cabela's and other companies make some very nice squids. That's not counting the companies that are manufacturing the outsized squids for offshore anglers who pursue tuna, marlin and swordfish.

Squids are used for cod, pollock, hake, wolffish, and other bottom dwellers as teasers rigged above large diamond jigs, or, big bucktails or large leadheads. Jigged over bottom structure, around oilrigs and over wrecks, the squid has accounted for lots of fish over the years.

In my opinion, the soft-plastic squid should be used in many more fishing situations. Like other soft-plastic lures that have appeared, their effectiveness and ability to catch numbers of fish through new and different ways of rigging, is still being discovered and improved upon. The fish love them, so why not use them more?

Basic Rigging

The first squids were relatively simple, but very effective. To make them catch fish, all you needed was a dropper rig tied about 18 to 24 inches above a bucktail jig. The leader to the squid was usually 18 inches to 4 feet in length. The squid's lightweight plastic body allowed it to ride high above the jig, and it had lots of movement. You could add strips of fresh squid and even live mummies to it to make it more appealing. Its long, lifelike tentacles made it a great fish attractor and catcher.

With the original squids, a fisherman was left to his own devices to figure out which hooks worked the best. Over time I tried all types and styles and models of hooks and finally settled on two different kinds. The first one was an English-style bait hook, also known as a Kahle hook. It's a thin-wire hook with a wide-bend style. Because of its wide bite, it has great hooking and holding properties. Its curved shank is great for rigging and hook-setting. The other popular hook was a 1/0 to 5/0 Matzuo hook or a Tru-Turn Bleeding Bait hook. The newer generations of these hooks are made of light wire, but are very strong and have super sharp points that allow the soft plastic to work better and act much more naturally than the heavier hooks of 20 years ago.

Now that squid are used by more anglers up and down the coast, they account for catches of weakfish, bluefish, sea bass, striped bass, channel bass and many other species. When squid jigging, I

Small to medium-size squid bodies rigged on a leadhead are a great soft bait for school tuna, little tunny and for casting to dolphin around weed lines.

find pink, clear, yellow, fluorescent green or pearl are just right for most situations.

Squid can also be placed on jigs or leadheads just like any other soft-plastic bait. They can also be used as a trailer and jigged off the bottom for stripers, codfish, pollock, hake and haddock. Remember to always use a metal jig as small as possible to get the rig down to the bottom. You will usually catch more fish with the smaller jigs, however, larger jigs with longer squids will usually account for the bigger fish. It all depends on whether or not you have the patience to wait it out for bigger fish to grab the larger imitations. In my experience in the charter business, most anglers usually choose more action and numbers rather than holding out for size.

You can make squids almost weedless and castable without a leadhead, by simply pushing a bullet weight or small egg sinker up inside the squid's hollow body cavity. Thread your line or leader through the sinker and place a small plastic bead between the sinker and the hook. When the hook is tied to the leader, the plastic bead prevents chafing of the knot. Next, run the leader up through the squid, then, pull the hook up inside the body. This is a great weak-fish rig to use at night during the spring. If you use a 1/4 to 1/2-ounce weight, you can cast it up against the shoreline for stripers that will gobble up a small squid in no time flat.

Boone Bait Company of Florida took the squid to another level by making a spinner-bait squid lure. The lure has big willow leaf blades in either gold or silver (chrome), and a leadhead with a plastic squid stretched over the leadhead. Bluefish love this lure when trolled in back bays or when they are on peanut bunker. With a marking pen, you can make an eye on the blades, or use stick-on fly-fishing eyes for added attraction. The gold-colored blades will wind up looking just like small peanut bunker that are now so plentiful in late summer and early fall.

Several years ago, a client of mine showed me a way to get more bonito and albacore to hit a soft-plastic squid when nothing else seemed to work. He took a 1-1/2-ounce pencil popper plug and removed all the hooks. He then tied on a 3 to 4-foot leader of fluorocarbon leader material to which he attached a 4-1/2-inch

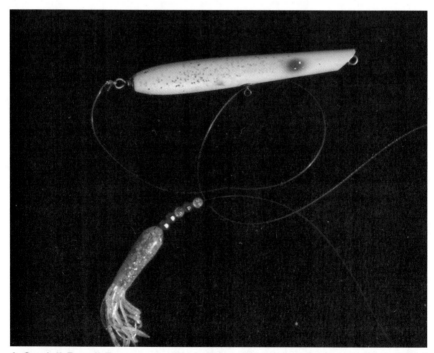

A Cordell Pencil Popper modified with a 3 to 4-foot leader at the tail end attached to a squid or large tube bait is a killer combo for inshore trolling.

This Atlantic bonito smacked a Mario's Squid draped on a bucktail and trolled on flat line in the wash just behind the boat.

plastic squid. Inside the squid, he placed a 1/8-ounce bullet weight pushed up inside to the top of the squid's head. He would then troll this rig at around 2,000 to 2,500 rpm's so the pencil popper would skip, jump and hop over the boat's wake and the white water. He told me, on more than a few occasions that he and his partner would land a dozen or more albies with this technique, as he was reeling in his fifth on my boat. It really is a great technique for taking finicky bonito and albies, especially when they are zooming from one spot to the next every few seconds and you can't keep up with them. That is the time to troll.

Although tube baits were discussed in another chapter of this book, the bigger tubes like the Tora Tubes and the giant 5 to 8-inch tubes really look like big squids. The 8-inch tube bait from Lindy's Old Bayside Lures is one of the most colorful squids I have seen. The plastic is clear with a tint of red, purple, brown and light green. It looks just like a real squid. If you add some eyes to it by gluing them on, you have one heck of a squid imitation.

Mario's Squids

In this family of squids we will include a product called Mario's Squid Strips. Available from 4 to 13 inches, they will attract most species of fish. These squid strips are scented, so they add a trail of smell that can be honed in on by most predators.

Mario's Squid Strips can be added to the following lures to make them even more effective: jigs, metals, bucktails, parachute jigs, diamond jigs, cod teasers, umbrella rigs, hex heads, Green Machines, and the backs of plastic shell squids. That is one versatile piece of plastic to have handy.

When fluke fishing, use them on bucktail jigs for greatly added motion and attraction. Choose a color combination that will attract fish according to the day's conditions. On bright sunny days, choose red hologram, silver hologram, violet, white, and pink. On cloudy days, choose chartreuse or emerald chartreuse. These two colors will work on foggy, overcast days as well as low light conditions.

Bucktails and a Mario's Squid Strip are a great combo for casting to tuna and dolphin or for light tackle trolling.

For striped bass, you have many options to choose from. Sizes from 4 to 7 inches are the key for most fish and fishing situations. Other popular colors for stripers are white, pearl white, emerald chartreuse, and black. For anglers who fish wire line with parachute jigs, you will find the red hologram, 7-inch model to be extremely deadly. Red hologram works best just at first light or just prior to dusk, as the sun begins to set on the horizon.

Near my home waters, Captain Kelly Smith of the Sea Devil II, guided an angler using a parachute jig with a Mario's Squid Strip to a monster striper of 58 pounds. For many experienced captains, the Mario's Squid Strip has replaced other traditional teasers on the tails of jigs and other lures.

The 4-inch Squid Strips can also be rigged on a single hook and cast towards rocky banks, grass beds and other structure for stripers as well. Use them with a light- to medium-action spinning rod and 10 to 15-pound test line for the best results. These are excellent on shallow water flats in the spring as well.

Northern offshore species like cod and pollock also like squid strips. The violet and red hologram colors are highly effective when used in conjunction with diamond jigs as teasers rigged above the jigs. Four to 7-inch sizes are preferred.

If you fancy sharks and shark fishing (who doesn't?), the long 13-inch strips are just what the sharks like to see floating off a fresh piece of meat. Many times, you can't find fresh squid that is big enough to use as strip bait when sharking; these plastic imitations fill that void nicely. Over the years, violet, chartreuse or blue/green colors (the latter looks like a mahimahi) have worked very well on sharks.

The Rhode Island state record dusky shark was taken by Captain Bill Brown on the Billfish in 1998 while using a 13-inch violet squid strip. He then followed that with a 526-pound thresher shark landed in 1999, another state record. That's one heck of an accomplishment for a piece of plastic.

Some tuna fishermen are finding these long, thin, lifelike soft-plastic squids are great on tuna as well. Try the 13-inch size in violet, black or red. It adds a lot of action when used along with 18-inch shell squids. The buoyancy of the Mario's Squid Strip adds to the realistic movement and appearance of the bigger squid, while the colors mimic the chameleon-like capabilities of the squid. The violet color is translucent, which acts like the true color of the squid's ink when it's frightened and trying to escape.

This hefty fluke fell for a leadhead rigged with a chartreuse shad body and fished over an inshore lump. Striped bass love shads, too.

CHAPTER TEN

SHAD BODIES

The plump profile and seductive swimming tail of a shad-body lure makes a presentation that is hard to resist by most gamefish. At one time, shad-style lures were only available in small sizes, but eventually the jumbo sizes came on the market to round out the selection. The small shads of 3 to 5 inches are very popular with inshore fishermen for catching school stripers, flounder, scup, (porgies), seatrout, sea bass, bluefish, weakfish, redfish, snook, drum, baby tarpon, jacks, mackerel, bonito and albacore and many other species.

Shads are not just available in the traditional leadhead, soft-plastic tail configuration. Today's anglers also have the remarkable swim baits from Storm, Tsunami and others that have a built-in foil holograph to reflect light. The swim shads have the weight of the lure molded inside the bait itself. The only part that is exposed is the eye of the hook and the hook shank itself. These newer, tougher plastics are even tough enough to survive repeated strikes from toothy critters such as bluefish and barracudas.

Larger versions of the shads are very popular with striped bass trollers, and big shads are now being used by offshore fishermen seeking battles with tuna, dolphin and billfish. The largest of the swim shads, with their molded-in hologram foil and weighing several ounces, are an ideal bait to use when jigging tuna in a chunk slick.

Shad-body plastics are among the most widely used of all the soft lures, and with good reason: they catch fish!

Small Shads

The most popular shad bodies are the 3 to 4-inch sizes. They get the most use from the majority of anglers, and will cover most of the inshore fishing situations all along the Atlantic and Gulf Coasts. The wide profile resembles a variety of important baitfish, so the shad body has really found its niche in inshore saltwater fishing.

During the early part of the season, when the majority of the forage found in coastal rivers and bays is small, the 3 to 4-inch shads are superb baits. They are great for tossing up against grassy banks or shoreline structure, or cranking them over a mud flat, or in a river system where holes and bends hold gamefish. Shad bodies in this size range are extremely versatile and are as effective on saltwater flats as they are down deep in offshore rips. You can cast them from a boat or from the shoreline just about anywhere you can reach the water. It is one bait that really doesn't require a lot of experience, as the action is built into the bait itself. The paddle tail does the work. All the angler has to do is cast out and reel back in.

As a guide, I get to fish with people of all skill levels. Shad tails make even a rank beginner into an accomplished fisherman. I can show someone with little fishing experience how to use it to catch fish in just a few minutes. The lure really does all the work on its own, provided you have rigged it properly and selected the proper size jighead. The shad's vibrating tail section sends out sound waves and the necessary action to trigger a gamefish attack. It really doesn't get much easier than that.

I have used plastic shad bodies in Florida, the Caribbean, Mexico and even in Cuba in 2000 when we went on a research trip with world-famous Lefty Kreh. Lefty had been invited by an Italian outfitter who ran a big outfitting lodge off the coast known as The Garden of the Queens, or in Spanish, "Jardines de la Reina." Those fish had never seen our plastic lures. We used up an awful lot of soft-plastic lures and caught a wide variety of species doing it. After the 10 days were over, I believe the 10 anglers accounted for 16 different species of fish in these pristine waters.

Early-run striped bass and weakfish are easily attracted to the 3-inch sizes in white, yellow, black, red/white, purple and bubblegum. The lures are best fished on the smaller size jigheads from 1/8 to 1/4 ounce. There are dozens of jigheads to select from, but choose one that does not have a thick collar that could rip or split the shad body while rigging.

When the head of the shad goes up against the back of the jighead, it should fit evenly and snuggly against it. This may require that you cut a small piece off the front tip of the shad body so it fits correctly against the back of the jighead. The better the fit, the better the bait will work in the water. The arrowhead shape of most

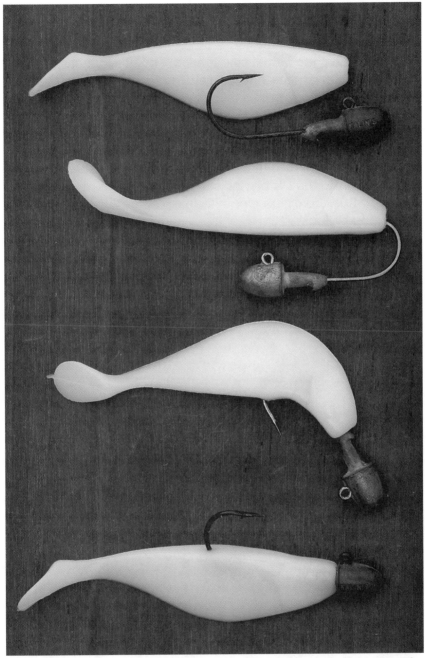

To rig a shad body, lay the leadhead next to the shad to determine where the hook point will be positioned. Insert the hook point into the nose of the shad body, then push the shad body along the hook shank and around the hook bend until the hook point exits the body. Slide the shad body up against the back of the leadhead.

191

jigheads used for shad bodies allow for an aerodynamic passing of water over the jighead's surface as well as the shad body itself. If this is done correctly, the shad is much more effective.

Always select the proper size jighead, and one that has a quality hook capable of holding a trophy fish. Many of the smaller jigs have hooks that are much too light for saltwater angling. Even if you have to pay a few more pennies for a better jighead, it will be worth the extra cost in the long run. It will result in more fish and less straightened hooks.

Jigheads equipped with a shorter hook shank are best for shad bodies. Refer to the chapter on jigheads and all the various types, styles and hook configurations available. This section explains what you should be looking for when selecting a jighead in size, weight and shape and what you should avoid.

Small shads can also be used to arm umbrella rigs for trolling. When the umbrella rig is rigged properly, the entire lure looks just like a small school of baitfish packed in close together and trying to escape. The rig has proven extremely effective both in inshore and offshore

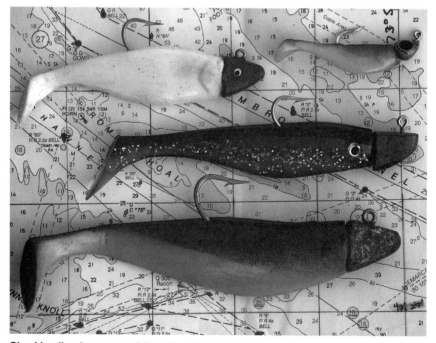

Shad bodies have a paddle tail and plump body shape that perfectly imitates mullet and peanut bunker. Snook, gator sea trout, striped bass, cobia, redfish and weakfish will attack a plastic shad lure with enthusiasm.

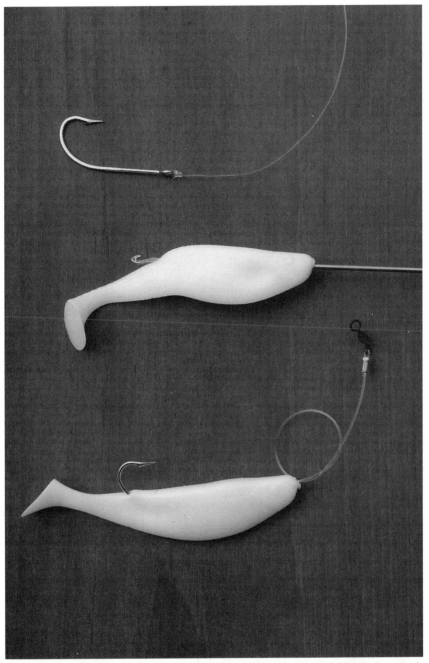

Tie a mono leader to the hook. Push a rigging needle through the bait, attach it to the mono leader, then pull the leader and hook into position inside the bait. Attach a barrel swivel to the end of the leader. The mono leaders add extra motion when shads are rigged on umbrella rigs. These are hot for stripers on the troll.

applications, and no doubt would also be effective down south.

Umbrella rigs come in a variety of sizes. There are mini-umbrellas that hold only four or five shad bodies instead of the regular eight to nine-bait models. They are good when fishing in shallow water situations, and do not need to be trolled on wire line or lead-core line outfits to be fished effectively. You can use braid or even straight monofilament for trolling.

Fishing Tips

When casting small shad bodies to a specific target (e.g. a point, rock formation, or underwater ledge), allow the jig to fall to different levels to determine the depth at which the fish are holding and feeding. Almost all of your strikes will come as the jig and shad are falling. From day to day, the depth where bass hang will change, as also happens on a changing tide.

The best retrieve system is one that works in many types of different actions as you reel it back in. A stop-and-go retrieve, allowing the jig to fall momentarily is good, as is fast bursts forward followed by a slower rate of reeling in. Lifting the rod tip occasionally will also work on fish that aren't sure whether they are going to eat your lure. Whatever method or retrieve you use, pay close attention and make a mental note of when a fish strikes so you can duplicate that retrieve on the next cast. As soon as you don't get any more hits, go back to mixing up your retrieve motions to find a combination that works.

Some of these baits will have a tendency to turn over on their sides like dying baitfish when you stop reeling in. Once you begin to reel again, they right themselves and come back up straight on plane. This is a very effective technique to use. The one thing you do not want to do is reel in the bait in one continuous straight line. You may catch fish once in a while doing this, but not nearly as many as you will varying the speed, depth and motion of the lure.

It will pay off big time if you are prepared with several different colors. Stick with the basics once again and you won't go wrong for 90-percent of your fishing time. White, yellow, chartreuse, black, blue/white, green/white, and red/white will work under almost all conditions and all situations. Have those colors available, and when they don't work, go to different shades or combinations of shades or another lure altogether.

Shad bodies are good candidates for adding rattles for that extra dimension of sound, especially the 4-inch models. You can also add stick-on or glue-on eyes to the bodies, or use color waterproof marking pens to add gills and eye color. You can add small stinger hook trailers to the tail section to get those short strikers when the fish aren't very aggressive.

Big Shads

With the welcome resurgence of the East Coast striped bass population, matched by growing population of alewives and many year classes of bunker (menhaden) in recent years, it was only a matter of time for some companies to start manufacturing the larger size shads from 6 inches up to giant shad bodies measuring nearly a foot in length.

For a time, the largest soft-plastic shads measured only 4 to 5 inches. Manufacturers stepped up to the plate with jumbo shads

This school striper belted an umbrella rig armed with chartreuse shads trolled on wire at the start of the spring fishery.

designed specifically for trolling. They are so popular that along some parts of the coast, umbrella rigs are now called shad rigs, because they are almost always rigged with plastic shads, not surgical tubes. They developed plastic imitations that had just the right flexibility, a lifelike profile, ease of rigging, and the right blend of durability and cost. Over the years, many companies have tried to fill this need of soft-plastic junkies who like to troll, and some have come quite close in molding some excellent super shads.

When the first huge shads appeared, many anglers scoffed at their ability to produce fish and to withstand the rigors of fishing, but it didn't take long to put those fears to rest. Today, big shads enjoy wide acceptance and are considered true fish-catching machines, the likes of which have been hard to duplicate with hard-plastic baits.

After a few knowledgeable pros got their hands on the larger shads and began experimenting with them, they opened the eyes of many anglers as to how effective they could really be. One of the first really good large-size baits I used was the Mann's Bunker Imitation. This thick, heavy plastic, molded shad-type body bait has fins, molded-in doll-eyes that rattle and move, sits upright when in the water when fished on a limp line, and has action like you can't believe. To watch it take its natural position in the water as if it were really alive is quite a sight indeed. I never knew it could do that until I tossed one in the bathtub one evening when my grandson was over. I noticed it didn't turn over on its side like other baits did. So that spring, I tried the same thing on the boat when I was fishing to see if it would stay in an upright position when falling. As long as the bait was rigged properly with either a jighead or a big hook, it stood up in an upright position as it went to the bottom. The lure comes with a 3, 4 or 5-ounce jighead so it can be rigged for trolling, casting or jigging. It can be three-way fished in rips or used on umbrella rigs for larger fish offshore. It is one very effective piece of plastic.

The 9 and 12-inch shads from several manufacturers have also become very popular with charter skippers up north. They are so effective that some fishermen prefer to use them instead of live bait in the spring. They feel the plastics work just as well as the real thing, and no time is wasted collecting live baits at a local brook or pond trying to catch buckies (blueback herring) for a day's fishing. Almost nothing beats the real deal when it comes to trying to fool any type of gamefish, but the popularity of soft-plastic baits gives some idea of how important they are becoming. They are accepted as a viable tool by pros that specialize in fooling big fish.

To rig either of these larger size baits is simple as long as you make sure the bait sits straight when positioned on the jig hook. You don't want it to have any bends, crimps, twists or bumps in the body to make it look unnatural in the water. Improper rigging will cause the lure to twist, which in turn will kink and twist your fishing line.

To hold these bigger baits in place, it's a good idea to glue them on the hook shank or the jighead so they don't move a lot or tear a hole in the head. I like tying some rod-wrapping thread onto the shank of the hook so the glue and the plastic has something to grab onto when gluing.

Tune-Ups

You will soon find out this fake stuff can and will work almost as well as the real thing. When striped bass are migrating up the rivers in the spring to feed on migrating alewives or herring that are ascending to spawn, the stripers find them (the soft plastics) just as

Like all soft plastic baits, shads can be modified with colors and extra scent to make them even more effective. Store the bodies in a Ziploc bag and squirt a few drops of scent into the bag.

197

tempting to eat as the real thing at times. This can be especially true when the run of buckies first begins and again when the runs are coming to an end, and there aren't many natural baits around. As good as they are, fishermen always find new ways to modify the lures or tweak them to help catch more fish.

One of the first things you might want to consider with these bigger pieces of plastic is to place them in a Ziploc bag and spray some type of scent in the bag and seal it shut. I'm sure that if you have ever handled a piece of new plastic, or taken one out of the bag to rig, the very first thing you smell is rubber and chemicals. Well, guess what? If you can smell it, just imagine how it smells to a fish that has the ability to smell in parts per million at great distances. It just has to stink to high heaven. Once we started to marinate our lures, we quickly saw a rise in the number of strikes we were getting. I'm not going to say which scent worked better, because I really don't know. What I am sure of is that almost any type of scent placed on these big lures is better than none and will improve your odds of getting the fish to bite. It also has the added advantage of masking your scent as well.

When the mullet run is on, snook have a hard time resisting a well presented shad fished on a leadhead.

Next, on many of the plain models of the big shads, we usually glue or screw in plastic eyes. Eyes add a very natural, lifelike appearance and appeal to the lure that fish just seemed to be drawn to. That's why so many fly fishers use big eyes in their patterns. A waterproof-marking pen can add traces of red around the gill area and the throat to imitate a bleeding bait.

You might want to consider trying to custom pour your own jigheads to fit specific fishing situations. I have a few friends who do that, and the special jigs they pour in both size and weight do not exist on the commercial market. The rigs and bait can be fished from three feet of water on down to over 70 or 80-feet of water or more. They fit a very particular niche when fishing for striped bass or summer flounder, and the jigs work terrific. There are so many items that you can buy today to pour your own jigs, it is mind-boggling.

Many anglers will add a stinger hook when fishing the 9 and 12-inch shad bodies. Add it so it makes it back to the tail section just before the thin part of the tail. If bluefish are present, this will be absolutely necessary as they will just bite the tail section clean off, and for some reason, they don't return for the rest of it most times.

To rig a stinger hook on mono, start by crimping the hook to the eye of a 2/0 treble hook, 3X strong. Next, push a rigging needle through the body of the bait to where you want the stinger hook to be located. Pull the mono leader through the bait until the treble hook shank slides inside the bait. Crimp the leader to the hook eye of the jighead. Almost all of the fish that take the stinger are hooked in the mouth and not down in the gut, and can be released easily. When using wire, make sure it's flexible enough so it doesn't impede the motion or action of the plastic lure. The bait will work best with the treble positioned in front of the tail so it doesn't interrupt the swimming action of the tail section as you cast, retrieve or troll.

Ripping Shads

Plastic shads are also referred to in many articles and books as swim baits. The shads can be ripped through the water at lighting speed to induce strikes from many species of gamefish. When your quarry is not very aggressive, this is often the ticket to many more strikes and hook-ups.

When fished quickly in this fashion, they account for bluefish, Spanish mackerel, dolphin, barracuda, bonito, albacore or small school tunas. Fish them with a relatively fast retrieve with twitches of the rod tip to make it dart forward and rise up as if it is being chased. This will allow you to cover a lot more water so you can tune-in on those aggressive fish. It's also nice having only to deal with one single hook and not a bunch of trebles. Take it from someone who's been to the hospital more times than he'd care to admit.

Rigging for speed-ripping requires the same precautions and rules to be followed as if you were rigging it for any style of fishing. Make sure the jighead matches the size and shape of the plastic shad being used. If you don't, you will certainly notice that the lure will turn over and not ride properly. This is especially true when ripping the shad at high speeds.

Lunker City Lures has introduced a shad body called the Salt Shaker, which is slimmer and narrower in the body than most other shad baits. The heads on these shads are already cut flush so they fit the jighead perfectly when rigged. This allows the bait to be ripped very fast without fouling or turning over on its side.

Match a shad body to a light-weight jighead when wading the flats to catch stripers, like this big schoolie being released by the author.

Power-cranking or power-ripping will let you cover a lot more water in a shorter period of time to find those aggressive fish. This technique has been effective on freshwater bass for decades and works just as well in saltwater as it does in freshwater.

When seeking bigger fish, these large shad bodies can be trolled individually on braid, mono, wire or lead core or rigged on downriggers or used on umbrella rigs to present to a school of huge baitfish. Use eyes, rattles and marking pens to tune them up.

Three-Way Rig

Big, rubber shad bodies from 6 inches to almost a foot in length and the giant Tora Tube, can be three-wayed across the bottom just like live or cut bait and in many cases it is just as effective—if not more so.

Three-waying big soft plastics over bottom structure or in deep holes, reefs and over wrecks requires the use of proper equipment to get the job done. A rod of 6-1/2 to 7 feet and of medium heavy action to heavy action is the best rod choice. You need the power to set the hook once you get a hit. A conventional reel is definitely the way to go with big baits. We use Penn International 900 series and spool them with braided line such as Power Pro or Tuf Line that is very strong, sensitive and has a thin diameter in relation to test strength. This helps get the baits to the bottom faster since there is less water resistance on the line. The ability to detect strikes with this line is amazing. The best rod I have found is the St. Croix Muskie series. This rod is 6 feet, 9 inches and made from E-Glass. It is light, powerful, and has power in its butt section to lift heavy fish.

To rig up, start with a good quality three-way swivel. Tie on a length of mono leader material that is lighter than the main line. In case you get hung up it will break free and you won't lose your whole rig. Usually a 2 or 3-foot leader is sufficient to attach to your weight. On the second eye of the three-way swivel, attach the main line from your rod. For the third and last eye, tie on a leader of 4 to 7 feet with fluorocarbon leader material and attach your big bait to it. Because you will be fishing over rocks and reefs and the bait will be getting pulled, hit the shank of the jig's hook with some Super Glue to hold the lure in place.

Other big shads like Storm's WildEye series have weight built-in or molded into the bait already. The bait hugs the lead tightly since

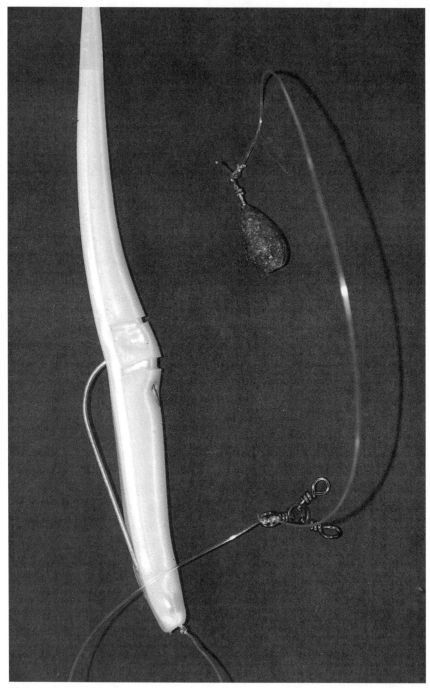

Most soft baits can be rigged for three-way fishing. This Slug-Go is rigged on a 24-inch leader tied to a three-way swivel about 12 inches above the weight. Jig it while drifting and it comes alive.

it is almost one piece. Since its introduction a few years ago, it has made a real impact in the striped bass fishery.

When three-waying, you want to fish over and around reefs, ledges, underwater humps, rockpiles, and areas where the greatest possibility exists to find fish. To three-way properly, you really need to have excellent electronics. Quality electronics are vital not only to finding fish-holding structure, but being able to see what is living on or near it as you drift over the area. A good GPS system is also helpful so you can get back to the spot where you found them. If you find them and can't get back, that's a lot less fish you'll catch.

Shad bodies of 6, 8 or 12 inches (or more) make excellent three-waying jigs. At times they are so good they may produce better than live bait.

**Mister Twister invented the soft baits with the famous twister tails.
They've proven successful on snook, trout, reds, weakfish, fluke and stripers,
like this one.**

CHAPTER ELEVEN

MISTER TWISTER TAILS

Twister tails are one of the oldest and most popular saltwater soft-plastic baits. They are one of the most versatile soft baits, and have been used by fresh and saltwater anglers to catch fish for many years. The original lures were designed by Mister Twister, an innovative Louisiana lure company responsible for helping to make soft lures so well received by the saltwater fishing fraternity. So popular have Mister Twister tails become that any soft-plastic lure with a curly-tail shape is called a twister tail by most fishermen. The term has become generic for this style lure.

Twister tails come in a wide range of styles and colors to duplicate just about any bait imaginable. Their main feature, and what makes them so appealing to a wide variety of gamefish, is the long, thin, sickle-shape tail section, which gives the lure its natural-looking action. When retrieved, the lure has a wild swimming action as the tail section fans back and forth, giving off vibrations as well as motion for fish to key on.

Twister tails come in sizes that range from tiny 2-inch creations that appeal to winter flounder, southern snappers and spike seatrout to big 10-inch lures capable of fooling a hungry tuna. In particular, the 2-inch model can be used in the springtime for the cinder worm hatch and can be cast on a fly rod. The ones with split-tails are also very effective on the worm hatch in red, red/black, orange/black, and pink/red. Just thread on a number one (#1) short shank hook, thread it on and toss it out. For the most part it seems that the 4-inch twister tails are the most popular.

Bodies of twister-tail lures are sometimes smooth and sometimes have rings around them. The ringed bodies are said to hold air and give off bubbles once they hit the water.

Getting real fancy, some twisters now have double and even triple-tail designs. Some have holes punched the length of the tail so water passes through it when it's retrieved, creating some extra sound vibrations.

There is such a wide array of colors available today that it is almost impossible to not be able to find a color or color combination that will work. From northern waters on down to warmer southern waters and even the Gulf states, there is a color for the species that inhabit those regions for both inshore and offshore. Of special interest are white, chartreuse, yellow, black and red. Multi-colors will often have a contrasting tail color such as white with a fire-red tail, yellow with a purple tail or purple with a lime green tail. These color combos offer exciting possibilities to attract strikes from gamefish.

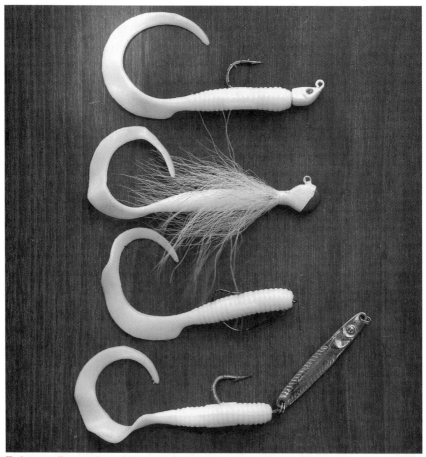

Twister tails are rigged the same as other soft baits, and they come in a variety of sizes that catch spike-size seatrout to big tuna.

Rigging Tips

The 4 to 6-inch twister tails are probably best known for use on the back of jigs as trailers, or ahead of lures as a teaser. Depending on the style of jighead chosen and how that jig is dressed (how much hair or nylon fiber is on its collar) will depend on how you apply the twister tail to it. You will also need to choose the size and tool shape that will work the best according to fishing conditions.

Problems arise when you choose a tail that is too thick, too long or too heavy for the jig. This will cause the jig to become overpowered by the large tail, and it won't ride correctly in the water. Too large a bait will also cause the bucktail or the synthetic fibers to flair out of proportion and away from the body of the jig giving the jig an unnatural appearance. Selecting the right size or the proper size tail is critical to your fishing success.

One way to solve this problem is by adding a stinger hook to the jig's hook and threading a twister tail onto the stinger hook. When this is done properly, it gives the jig a jointed body effect and provides a ton of extra action to the tail. You could also use a pair of scissors to trim the hair on the jig from the inside area around the hook. I have tried this method and do not care for it too much. Many jigs are tied in different proportions and degrees of thickness with the hair and fiber material. I have found you can mess up the jig totally when you take a pair of scissors to it. The stinger hook method is a much better option.

Twister tails can be rigged and used by themselves, especially the new larger or jumbo sizes available in 8 to 10-inch. These huge twister bombs, as we refer to them, lend themselves to a wide range of applications for many different species as well.

One method is to rig them weedless style by burying the hook point just underneath the body, then toss it into rock-infested areas to draw stripers and other fish to it. It can also be thrown underneath mangrove bushes, into thick patches of eelgrass, saw grass, river grass beds, or up beside pilings and docks. Use a 5/0 to 7/0 hook to make it work properly.

For fly-fishing, the 2-inch baits should be rigged on a Tru-Turn Bleeding Bait hook or an Eagle Claw hook and fished on a 9 or 10-weight fly rod with a floating fly line when the cinder worms are hatching. Allow the lure to drift if possible and hold on for some smashing strikes. The action of the tiny tail section leaves the same telltale wake on the surface that worms do when they come to the surface during their spawning cycle.

Fishing Tips

Your tackle selection here is going to be the same as when fishing other baits of similar size and proportions: it has to be in the heavy category. The best example is you wouldn't use the same tackle to toss and fish the 3 to 5-inch twister tails as you would if you were tossing the 10-inch mega sizes. It just does not work.

Light spinning or baitcasting gear can be used for most of the 2 to 4-inch size twister tails, but many anglers like to work the lures with stouter tackle. They believe a stiff rod helps impart more jigging action, and the rod has the muscle to haul a fish out and away from bridges and dock pilings. This is especially true when fishing with the larger tails, which can attract strikes from larger fish. A rod with a stiff action is more effective with heavier lures to allow better casting and increased ability to work the lure correctly. Stout tackle also has more power to set the hook and drive the hook out of the plastic and into the fish's jaw in one swift movement. A 6-1/2 to

Because of the fluttering tail action, weakfish just can't pass up a curly-tailed soft bait.

Florida Keys flats fishermen use twister tails to fool redfish, speckled trout, jacks and baby tarpon.

7-foot medium-heavy action rod with a baitcasting reel such as a Penn 965 International or a St. Croix Avid 250 loaded with braided line, are ideal choices.

Inside river systems where there are bridges and pilings, rig the twister tail with a single hook and some weight in front of the head. Throw the bait up against bridge abutments, piers, under docks, against pilings and other wood or cement structure. Bounce it off the structure and let it sink slowly towards the bottom. During the morning hours before the sun gets too much above the 10 o'clock position, most bridges will retain a shadow line. This shadow line works the same way as a shadow line at night, even though the sun is shining. The fish will key-in along the edge of the shadow to feed until the sun is overhead and they drop down to deeper water. If you fish this edge with the proper lures, you can catch some very nice fish.

Twister tails that have a round body, such as the Magumbo Grub, can be buzzed over the surface of the water to cause a commotion the likes of which you have never seen. The strikes this bait generates are nothing short of heart-stopping. These big twister and grub-style tails can also be used like a popper on the surface, provided you use the right gear. Both the 10-inch Magumbo and the 8-inch Power Grub can be fished in this manner very effectively.

You can also choose undressed plain jigheads to rig twister tails on. These can then be fished from just beneath the water surface to depths as deep as 100 feet or more. Once you cast the jig and tail, you simply raise and lower the rod tip as you reel the lure back towards you allowing the tail to do its job.

Twister tails have been used as teasers rigged above a big jig, such as a diamond jig for cod, pollock, halibut, grouper, and other species over offshore wrecks and high spots. They have accounted for some very nice fish. They can also be used effectively when drifting for fluke during the summer. Twister tails of 6 to 8 inches in white, chartreuse, and pink are great attractors when fluking on the inshore and offshore grounds.

Twister tails can be used as replacements on umbrella rigs and trolled for stripers and blues. Check out the motion and action of an umbrella rig rigged with six twister tails as it moves through the water. It just begs to be eaten!

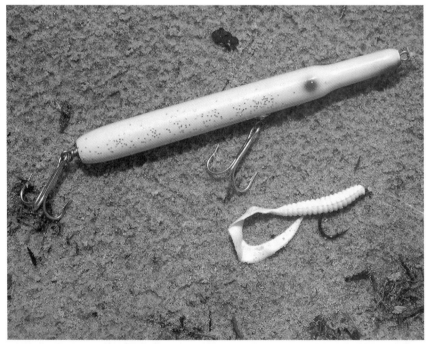

A Mister Twister fished as a teaser ahead of the main lure is a dynamite way to fool striped bass in the surf.

If you use your imagination, you can get fancy and stick plastic-worm rattles inside the body of the twister tail. Just use a plastic-plug puller, insert it into the body of the tail's grub section and pull out a slug of plastic. Then insert your rattle in the newly created hole. Before I place one inside, I usually drop in a couple of dabs of glue inside to hold the rattle and keep it from slipping out during casting.

In the early spring when the fish are shallow, I rig two twister tails in tandem and troll them in tight up against the shoreline on a mono flat line. Use a big 8 or 10-inch grub tail for the front section and a 4, 5 or 6-inch tail on the back end. The trailing twister tail is rigged so the hook is close to the body's tail section in case the fish are hitting short that day. You can also rig up a stinger hook rig with a smaller hook trailing the larger hook in the head portion and place it just at the spot where the tail meets the meat of the body. I usually use a number one or 1/0 hook for this purpose, as it doesn't interfere much with the lure's action.

Try mixing the color combinations so every angler onboard tries a different color. Start with white/yellow, white/chartreuse, white/black, black/watermelon or white/bubblegum. When fished close to shoreline cover, they can spark tremendous strikes when the fish are aggressive especially during the early morning hours just as the sun is coming up on the horizon.

When using just plain hooks, try wrapping a few with rod-wrapping thread before tucking them inside a hunk of plastic. The thread on the hook shank will allow the plastic to hold the hook better and it also gives you someplace to add some glue if necessary to hold the hook in its proper position. Doing this also stretches the shelf life of the plastic.

A fake shrimp fooled this crevalle jack into striking. Imitation shrimp, crabs and baby lobster-like baits are the go-to lures for many saltwater anglers.

CHAPTER TWELVE

SHRIMP, CRABS AND LOBSTERS

Three of the baits most commonly eaten by gamefish are shrimp, crabs and lobsters. While the natural baits are good, they are followed closely by soft-plastic imitations that look so real you think they might swim away! These three soft plastics fill a void that hard baits just can't match.

The soft-plastic shrimp has been around for quite some time and was first of this trio to be manufactured for sport fishing. Plastic shrimp have progressed a long way from the original simple shrimp molds into the elaborate clones that are produced through today's technology. The D.O.A., Rip Tide and Snappin' Shrimp are extremely lifelike and have a terrific fish-catching reputation.

Shrimp baits have been used for many years in southern waters, developed essentially for southern seatrout and redfish. Their appeal in the sport fishing world is well-known and very broad. They will catch striped bass, bluefish, weakfish, fluke, seatrout, redfish, snook, tarpon, jacks and just about any species of inshore gamefish that swims in saltwater.

As the appeal of shrimp baits grew, it was only natural that manufacturers expanded their production into lifelike crab baits and crayfish or lobster imitations. Some of these baits have built-in scents, and all have great appeal to a wide variety of gamefish. Fishing with shrimp, crab and crayfish/lobster plastics has opened new possibilities to lure fishermen.

Fishing With Shrimp

Shrimp are sometimes thought of as a southern bait, but they are just as abundant along the northern coast. When fishing with imitation shrimp baits, chumming with the real thing can be a big help. Shrimp are often present in good numbers at local marinas or docks, and can be seined or scraped off pilings with a fine-mesh net. Grassy areas are the best bet. Outflow areas of creeks, back coves, back bays, rivers and small estuary streams also hold lots of shrimp.

Many of the imitation shrimp are pre-rigged with the hook molded into the body of the bait. All you have to do is tie one on and make a cast. Others are unrigged and must be mounted on a jighead, or rigged with a weight at the nose.

One of the more popular methods that originated in the southern fishery is to fish a shrimp beneath a popping cork. Although the method looks amazingly simple, it can be very effective. Popping corks are 3 to 4-inch pieces of cork with a hollow head, a hole down the middle of the cork and a 3 or 4-foot leader of heavy mono, running from the head to the end where the shrimp goes. Some have beads at the head, some don't. In the top of the head, I like to place a Worth Popper snap, so you have a solid place to attach your line and get a good solid knot attachment. The rig is very effective on seatrout and redfish but it also will take striped bass, weakfish and bluefish up north. In our area, it is used mostly to catch snapper blues in the harbors and coves off the bay. Unfortunately, despite its potential, the popping cork has never really caught on in the northeast. The popping cork also works with other baits as well; it doesn't necessarily have to be a soft-plastic shrimp that you tie on the bottom portion of the leader.

In New England and the Mid-Atlantic region, the grass shrimp has made a tremendous comeback in numbers, and in the areas they now inhabit. As waterways have begun to recover species diversity from industrial pollution and waste, shrimp have returned in amazing numbers to areas they were once plentiful.

During the early spring, the first bluefish to show up in our bays, feed heavily on the tiny shrimp. The fish, known as harbor blues, are usually 1 to 3-pound juveniles that invade the bay areas in big numbers. Many that are caught spit up a handful of tiny shrimp.

For New England surfcasters, the popping cork rig is very similar to the egg and jig float combination that is so popular in the surf

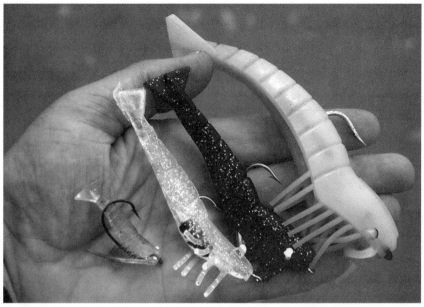

They look good enough to eat! Plastic shrimp are a favorite bait in Florida for snook, trout, baby tarpon and reds, and they also catch school stripers and weakfish up north.

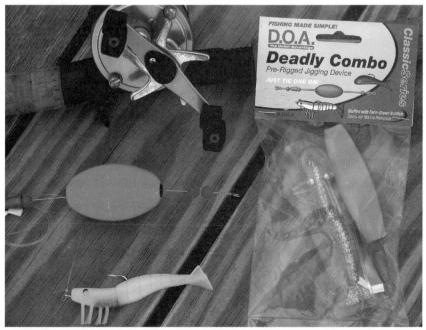

Float rigs are popular with bay anglers seeking weakfish and seatrout. The float is rigged so it pops and makes a metallic "clacking" noise when the rod tip is jerked, attracting the trout to the shrimp.

during the spring for schoolies. Although not quiet as heavy as the wooden egg float, the principle is the same with popping corks.

I like leaders of fluorocarbon leader material so they literally disappear in the water. A leader of 18 to 24 inches is fine. Cast the rig out, let it settle a bit, pop the cork two or three times, then stop to allow the shrimp to fall. Repeat the process until you are back to the boat or shore.

We have found this combination deadly in the spring, and early summer on shallow water flats, in back bays and coves, in estuaries, rivers and over sandbar areas where shrimp gather.

When using the popping cork rig, try making the leader close to the depth of the water you are fishing, but not so long that it lays on the bottom. Once you pop the cork, the shrimp will rise up behind it; once you stop, the plastic shrimp will sink back towards the bottom. You want it to ride just above any bottom weed, or obstructions so it is always 3 to 6 inches off the bottom and visible to the fish. On sand flats or over mud flats, this technique is deadly on early run striped bass.

Most of the gamefish we pursue can become very selective at times in their eating habits, especially when there are lots of shrimp bait available or other food supplies. At times like these, when sand shrimp emerge from their burrows, the stripers will key-in on them and eat nothing else. They will pick off one shrimp at a time off the surface just like a trout would feed on a hatch of bugs. Many times, you will only hear a slurp or a pop, a sure indication they are feeding on sand shrimp close to the water's surface.

Sand shrimp are grayish in color and about 2 to 4 inches in length. They come out of their burrows individually, and usually are seen singularly on or just beneath the water's surface. If you aren't looking very closely and paying close attention to them, you can easily overlook their presence. The best days to see them are calm, foggy days, with high humidity and no wind. That is usually when most shrimp come to the surface. It's during this time that the popping cork and shrimp combo work great.

Some of the new shrimp lures come already weighted and can be fished on their own. Just cast them out and snap and hop or pop the rod tip so the bait jumps, darts, and hops like a real shrimp. Other types of shrimp lures, like Berkley's Power Shrimp, Snap Tails, and Scamps, can be rigged on a jighead or worm hook and fished deep or near the surface.

Tube baits from 2 to 4 inches, small curly-tail grubs and flat-tail grubs can also be used to simulate the shrimp. It all depends on where and how you are going to fish, and how deep the fish are holding.

If you combine the plastic shrimp with fresh shrimp chum, you can really do well in drawing the fish to the boat and your artificial offering. With lots of live shrimp in the water, the new duplicates are easily mistaken for one and eaten. If you spray them with some shrimp scent, they'll work even better.

You can get a supply of shrimp for chum with an 8-foot seine or a fine-mesh net. Marinas are one of the best and easiest places to find lots of live shrimp. Just take a fine-mesh net and scrape it underneath the docks and across the foam that floats the docks. In no time at all, you'll have plenty of shrimp for chumming.

Crab Baits

The introduction of the soft-plastic crab is a relatively new occurrence, but these new creations are making up for lost time. They catch all types of fish from bottom-hugging sea bass and tog to stripers and weakfish, seatrout and snook.

Imitation crabs have come a long way and they look so natural they are easily mistaken for a live one. Striped bass and weakfish eat them up north, and permit, bonefish, reds, snook and trout eat them down south.

Northeast crabs came into their own for two reasons in my opinion. First, fly anglers began to notice that crabs had hatches just like the cinder worms did. It usually happens in early summer on very calm, foggy mornings, on an outgoing tide when they emerge from the rocks and drift in the current by the hundreds of millions. It is quite a sight if you have never witnessed it yourself.

Since the green crab and a few other crab species were introduced by accident to our waters from ships coming in from overseas and dumping their bilge water into our waters, the crabs have proliferated in amazing numbers. The problem is they have very few, if any, natural enemies here in this country.

We now have the green crab, rock crab, lady crab, calico crab and the blue claw that are common in our waters in the northeast. When these hatch, they are about the size of the head of a pin. Even fly fishermen have a very difficult time matching such small bait and worst of all they are around by the tens of thousands. The fish just open their mouths and suck them in by the hundreds. So getting a fish to focus on just one particular fly or piece of plastic is a difficult task at best—but not impossible.

A second reason crabs are getting more angler attention is a change in the striped bass diet. With fewer large baitfish present in recent years, stripers have begun scouring the bottom for other food sources.

The fish, it appears, are becoming increasing more bottom-oriented, as there is a lack of big baitfish such as menhaden, squid and mackerel. At the same time, the explosion of the crab population

Even finicky bonefish can be taken on imitation shrimp. Let them settle to the bottom after the cast. Retrieve with short, slow hops so they look alive.

in our country, especially in the northeast, has provided an easy meal for foraging stripers to easily feed on. Why wouldn't they take advantage of this free meal? I've found crabs almost 3-1/2 to 4 inches across the shell top inside their stomachs while cleaning bass.

It was only a matter of time before a few of the more enlightened companies, such as D.O.A., would try to produce a crab imitation that would appeal not only to stripers, but weakfish, seatrout, snook, tarpon, redfish and other gamefish that feed on crabs on a regular basis.

One of the very first plastic crabs I saw was from Bass Pro Shop. A friend of mine gave me a few to try on the flats, as he was having some great success with them. The crabs were just a simple crab shape with an extra long piece of plastic off the side for rigging. I used it some but I could not gain any confidence that a fish would actually be stupid enough to try and eat it.

That's when I found the Rip Tide crab. Rip Tide is the saltwater division of Culprit Lures, who make all types of saltwater plastics. They answered requests from the Redfish Tournament anglers for a realistic crab pattern they could use while fishing tournaments. Rip Tide answered their request and developed one of the most realistic crab patterns on the market today.

Before you scoff at the crab, remember they laughed at Herb Reed's Slug-Go when it came out. No one is laughing anymore. I believe this crab will eventually be in the same category, once anglers figure out new ways to present it to gamefish. As it gets used by more and more fishermen from north to south, it will become part of their regular offerings while fishing.

The one big drawback is this bait has to be fished very, very, very, slowly. And you need to pay close attention to your line and what is going on while fishing it. Crabs don't normally move in feet per second, it's more like millimeters per minute. Therefore, the slower you fish it, the better your chances of being successful.

The crabs made by Rip Tide come in 2 and 4-inch models so they cover the most fed-on size by gamefish. The crab can be rigged in a number of ways. A plain hook of appropriate size will work fine in the 2-inch model. I use a hook from 1/0 to 3/0 in black chrome like the Matzuo O'Shaughnessy model. The 4-inch version warrants a 5/0 to 6/0 hook. You could use a weedless worm hook as well since it will be on the bottom most of the time, or the Mustad or Mister Twister weighted worm hooks with keeper wires on them.

For deeper presentations, you can attach a jighead. Hook it in the side, right behind the legs on either side of the plastic. This rig can be fished in and around rocks, drop-offs, and mussel or oyster bar beds crabs frequent.

Remember you need to fish this plastic imitation slowly. That means s-l-o-w-l-y, at a snail's pace to be effective. The bigger 4-inch models will float just beneath the water's surface with only a hook in it.

The unique thing about this bait is that the methods to fish them and the techniques that work are still being discovered. When all is said and done, crab imitations will no doubt take its place among other soft plastics as being a very productive lure for many types of gamefish.

Crayfish And Lobsters

You can call them crayfish if you like, since they do come from the freshwater fishery and are sold nationally as crayfish, crawfish, or crawdads. I prefer to refer to them as baby lobsters. The ones made by MadMan Lure Company are so realistic looking that it is almost impossible to tell them apart from the real ones. I placed one in a tidal pool with a real lobster of similar size and dared friends to grab the plastic one, giving them only five seconds to make up their minds. No one wanted to stick their hands in the pool in that short period of time, for fear of grabbing the real one.

Maybe you don't believe a self-respecting striper would stoop so low as to eat a rubber crawfish, would they? Well, I look at it this way: during the needlefish craze of the early to mid-eighties, I refused to believe for the longest time that a striper would eat a piece of long wood with no action. It was totally alien to what I had been taught. This was the smartest fish in the ocean. No stick would fool them. They would figure it out in a hurry. Well, twenty to twenty-five years later, anglers are still catching striped bass on needlefish plugs of both wood and plastic, so it shows you just how little we knew.

Stripers are foraging on the bottom like never before. Once again, ask someone who takes a fish or two occasionally and cleans it. Guess what they are seeing inside the stomach besides a lot of crabs? Yes, that's right, lobsters of 3 to 7 inches and sometimes in numbers, not just one. Bass are eating these things like they are going out of style.

Small lobsters and crabs can be found on sand flats, over oyster bars and mussel beds, boulder fields and deep drop-offs. Once again, the most likely reason that more anglers aren't using these types of soft plastics is they don't know about them, have never seen them, or it takes too much in the way of patience to fish them properly. If you retrieve too quickly, you probably won't get any fish to hit your offering.

A long, slow steady retrieve is required with quick 2 to 3-foot sweeps of the rod tip to move the bait quickly like a live lobster would, trying to escape. Once you complete this move, go back to a slow, steady retrieve. Lobsters will move quickly with one push of their fantail, but most times they are simply moving slowly across the bottom looking for food.

The first thing you need to do is to get yourself some MadMan crayfish in red shad, brown/orange, or crawdad colors. There are other imitations out there, but I find this one the closest to a real lobster as you can get.

You will notice a hollow cavity in the belly of the bait. Inside this cavity you are going to insert a piece of foam. The long, cylindrical foam bodies that are available for fly rod poppers work great. Before you get it inside, punch or drill a hole through it so you can get a leader through it. A Dremel tool is great for this job. Some anglers just push the foam inside and then connect the leader to the eye of the hook without foam. It really makes no difference as long as the lure rides properly and doesn't spin or turn over unnaturally.

Now make a 12 to 18-inch leader of fluorocarbon leader material. At the end, tie on a SPRO swivel. Above that, thread on a barrel sinker or an egg sinker of appropriate weight for the depth of water you will be fishing. You only want enough weight to continually maintain contact with the bottom. Your main line is attached to the other eye of the SPRO swivel, sort of like a small Carolina rig.

Cast it out, let it settle to the bottom and remain still. The foam should lift the crawdad up and off the bottom while the sinker goes to the bottom. Reel in s-l-o-w-l-y, with a steady motion, letting the sinker kick up mud, dust, sand and weed as you crawl it along the bottom. After a few feet, sweep the rod tip up and back to a vertical position in one even, quick movement. Then stop, and regain any slack in the line. It's a deadly technique for stripers.

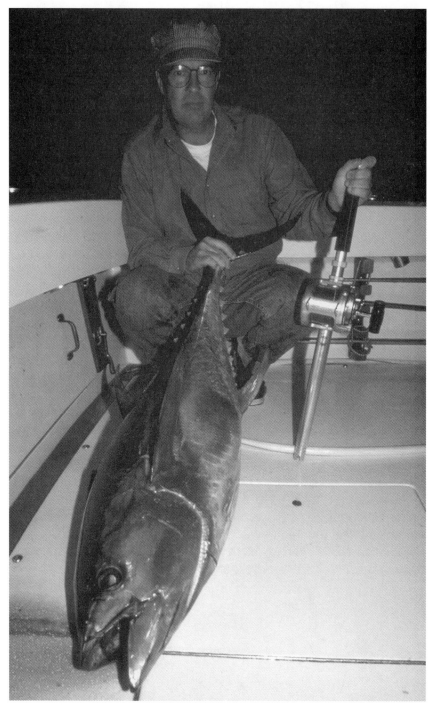

Jumbo shads, twister tails, Fin-S Fish and Slug-Go baits will fool yellowfin tuna. The strike is jolting and the battle exhilarating on stand-up gear.

CHAPTER THIRTEEN

PLASTIC BAITS OFFSHORE

Some of the finest, most challenging gamefish that swim the world's oceans are found in the blue waters far offshore. The cast of characters includes yellowfin, blackfin, bluefin and big eye tuna, and longfin albacore, plus the inshore tunas such as little tunny, skipjack and bonito. Large or small, they are exciting and physically demanding fish to catch. Anglers also find dolphin, those beautiful gamesters that range from pint-size grasshoppers to hefty bulls of 35 pounds or more, in the same neighborhood as tuna. White marlin and southern sailfish are also readily caught on plastic baits in these same waters, shark anglers are also using soft-plastics to fool mako, thresher and blue sharks.

Soft squids were the first plastic lures to become popular with offshore trollers, especially when rigged as a daisy chain or on spreader bars. They'll catch everything from big blue marlin and giant bluefin to the smaller tunas found closer to shore. Dolphin and white marlin love them too.

As offshore anglers experiment with soft-plastic lures, some exciting new ideas are being introduced by innovative skippers. Manufacturers also seem quick to explore these new fishing opportunities, and special soft-plastic lures designed from the get-go for offshore fishing are becoming popular.

Offshore techniques include casting to small tuna in a chum slick or casting to dolphin around a fish pot, trolling along structure edges, jigging in deep water and drifting for sharks. Rigging methods and lure choices vary widely depending on the angler's strategy; casting, trolling, jigging or drifting. Casting new lures and new techniques catch plenty of fish, so let's take a look at what the offshore clan is using to get more strikes.

Which Color?

The old timers use to tell us that the best color lure or jig for the albacore and the bonito was yellow. Their second and third choice was also yellow. As long as some part or portion of the lures, tin or jig had yellow in or on it, the lure would catch both species. That theory is over 45 years old and it still holds true to this day. Day in and day out we catch more bonito and albies with something that is yellow than almost any other color in the neighborhood of four to one.

We must remember, however, that the old timers of years past didn't have the color selection to choose from as modern anglers do. Back then everything was pretty basic. It was mostly white, blue, black, yellow and some reds or a combination of those colors. Today there's an amazing selection of colors. Some are bright attractors, others are lifelike imitations. I can't imagine my father trying to decide which lure to buy today in a sport shop. He'd be totally confused looking at the selection to choose from.

There's no single color that is best for offshore, and the well-prepared angler will have a selection on hand. Yellow is still a perennial favorite, and pearl white is a close second. Just like on the inshore grounds, offshore anglers will choose from a variety of bright, dark and lifelike combinations. The point is—bring a selection of colors, along with various sizes of plastic tails. You just never know which color or size will be today's winner.

Casting For Fun

Small tunas, such as bonito and false albacore can be taken on simple stick-type lures such as Slug-Go baits, YUM worms and Bass Assassins with just a standard worm hook imbedded inside the bait's body. Cast this light lure out where fish are feeding on the surface and race it back towards you as fast as you can. The strikes will be explosive and arm wrenching.

When working a chum slick, cast the lure out, let it settle and then begin a hopping retrieve. This technique is usually a sure bet with 3-inch shad bodies such as Mister Twister Sassy Shads and the smaller Berkley Power Shads. Fish them on a leadhead jig to cover the water column from the top to the bottom. Let them sink after a cast to go deep, or start retrieving right away to attract surface strikes.

Medium size soft-plastic baits can be jigged for tuna or cast into weedlines or around lobster pot markers for schooling dolphin.

Recently, anglers experimenting with the YUM worm and the Gary Yamamoto Senko Worm in white, white/green and watermelon have had great results with surface-feeding fish. These worms have a shimmy-and-shake action that drives saltwater fish nuts. It's not unusual to see four of five gamefish attack the lure at the same time.

Swim baits, shad tails, slender jerkbaits and curly tails will all take small tuna in a chum slick. Vary the weight of the leadhead to get the desired water depth. Small dolphin, often found around fish-trap or lobster pot markers, are suckers for a soft tail retrieved with a hopping action.

Squids can also be cast effectively for offshore species. The rigging set ups are the same as we discussed in chapter nine. Casting squids to dolphin hanging near a lobster pot marker, some floating debris or a weed line is great fun, especially on light spinning tackle. To get the fish on a feeding frenzy, toss a few small chunks of butterfish, ballyhoo or natural squid toward the dolphin school. Once they start whacking the baits, toss the plastic squid into the action and hang on—the hook ups are usually fast and furious.

The Trolling Game

Plastic squids are best known for their fish catching abilities when trolled. Although they can be presented as a single lure, most blue-water fishermen rig them as daisy chains—a string of several squids on a single leader. The sizes of the squids can vary from small 3 and 5-inch sizes for inshore species such as little tunny, school bluefin and bonito, to hefty 9 and 12-inch sizes for bigeye tuna, giant bluefin, blue marlin and yellowfin. "Rubber" squids, as captains call them, are so effective, that many skippers rig them hookless and run them on special lines off the outrigger lines. The teasers are let out and hauled in by hand and are not attached to rods and reels (although the teaser lines can be wound onto reels especially dedicated to the teaser lines and clamped to the tower or railing of the boat.

Small plastic squids can be enhanced with an additional vinyl skirt slipped over the front of the squid. The added color and motion are often very effective.

Here is a rig and a method that I learned from one of my clients one day when chasing albacore with not too much luck. He told me how he rigs a 4-inch plastic squid in pink or chartreuse on a 4 to 5-foot fluorocarbon leader. Inside of the soft plastic squid he inserts a small bullet weight, the type used in largemouth bass fishing when fishing plastic worms. At the top of the rig he attaches a 2-ounce pencil popper with all its treble hooks removed. His preference is the Cordell Pencil Popper because it has a built-in rattle chamber that helps attract fish. He then trolls the rig behind his boat in the boat prop wash at around 5 to 7 knots or so. It works like magic and raises a lot of fish.

I took his idea one stop further and made a mini daisy chain using six to eight squids and rigged one in back of the other on a long leader. Crimped in place with a foot or so in between each squid, it makes an impressive lure presentation. I like to place several red, yellow, pearl or green plastic beads inside the squid bodies to get some added glow and color. As in the original version, I attach the Cordell Pencil Popper at the top end of the chain.

Larger squids have been used as a daisy chain on a single mono leader for many years. An expanded version is the spreader bar rig which adds a stainless steel or titanium bar across to the leader about one quarter of the way down from the forward end of the daisy chain. Spreader bars add up to eight or more additional squids and provide a top-water show that rivals a small pod of live natural baits.

Big shads can be rigged for trolling. Add a skirt for additional color and motion. They work real well when positioned on flat lines.

Daisy chains can be fished on flat lines close to the swirling water of the boat's wake just a few feet off the transom. An alternative position is on the second or third wake, also on a flat line. The last alternative is to run the daisy chain off an outrigger. Trying to keep all the squids in the water so they splash effectively may require that the outrigger clip be positioned halfway up the outrigger halyard, instead of all the way to the top. Too high and all the squids will leap clear of the water in a very unrealistic appearance. Squid spreader bars are usually fished off flat lines or directly off the rod tips. They have too much water resistance to be held in an outrigger clip.

Large shad-style plastic tails are becoming more popular with school tuna, longfin albacore and dolphin trollers. The wobbling paddle-type tail has great action and a small vinyl skirt can be added to the front of the shad body to add additional motion and color. To keep the lure below the surface, hide an egg sinker under the skirt. The added weight will make the lure track straight and true in the trolling pattern.

A plastic squid daisy chain in action. The commotion calls in tuna and billfish because the lures are extremely visible to gamefish.

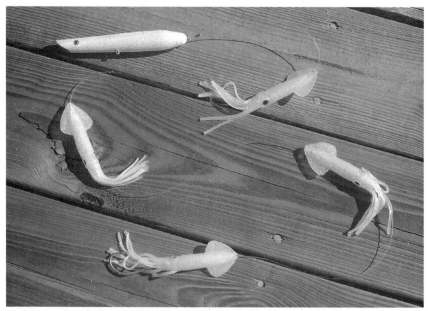

Here's a daisy chain of vinyl skirts fished behind a pencil popper. The incredible splashing from several lures attracts tuna like kids to ice cream.

Ballyhoo Baits

Manufacturers such as Calcutta, Mann's and Mold Craft now manufacture some remarkable soft baits that very closely resemble "the real thing, baby." They can be rigged as single baits and dressed with a skirt to add color, or they can be rigged as a dredge, a huge umbrella rig affair that is used to attract sailfish and marlin while power drifting with live baits. The dredge looks like a massive ball of bait near the boat and attracts billfish with amazing success.

To prevent the soft baits from tearing apart, the hook is usually pulled through the bait until the hook eye is exposed at the front, or nose, of the bait. This is especially easy to do when using relatively light 80 to 130-pound leaders for sails and whites. The tag end of the leader is pulled through the bait from the nose to a point just behind the gills. The hook is then tied or crimped in place and the leader is pulled forward until the hook seats correctly just as when rigging a natural ballyhoo. A lead weight can be added to the leader at the nose to help the bait swim better.

An added advantage of fake ballyhoo baits is the ability to change colors. Bright yellow, chartreuse, pink and pearlescent are easy to see, but dark baits, especially black, show up vividly against the light blue background of the sky. When a fish looks up from its watery domain, a dark lure is very easy to spot. That's why many trollers use black, purple or red baits, or they drape a dark color skirt over a bright body.

Most boats will troll several baits, four or five at minimum and up to nine or more on larger boats. It can pay off with increased catches if the colors are mixed to offer the fish a variety of dark and light baits. If one color is attracting most of the strikes, then the crew can add more of that special fish-catching color to the trolling pattern.

Deep Jigging

The heaviest swim shads, leadheads and jigs can be very effective on members of the tuna tribe. Depending on the water depth and the level at which the fish are located, leadheads of 2 to 8 ounces can be used to pull plastic baits down to the feeding level of the fish.

The jigging action that works best requires a quick upward sweep of the rod tip, then lower the tip to let the jig settle down deep. Lift the tip smartly again to make the bait zip toward the surface. This

Huge leadheads and jumbo tails plummet to the depths where yellowfin tuna feed. When chunking, if tuna are holding at 10 to 20 fathoms below the chunk slick, drop a big soft bait down to grab their attention.

alternating upward sweep and drop down makes the jig dance very nicely and yellowfin, bluefin and bigeye tuna can't seem to resist. Most strikes will come at the end of the drop down so as the next rod lift is attempted, the fish is immediately hooked. Hang on! It will be quite a ride for a few minutes.

If the tip-sweep doesn't seem to catch the fish's attention, the reel-and-drop technique can be a good alternative. After the swim bait or jig has been dropped down to the desired depth, the reel is engaged into gear, the rod tip pointed towards the water and the angler simply cranks 10 to 15 turns of the handle. After cranking the bait up, the reel is free spooled to let the jig fall back down to the feeding depth. Re-engage the reel, crank, then drop back down. This technique works well, but the angler has to pay attention to be sure the leadhead does not drop down below the level at which the fish are located. The leadhead can often be seen clearly as a scratchy line on the display screen of the colorscope or fishfinder, so keeping track is not usually difficult.

Stand-up tackle is usually employed, with 30 to 50-pound gear the most popular at the distant canyons, and slightly lighter equipment getting the nod for schoolie-size fish. Avoid hardware such as snap swivels, but a leader can be added via a small SPRO barrel swivel. Use a double improved clinch knot from the main line to the barrel swivel, and a four-turn clinch to add the heavy leader of about 4 to 6 feet in length. Tie the lure directly to the leader with an improved clinch knot.

Drifting For Sharks

There are several good books that describe the best techniques for catching sharks. In this book, we'll just concentrate on how to improve the bait presentation by adding some soft plastic tails to the menu. Most sharkers fish for these toothy critters while chumming and drifting over changing bottom structure, or along the edge of a water temperature change. Fillet baits are proven winners and are used by many shark anglers to attract bites from sharks called into the chum slick. Mackerel, menhaden, bluefish, shad, little tunny and skipjack are among the preferred choices.

Adding the largest filleted mackerel or whole herring, adds an extra dash of color and motion that sharks find irresistible. Mario's Squids can also be fished alone with no natural bait because just the color and motion of the tails will attract strikes.

Natural baits can be improved upon by adding a large Mario's Squid Strip to the natural bait. The two-tailed soft-plastic squid adds color and motion to the visual package. Mako and thresher sharks have a hard time resisting this bait and soft plastic combo.

Small sharks that enter the slick and are visually seen near the surface can be caught by casting a leadhead and plastic tail lure just ahead of the shark. It has to be close so they can see it, but not so close that fish are spooked. Rig up with a short length of wire leader to avoid being cut off by their sharp teeth.

On the flats in Florida, plastic baits are a proven lure. Use a 3/8 to 1-ounce leadhead, depending on the water depth, and add a bright yellow, red or green shad tail. Cast on light spinning tackle or a light seatrout-style casting outfit and these fish are great fun to catch. They run fast and far, pull hard and give a very sporting account of themselves.

Tackle Tips

Choices for tackle and gear offshore are wide ranging to say the least. We are living in an age where tackle has reached sophisticated proportions in all areas. Spinning gear for the smaller tunas consists of reels like the Quantum Cabo 40 or 50 series or the Penn 550 Slammer. Load these reels with a super braid line and you will have enough line capacity to catch most any of the smaller tunas such as albies, skipjack, school bluefin and bonito. A 7 to 7-1/2-foot light to medium-action spinning rod is great for the lighter lures and jigs as you can make long, accurate casts with even the lightest weight plastics. Don't be afraid of going too light either. Anglers are catching these fish on fly tackle. As long as your equipment is in good working order, you have good line, a drag system that is smooth and you take your time and fight the fish properly, you can land almost anything on light tackle.

For large school and medium tuna, such as yellowfin and blackfin, you should have tackle that is a bit heavier. An outfit in the 20-pound class range should be sufficient for most fishing situations. Look for reels that can handle 17 to 25-pound test line like the Cabo, Penn, Shimano, Okuma and Daiwa medium size levelwind reels, or small lever drag reels, and you will have a lot of sport, yet still have plenty of power to land these scrappy fish.

With the larger size tunas, most offshore veterans use larger lever-drag reels capable of handling 30 to 80-pound line rods with roller line guides and aluminum butts. If you fish from a small boat, stand-up gear can be employed instead of the traditional, but longer, trolling rods.

Small plastic baits are nearly weightless and can be effectively fished with fly tackle. It's a fun way to add some extra sport to your fishing experiences.

CHAPTER FOURTEEN

FLY ROD PLASTICS

Several years ago, my son and I introduced soft-plastic lures to some of our more enlightened and progressive clients willing to try new ideas and techniques. I must admit that there were some who became down right belligerent about flycasting with plastic baits. The argument over what is and what isn't acceptable as being a so-called "fly" is, in my own humble opinion, ridiculous. One could make the same argument over many of the standard fly patterns on the market today that they are not actually flies, but fall into some other not-yet-classified category of fishing tackle. The first would be the Clouser Minnow. Today it is accepted as a great fly, but one could argue that it is really a jig and not a fly at all.

So let's cut to the chase and say we enjoy catching fish and using new ideas and tactics to do it. We enjoy sharing these ideas with others that would like to try them and really don't have the time to argue fishing philosophy. We prefer to have our rods bent and drag screaming than to stand shaking our finger in someone's face or pointed up in the air.

In our fly-fishing guide business we have always used what is considered pretty big flies by most standards. We have been doing this for many years, long before it became fashionable. Some of the flies we created were 10 to 12 inches, but big flies caught big fish. Some had Clouser eyes so big that if one hit you in the back of the head, it would knock you out.

One morning while casting with a client over a deep oyster bed for big stripers, the customer made a comment on the huge fly he was trying to cast, just as the fly and line became wrapped around his back. He simply stated that he could have tossed his partner's

Slug-Go just as easy as the fly that I had given him. That started me thinking.

For more than a few years, light tackle anglers had been doing very well, sometimes even better than the fly guys, especially during the cinder worm hatches in the spring. The lure they were using was a 3-inch Slug-Go with favorite colors such as bubblegum pink, red shad, purple or black. The Slug-Go was the perfect imitation for the small worms as they came spiraling to the surface in their mating ritual dance.

I decided to try a small Slug-Go on the fly rod and see what it could do. I rigged my 10-weight Thomas & Thomas Horizon rod with a Rio floating fly line and using long-shank bend-back hooks "tied-up" with several 3-inch Slug-Go tails in bubblegum and clear metal flake. The match of this size plastic to the 1/0 bend-backs was perfect. The bend in the hook caused the plastic to lie perfectly straight along the hook shank and the bend underneath was the perfect keel to keep the lure upright and working properly. I was totally surprised to find how easy it was to cast this "lure fly." Both colors proved to be more effective on the fish during the hatch than almost any worm fly I had

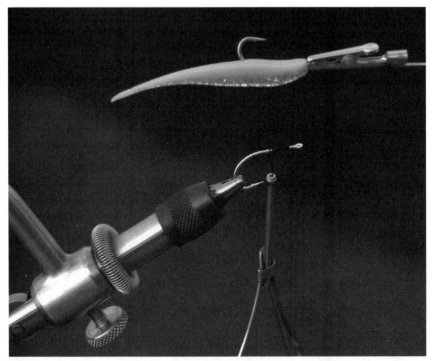

To keep the bait positioned on the hook, wrap the shank with fly tying thread, apply a drop of Super Glue and then slide a Fin-S Fish into place.

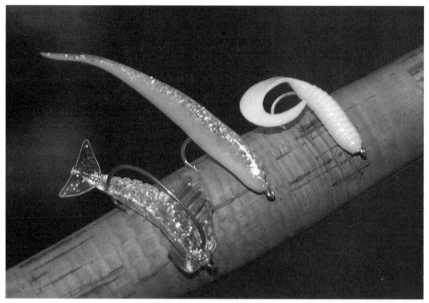

Small imitation shrimp, Fin-S Fish and curly tails are all good candidates for fly fishing.

ever used. The tiny Slug-Go had the same darting, diving action as the worms did when they come to the surface; the floating line kept them on top where they needed to be.

That size Slug-Go matches perfectly to a 1/0 or 2/0 long-shank bend-back hooks. Several manufacturers offer these hooks, or you can take a standard hook and bend the shank slightly in a vise. I like the Gamakatsu, Matzuo, Mustad and Tru-Turn O'Shaugnessey hooks that are light in weight, made of thin wire and very strong and sharp. Having the sharpest hook possible is a great advantage when using plastic on a fly rod. You need quick hook penetration when you set the hook.

"Tying" A Soft Plastic

Because of the mechanics involved in using a fly rod and the casting motions needed to get the lure out there, you really have to secure the soft plastic to the hook shank. First, wrap the shank with two or three wraps of fly tying thread. I like 3/0 flat waxed thread for this. This will provide a very good base for holding, grabbing and gluing the plastic in place so it doesn't slip while casting. The best thing you can do is to tie up some of these hooks before you set out to go fishing. Place them in a small Plano box or a Ziploc bag and they will be ready to use in a moment's notice.

Remember, when rigging these lures and getting them ready to fish, you can add flash to them, extra weight like Jiggy Heads to take them down deeper, Clouser eyes, stick-on eyes and more. Don't be afraid to try new things. You just may come up with a hot new presentation.

Fishing Tactics

If you are fishing in an area with current, the Slug-Go works great when you allow them to drift freely in the current when stripers are feeding on cinder worms. Very often the best technique is to not give any movement to the fly (in this case the lure) except for a few light twitches. The lure will move along in a much more life-like fashion. You now have the advantage of a molded plastic bait imitation that would actually be very difficult, if not impossible, to cast on regular spinning gear, with the delicate presentation of a fly rod that handles this lure with ease.

Another productive soft plastic that we have had great success with on the fly rod is the 2-1/2-inch Fin-S Fish in white, yellow and black. The Fin-S Fish is one of the most popular and most-copied soft plastics on the market. Its darting, tail-flipping motion drives fish wild. It is very good when fished on sand flats or in back coves during spring, when bait tends to be small.

Rig this bait in exactly the same fashion as you would the Slug-Go. If you can find those bend-back hooks, they are the best. If you can't, go with a straight-shank hook like an O'Shaugnessey. In either case, the same rigging principles apply. The lure needs to hang properly in a straight line on the hook's shank without twists, kinks or bumps, so it floats and moves naturally.

These two soft plastics are not the only soft plastics that you can use on a fly rod. From Optimum Bait Company of California comes one of the most realistic silverside or spearing imitations I've ever seen. It comes from 2-1/4 -inches to around 4-inches and has an amazingly life-like finish with molded-in 3-D eyes.

The Mojo Lure Company, also from California, has a small eel-like soft plastic known as a "Reaper" that is used in freshwater finesse fishing situations but will work in the salt just as easily and effectively. They are long, thin and also loaded with amazing natural action. We have taken so many stripers and weakfish with these smaller plastics on our fly rods that it is hard to keep count. On many occasions now I put one of them on before I tie on a fly.

From Tsunami, try their amazingly realistic eels. They are great in the small sizes. These small baits are best rigged with a #2 Eagle Claw short shank hook (a Tru-Turn Bleeding Bait hook in red is even all the better). The larger 3 to 4-1/2-inch models will take a #1 or 1/0 hook with no trouble at all.

Small plastic worms, some of the smaller tube baits, and small curly tail grubs, Red Gill teasers, shell shrimp and even 2-inch shad bodies can all be deadly when fished on fly tackle.

Fish them on floating lines, intermediate or sinking line and rocket them out with shooting head systems. I prefer the shooting heads since they offer the most distance with the least amount of work once you get use to casting them. Any good 10-weight fly rod will work fine. I believe that a 10-weight rod is best because it has the necessary power to toss a little bit heavier bait/fly, and also has the backbone to handle and land big fish. It also has the power to be able to deal with the wind, an eternal problem in any bay or ocean setting.

I'm sure that some of the more dedicated fly-rod anglers will be upset with this section, but if it gets you more fish and you are having a good time doing it, why worry about what anybody thinks? After all, isn't the name of the game to catch fish and have fun doing it?

Soft-plastic baits are an essential lure for guides, captains and local "sharpies" who depend upon them to make consistent catches of trophy fish.

CHAPTER FIFTEEN

WHAT THE PROS SAY

Guides and captains who make their living on the water need reliable tackle and good lures. Soft-plastic lures are a favorite of many of these veterans, and with good reason—they catch fish day in, day out.

To get their first-hand opinions, I personally interviewed a wide selection of captains who use soft plastics in their fishing businesses on a daily basis. I wanted to know how other captains and professionals felt about soft plastics, what they used, special tricks they employed and how these lures have become so much a part of their fishing success.

Their comments are interesting and provide readers with a window into the world of the professional. Hey, if it works for them, it should work for you, too!

Capt. Fred Bowman
Bottom Line Charters
Wakefield, Rhode Island

Capt. Fred is one of the best in the business, and his tube lures have become famous all across New England. His season starts in early spring in the waters of Block Island Sound around the middle of May. The early-run striped bass are then migrating up the coast following schools of alewives and bunker. During this time period, he takes big stripers consistently by trolling deep with a wide variety of soft-plastic lures that replicate the forage fish the striped bass are feeding on.

Fred likes a shad body up to 9 inches in length, fished on a 3-ounce leadhead jig with a huge 10/0 hook molded in the head. This combination is fished on 300 feet of wire line in Block Island Sound trolling down deep in the rips and heavily structured bottom areas. He likes the Storm Wildeye Shads and Mister Twister Sassy Shads in 6-inch sizes for trolling both inshore and offshore areas. The big, wide paddle tails provide lots of irresistible swimming action that striped bass can't resist. When trolled, jigged or drifted in areas where the bass take up feeding positions, the shads are superb fish catchers.

Fred says, "I also like to fish the 4-inch and the 6-inch shad bodies on umbrella rigs. I usually rig two 6-inch shads on 80-pound test leader material and trailing back about 24 inches from the frame. On the other two arms of the frame, I run two 6-inch shads on 8-inch 80-pound leader with no hooks. These two baits act as teasers and are attached by a large snap swivel. On the inside of the frame I use the 4-inch shad bodies with the body snugged up close to the frame, and held by snap swivels. This rig is a good representation of the schooling patterns and habits of both menhaden and alewives. I've taken stripers to 53 pounds with this rig."

As the summer gets closer and the water gets warmer, and most of the herring and menhaden are gone, Fred switches tactics over to another type of plastic that is known as trolling tubes. Trolling tubes are made of plastic PVC material that is dyed in various colors. He usually makes them around 30-inches in length. His two favorite colors are amber and red. The lure is also trolled on wire line in deep water around Block Island and it has been known to locals and others as tube and worm fishing.

The tube rig has two hooks on the end. One is attached to the wire running the length of the tube itself; the other is a stinger hook attached to the first hook. To the stinger hook, a live sea worm is added, or a plastic Berkley Power Worm. These scented baits have fooled many a big bass over the years including two fish of 63 and 61 pounds.

"These tactics work," says Fred, "and I wouldn't go to work without them in my tackle box."

Mark Nichols
D.O.A. Lure Company
Palm City, Florida

Mark was a shrimp and a crab boat operator before he became a lure manufacturer. He told me he firmly believed that his crabbing and shrimping experiences gave him the knowledge to make his very first soft plastic lure, the D.O.A. plastic shrimp. From the first prototype, he worked on the lure for another 10 years to get the bait just right. It had to look, feel and swim just like a real shrimp. He did such a good job that anglers all along the coast use these lures for a wide variety of gamefish.

Mark Nichols created D.O.A. (Deadly On Anything) Lures and his extensive testing and refinement offers fish-catching products that are used by pros, guides and captains all along the Gulf and East Coasts.

When Mark said, "Soft plastic shrimp are not used nearly enough along other parts of the coast," I assumed he meant New England. He actually meant the entire East Coast. He's fished New England waters and taken hundreds of striped bass on his 3/8-ounce shrimp imitation to the amazement of others who were watching him fish. He's also done it in many other states along the coast. Shrimp are found all along the coast, but most tackle shops outside Florida don't sell live shrimp for bait. Because of this, anglers in these areas don't think shrimp will catch fish. Wrong!

According to Mark, the success of the lure is all in the techniques used. Fishing these imitations properly makes all the difference between success and failure. Mark likes to use soft-plastic lures when the sun is out and it is very bright. His experience has shown that this is when soft plastics are at their best. The brighter the better. Soft plastics in his opinion will catch almost anything that swims and it doesn't matter where you are fishing either. In the Atlantic, the Pacific or in the Gulf, plastic lures will work when rigged and used properly.

Mark almost never uses any live or cut bait anymore, preferring to fool his fish with his soft-plastic imitations instead. He has made quite a name for himself in Florida in capturing some pretty big fish on his products, which cover the gamut from shrimp and crabs to innovative swim baits, and leadheads and all types of tails. He noted that he takes an awful lot of pride in his company's name Deadly On Anything (D.O.A.) and loves to show people how to catch more fish with his lures. He is constantly in demand to do seminars to share his knowledge.

He uses super braid lines because of the added sensitivity to feel strikes, and also because of the small diameter, but heavier pound test line can haul a big snook or striped bass away from a bridge piling before the fish gets to cut you off.

"Let the lure sink," he advises. "Many fishermen begin their retrieve right away, yet the fish are not usually on or near the surface. Get the lure down and you'll get more strikes." Mark will use many retrieve actions depending on what he thinks the fish may want to see. He tries short hops, sweeps and jigging actions. His retrieve speed is often on the slow side. "The fish have to see the lure before they can strike at it," he says. Mark believes that fishermen should pay closer attention to their presentation and technique and they would hook and land more fish. Very good advice indeed.

Capt. Joe Pagano
Stuff-It Charters
Wakefield, Rhode Island

Joe Pagano has been chartering for many years and his specialty is striped bass at night. He calls it surf fishing from the other side. When I asked Joe what he uses he told me he likes the 4-inch shad bodies, Fin-S Fish, Wildeye shads, and Zoom Flukes.

Joe rigs these baits on jigheads and sometimes as droppers, especially when fishing for fluke or sea bass. The reason he likes them so much is simple, he says that they are very effective. The stuff looks exactly like baitfish and he strongly believes that the fish will hit and attack them when they turn their noses up to other lures and baits.

He likes the white/pearl Zoom Fluke for albacore fishing during the fall run and Fin-S Fish in a green silver color of four inches. He uses them with no weight and rigs them as you would a rubber worm and just has his clients pop them across the surface of the water. He has also caught triggerfish on these lures and mahimahi offshore next to floating pieces of wood or weed lines. Rig them on a small jighead and toss them next to high fliers as well. Joe also feels strongly that

Captain Joe Pagano is a firm believer in the power of soft-plastic lures to catch trophy-size striped bass.

soft plastics such as Bass Assassins are good wintertime or cold-weather baits.

On visits to Key West and other parts of Florida on family vacations he has taken along his small bag of plastics and taken snook, ladyfish, jacks and some big barracuda on light spinning gear.

In the springtime Joe uses the 3 and the 5-inch Storm Wildeye shad bodies when the herring are running. When fishing at night he has used and still uses the Zoom Fluke and the big Fin-S Fish for bass and bluefish. At times he rigs big Slug-Go baits on an 8/0 worm hook and pops them on the surface like a surface lure. Joe also likes the Mann's Jelly Hoos which look like a ballyhoo. Okay, it's not offshore, but he fishes them in front of breaking waves and across the surface for some super surface action.

During the worm hatch he has no problem using curly-tail grubs to attract bass, as he believes that the tail action excites them into hitting. American shad also hit the curly tail grubs in the smaller sizes in black, chartreuse and red.

Joe also uses the Senko worms that are so popular in freshwater right now. He doesn't rig them Wacky Worm style but instead rigs them like plastic worm and fishes it like a jerk bait up near the surface. Because this worm is somewhat heavier than most, it casts very well and the action is just amazing.

Joe states that he will continue to experiment with soft plastics as long as there are fish to catch. Let's hope that is a long, long, time.

Brian Horsley "Flat Out"
Sara Gardner "Fly Girl"
Nags Head, North Carolina

Brian and Sara own and operate a premier guide business and their reputation for putting clients into fish is famous. Their home waters are the inshore and offshore areas of the Outer Banks of North Carolina. Even though they specialize in fly fishing, they have to offer their clients a variety of techniques, and they use light spin and conventional when the situation demands. Many days you can't fish with the fly rod no matter how bad you want to. According to Sara, "Soft plastics are a big part of our light-tackle game plan, and we hardly use any type of hard-plastic baits anymore." About the only time they still use hard baits is as a teaser to draw fish close to the boat. This technique is especially effective with stripers and bluefish.

Captain Sarah Gardner is world known for her fly fishing guiding, but she and her husband, and fellow guide, Brian Horsley, also depend on plastic baits for their spin-fishing customers.

Soft-plastic baits are relatively inexpensive to purchase, they're easy to use by anglers of all skill levels and they are safer because you're dealing with only one hook. "Best of all," says Sara, "soft-plastic lures work in all sorts of situations on a daily basis."

Sara reported that she and Brian use a lot of Storm and Tsunami swim baits. In their neck of the woods they use soft plastics for almost everything that swims, including striped bass, bluefish, seatrout, amberjacks, albacore, small tuna and more. She says, "Soft plastics are effective on a lot of different species, and we use the same lure to catch three or four different species of game fish."

They use a lot of twister tails on their leadheads to get the lures deep, even when fishing the relatively shallow waters of the back bays. "Even when we see schooling fish on the surface, the jig get the lures deeper where the bigger fish are holding below the main school."

Both anglers agree that the light tackle aspect of their business and the use of soft-plastic lures have complimented their fly-fishing very nicely.

Bob Turley
North Coast Charters
Niantic, Connecticut

Bob is a light-tackle and fly-fishing guide from western Connecticut, and he uses a variety of soft-plastic baits. He has taken bass, blues, weakfish and even albacore on these lures. He likes Slug-Go baits, Mister Twister tails and big Fin-S Fish and big shad bodies. Favorite colors include white, yellow and black. One of his favorite is to three-way big plastics in the deeper areas of Long Island Sound. He finds that they are lethal for taking big stripers as long as you use enough weight to get them to the bottom and keep them there. According to Bob, the biggest mistake that most anglers make is not using enough weight to get the big shads down deep.

Bob likes braided lines like Power Pro and Spider Wire for this kind of fishing since there is little or no stretch and the small diameter of line helps get the lures deep. Instead of using an 8-ounce jighead fished on heavy mono, to get down deep he uses a 2 to 4-ounce jig with the braided line.

When he travels offshore he likes using plastic on daisy chains for tuna and other pelagic species.

Shell E. Caris
Shore Catch Guide Service
Toms River, New Jersey

When it comes to the New Jersey Coast, few surf anglers are as well-versed as Shell E. Caris (known as Shell E. to his buddies). From Sandy Hook to Long Beach Island, and back into Barnegat bay's sedges and wading flats, soft plastics play a big part in Shell E.'s professional and personal fishing strategy. Along with his partners, Jim Freda and Gene Quigley, Shore Catch Guide Service special-izes in fly, light tackle and bait fishing, and they depend upon soft plastics to deliver good catches for their customers.

Shell E. had been using Creme worms and curly-tails draped on bucktails for school stripers and weakfish, but he really got hooked on plastics about 12 years ago. As he tells it, "While fishing next to a buddy who was fishing live herring, I tried a large white Sassy Shad lure drifted along a sedge bank. At the end of the tide, the score was 10 fish for the shad and zero for the live bait. I've been a believer ever since." Today, Shell E. lugs around a backpack filled with tackle and lures, and a significant portion of it is dedicated to soft-plastic baits.

Among his favorites are the Fin-S Fish, Sassy Shad and Capt. Steve's Bass Candy, and he also fishes the Storm and Tsunami swim baits in 4 to 6-inch sizes.

"To get the most action from the bait, the best retrieve uses a lift of the rod, followed by a crank of the reel handle as the rod tip is lowered. This up and down swimming motion looks like a struggling or wounded baitfish and gets the attention of striped bass," says Shell E. "I like all-white as my favorite color, but some of the natural-looking colors also catch fish."

When fishing an inlet or an area where there is a strong sweeping current, Shell E. advises, "Follow the lure as the current carries it along, but retain the up and down swimming motion. Don't use a jerky retrieve." Depending on the current, he suggests using lead-heads in the range of 1 to 2 ounces for the best results.

"Rigging up with a braided line is a big help because it allows you to get the maximum sensitivity when working the lure. You also gain casting distance and plenty of power to set the hook because the line has virtually no stretch. "I especially like the no-stretch factor of braided lines," he says. "I usually fish with 30-pound test, which has

Surf guide Shell E. Caris uses a variety of soft baits to make sure his surf-fishing clients catch striped bass and weakfish.

the diameter of about 8-pound test mono. It's a good balance of casting qualities and hook-setting power."

To add a leader, Shell E. ties a SPRO 230-pound test swivel to the end of the braided line using a double clinch knot. A 30-pound fluorocarbon leader of about 24 to 30 inches is added. For leaders, he usually uses either a multi-color mono or clear fluorocarbon.

"The bottom line," says Shell E., "is that soft plastics help me get more fish for my clients, and when I just fish for fun. They work."

Henry Cowan
Cowan's Guide Service
Lake Lanier, Georgia

Henry guides his clients to striped bass, and catches them with a fly rod and light tackle. Henry likes the 5-inch Zoom Fluke in white, which many guides use as their go-to bait. He explained that the 5-inch Zoom imitation was a perfect match of the juvenile gizzard shad that live in Lake Lanner and that the stripers there really love the erratic action the bait has on the surface.

He recommends fishing plastics with a medium-action spinning casting outfit with 8 to 12-pound test line. The plastic bait should always be fished on a single hook. Henry likes using plastics first thing in the morning, then late in the afternoon or when the stripers are pushing shad to the surface and schooling up on a hot feed. He also cautioned that anglers will get more hook-ups if they only set the hook when you feel the weight of the fish. Reacting to the sight of the fish coming to the surface will usually result in missed strikes.

Henry also fishes saltwater and he commented on how the striped bass in freshwater are almost the same as those in saltwater. Their habits and feeding patterns are very similar.

Capt. Tom Koerber
Roccus Charters
Boston Harbor, Massachusetts

Capt. Tom fishes around Boston Harbor where aggressive clean-up programs have restored the area so it now supports all types and kinds of gamefish, especially the striped bass and bluefish during the summer. The harbor's big tidal exchange and its cool summer waters offer some very good fishing around the many islands and channels of the harbor.

Tom uses a custom-poured shad-shaped lure, usually in white. He tosses these baits on 7-foot St. Croix spinning rods with his reels filled with 10 to 14-pound test line.

He likes to rig Slug-Go baits and adds a corkscrew HitchHiker rig on the hook shank. An Owner 5/0 wide-gap offset-point hook is his preferred hook choice. The HitchHiker rig lets the lure ride evenly on the water, gives it a greater amount of action and attracts more fish, he believes. Tom says he also likes the mid-size to large Storm Wildeye Swim Shads.

During the fall run when the harbor and rivers are full of peanut bunker he switches to a 3-inch Mister Twister Sassy Shad to match the hatch. Depending on the size of the bait, he'll match the hatch with 3 to 5-inch Sassy Shads. All-white is again the color of choice.

Capt. Wayne Frieden
Reel Dream Charters
Scituate, Massachusetts

Capt. Wayne's favorite soft plastics are the 5 and 7-inch Bass Assassin. Wayne claims that the 7-inch model casts very well and is his go-to big fish bait, especially in the spring when herring are running. He uses jigheads weighing from 3/8 ounce on up to 3 ounces. He likes the pearl white color because it also has a realistic purplish glow that gamefish find appealing.

When peanut bunker are around, Wayne likes the 4-inch shad body for late summer and fall. He rigs them on 3/8-ounce jigheads, and fishes them in water of 4 to 18 feet deep. He likes the 3-1/2-inch Fin-S Fish in Arkansas shiner and rainbow trout colors to imitate a silverside.

Wayne tosses the large 7-inch Fin-S Fish in a smoke gray color on a big worm hook for bigger striped bass when fishing near channel edges.

Steve "Van Staal" McKenna
Quaker Lane Outfitters/ Surf Guide
North Kingstown, Rhode Island

Steve is known locally as "Mr. Van Staal," for his collection of Van Staal spinning reels. I have known Steve for well over 30 years and no one knows the shoreline of Rhode Island as he does. He has built a reputation of fishing the longest, walking the farthest, climbing the most difficult obstructions, wading the most difficult places, and

Steve McKenna has switched from live eels to Slug-Go baits because they consistently catch striped bass.

catching an awful lot of fish in the process. He has discouraged many a partner during his time on the water when they couldn't keep up with him any longer. Steve would fish in the hottest, wettest, coldest and windiest conditions, non-stop for just that ONE hit.

Over the years Steve has fished with some of the best surfcasters to ever walk the beaches or climb the rocky shoreline of the Rhody coast; such as Tim Coleman, former editor of the *Fisherman Magazine*; Pat Abate, owner of River's End Tackle Shop in Old Saybrook, Connecticut; Art Lavallee, Jr. owner of Acme Tackle Company and many others.

For years he was known as "Mr. Eel," because he refused to fish with anything other than a live eel when trying to catch a big fish from the surf. About four or five years ago, with some coaxing and advice from his friends Coleman and Abate, who had been catching some pretty decent fish on big plastic worms and Slug-Go-type baits, talked Steve into trying these new and innovative tactics. Here's what Steve had to say:

JRW: *Steve, did you ever think that you would ever give up fishing live eels for striper bass?*

SM: Honestly, Jim, I never thought I would. I sometimes can't believe that I haven't fished with a live eel now in almost four years.

JRW: *What replaced those snakes you loved so much?*

SM: Big 9-inch black Slug-Go plastics. In my opinion, they work just as well if not better than the real thing. I know that it's hard for some people to accept or believe, but it's true. I sometimes have a hard time believing it myself. I've had nights on the water where I was fishing next to guys who were tossing live eels and I was out-fishing them sometimes three to one.

JRW: *Have you tried anything else besides the big Slug-Go?*

SM: Yep. We use the new 7-1/2-inch sizes that are now available. We've used the Gary Yamamoto Senko worms with really good success and the new 10-inch YUM worms that have just been introduced with their Forktail Dinger. I'm also looking forward to trying those new 10-inch Bass Kandy Delights that you showed me awhile back. They look like they are going to be awesome as well.

JRW: *How have your clients responded to using soft plastics when you guide them?*

SM: Surprisingly they have been very receptive to the ideas and the techniques I've shown them. I'd have to say that I've opened up a lot of eyes to the use of soft plastics for big stripers.

Guiding from the surf is not easy, as you are probably already aware. Guiding is not an easy endeavor in the surf or from a boat. There are too many variables to contend with. So having an artificial plastic bait that works as well as live bait is a real bonus.

JW: *Do you thing you'll ever go back to using live eels again?*

SM: Well, you hate to say never, but given the situation with the eels right now and the possibility of having the fishery shut down in the future, I'd have to say that I'll be using those jumbo plastic baits for a long time to come.

Capt. Lynn Smith
C-Devil II
Charlestown, Rhode Island

Capt. Lynn Smith is one of the female pioneers of saltwater guides along the New England Coast specializing in both fly and light-tackle inshore fishing. Her husband, Capt. Kelly Smith, runs the C-Devil out of Snug Harbor Marina. When I talked to her about plastic lures, she gave me some valuable information.

"I use the Fin-S Fish, Mario's Squid Strips in the small size to 7-inch size, Curly Tail Grubs, Slug-Gos and swim baits. I use them to help me find fish that are active, especially when they aren't showing near the surface. It's better to have a client toss soft plastics when searching for fish than wearing out their fly-casting arm. Once we locate the fish, we break out the fly rods.

"When I fish around a rocky shoreline I like to cast Fin-S Fish and Slug-Go baits up against rocky shorelines, stonewalls, breakwaters and other visible structure that protrudes from the water. I have my client's cast up close into the white water wash so the lures act like wounded baitfish. The gamefish usually hit the baits very hard in those situations.

"For those times when I need to fish deeper, I go to the shad-body swim baits and fish them over rockpiles, grass beds, and deep holes and channels. The lure weight depends upon the depth of the water we are fishing, and how far we need to cast to reach it. Sometimes windy days require a heavier jighead."

"I like to vary the sizes and colors to match the type of baitfish present at the time. I also like a white bucktail jig with a white 6-inch curly tail grub on the hook. There is something about that combination that the fish just love. I think everyone should have at least a few in their boat all the time."

Captain Lynn Smith prefers soft baits such as Slug-Go, Fin-S Fish, curly tails and swim baits to fool a variety of gamefish, like this trophy weakfish, for her charter customers.

"A trick that works for me when the water is roiled or dirty is to add scent to the lure so the fish have another attractor to key-in on. Visibility can become a problem on some days and adding scent to the lures seems to help a great deal."

Bill Hurley
Striper Magnet Lures
Northhampton, Massachusetts

Bill designed the Striper Magnet Bait, a deadly lure marketed primarily in New England, but his rigging tips will be helpful to fishermen all along the coast.

A violet back and off-white belly is his favorite color combo for the 10-inch bait. He glues 10-millimeter doll eyes (black pupil with white background) to each side of the lure with a dab of Tower Hobbies CA glue, and speeds up the drying process with Tower Hobbies accelerator.

The 6/0 hook has a weight molded to the shank. The hook is placed into the belly cavity of the lure, then pushed forward until the hook eye protrudes from the nose of the bait. Once the hook eye is exposed, tie on a length of fluorocarbon leader material approximately 36-inches in length.

Next, draw the hook back through the lure and place plastic tubing or a soda straw around the hook weight. Do this by splitting the tubing or straw. Apply a liberal dose of CA glue to weld the soft-plastic lure body, the tubing and the hook as one unit. Pull the hook back into place so the hook eye again protrudes from the nose of the bait. Once dry, the result is very fishable and the walk-the-dog lure action is superb. It only takes about two minutes to make one finished lure— maybe longer if you aren't use to rigging your own lures.

This lure is totally different from almost anything that is out there at the present time and is very effective.

Ron "Big Fish" Whitely
Pro Angler
Florida

Ron was a pioneer experimenting with soft-plastic crab lures. We can all learn from his experiences. Ron began using plastic crabs in the early 1990s after seeing a lot of striped bass in the flats in Connecticut eating green crabs and ghost crabs. He believed there should be a way to fish imitation crabs, because crabs have always been favorite bait for fish like permit, tautog and stripers.

The first plastic crabs that he tried were called Cajun Crabs from Bass Pro Shops. Today there are a lot of different companies making soft plastic crab imitations and they are turning out some realistic reproductions.

As Ron was sight-fishing on the sand flats of New England, he noticed that a lot of fish were ignoring anything that he and his friends were casting. Many times the fish didn't even look when the lure passed over their heads because they were focused on the bottom. Baits fished along the bottom were producing strikes, so Ron stalked the fish to learn what they were eating. Sure enough, he saw what they were feeding on, crabs.

When striped bass, or other gamefish are not striking lures fished over their heads, when silver flashes are seen as the fish roll to feed, and when a fish that you do catch has red jaw from rubbing on the bottom, the fish are probably feeding on crabs. Whenever you encounter these tell-tale signs, the plastic crab lure is the go-to bait.

There are several ways to fish them depending on the conditions you are facing. In deep water, they can be put onto a jighead and dragged along the bottom very slowly. In shallow water a weighted worm hook is all you need to get it down and keep it close to the bottom. When fishing very shallow water, they work well just on a plain hook.

Retrieve action is critical to success. The best retrieve is slow and with a short hopping action. Let the crab sit for a few seconds. When a real crab senses danger it sits still and does not immediately try to get away as a baitfish would. Instead it holds its ground, spreads its claws and stands there ready to fight. The angler should wait for the fish to move up to the crab. A short twitch will usually get a strike.

There is a huge selection of plastic baits, hooks, jigheads, accessories and equipment available for the soft-plastic lure fisherman.

CHAPTER SIXTEEN

THE SUPPLY DEPOT

There is a huge array of soft-plastic lures on the market today, and what most fishermen see when they visit their local tackle shop is just the tip of a vast portion of the tackle industry. Each year at the annual fishing tackle trade show, new variations of soft-plastic baits are introduced and the innovations are seemingly endless.

Although you probably won't get to visit the trade show, there's an alternative way to search out all the latest stuff. Surfing the web for manufacturer's information can be an enjoyable and exciting trip. Visits to manufacturer's websites help you learn about lures you may never have seen before, and then you can try to figure out how to use them in your home waters.

This chapter is basically just a list—a long one, for sure—that covers the names, addresses and website addresses (or phone numbers) of as many manufacturers as I could find. Everyone on the list makes soft-plastic lures, jigheads, hooks or specialty products that support fishermen that fish with soft-plastic lures.

Since I have done a lot of freshwater fishing in my many years of guiding, I was always tuned into new ideas and new ways to use soft lures. Experimentation came easily to me, and I found many ways to catch more fish in the salt with soft-plastic lures. I urge you to keep an open mind and soak up some of the good innovations that are coming to the market today. Hopefully the accompanying list will help your journey—and help you catch plenty of fish.

The soft-plastic lure business is expanding rapidly and it's possible I missed several companies—new companies seem to spring up overnight! Let me assure you that the oversight was not intentional and hopefully anyone I missed can be included in future updates of this book. The companies are listed alphabetically for easy reference.

Soft Lure Manufacturers

AA Worms, Inc.
PO Box 176
29900 Rancho California Road
Suite 333
Temecula, CA 92591
951.676.4023
www.aaworms.com

Action Plastics
3927 Valley East Industrial Drive
Birmingham, AL 35217
800.874.4829
www.action-plastics.com

Barefoot Rods & Tackle, LLC
PO Box 450
Morrisville, NC 27560
919.596.5007
www.barefootrodsandtackle.com

Barlow's Tackle Shop
451 N. Central Expressway
Richardson, TX 75080
972.231.5982
www.barlowstackle.com

Bass Assassin Lures
232 SE Industrial Circle, Suite A
Mayo, FL 32066
386.294.1049
www.bassassassin.com

Bass Pro Shops
2500 East Kearney Street
Springfield, MO 65898
417.873.5000
www.basspro.com

Berkley
Pure Fishing America
1900 18th Street
Spirit Lake, IA 51360
800.237.5539
www.purefishing.com

Bimini Bay Outfitters Ltd.
43 McKee Drive
Mahwah, NJ 07430
800.688.3481
www.biminibayoutfitters.com

Boone Bait Co, Inc.
PO Box 2966
Winter Park, FL 32790
407.975.8775
boonebait@earthlink.net

Cabela's, Inc.
One Cabela Drive
Sidney, NE 69160
308.254.5505
www.cabelas.com

Calcutta Fishing (Big Rock Sports)
173 Hankinson Drive
Newport, NC 28570
252.726.6186
www.calcuttafishing.com

Canyon Plastics
602 Andy Devine
Kingman, AZ 86401
800.770.0575
www.canyon-plastics.com

Caribou Lures
PO Box 247
Montreal, Quebec
Canada
H4V2Y4
1.514.636.1112
www.caribou.ca

Castaic Soft Bait, Inc.
PO Box 6727
Nogales, AZ 85628
520.281.5108
www.castaicsoftbait.com

Classic Fishing Products, Inc.
PO Box 121249
Clermont, FL 34712
407.656.6133
www.culprit.com

Clatter Baits, LLC.
171 Cheramie Lane
Kentwood, LA 70444
985.229.8604
www.clatterbaits.com

Cotee Bait Co.
6045 Sherwin Drive
Port Richey, FL 34668
727.845.3737
www.cotee.com

Créme Lure Company
5401 Kent Drive
PO Box 6162
Tyler, TX 75711
800.527.8652
www.cremelure.com

DeLong Lure Mfg
955 Joliet Road
Valparaiso, IN 46385
219.465.1101
www.delonglures.com

Dezyner Baits
PO Box 2173
Lancaster, CA 93539
800.998.9676
www.dezynerbaits.com

D.O.A. Fishing Lures
1253 SE Dixie Cutoff Road
Stuart, FL 34994
772.287.5001
www.doalures.com

Doc Waters Lure Company
2303 RR 620 South
Suite 135-193
Austin, TX 78734
www.docwaterslures.com

F.J. Neil Company, Inc.
PO Box 617
1062 Route 109
Lindenhurst, NY 11757
631.957.1073

Fair Waters Company
17387 County Road 32
Summerdale, AL 36555
251.989.7575
www.fairwaters.com

Fish Trap Lures
4901 Morena Blvd
Suite 910
San Diego, CA 92117
858.273.6970
www.fishtraplures.com

Gambler Lures
1945 N.W. 18th Street
Pompano Beach, FL 33069
954.969.1772
www.gambler-bang.com

Gary Yamamoto Custom Baits
PO Box 1000
849 S. Coppermine Road
Page, AZ 86040
928.645.3812
www.yamamoto.baits.com
www.baits.com

Glowmates
PO Box 56596
Chicago, IL 60656
773.763.8737
www.glowmates.com

Harry-O's Baits
PO Box 91173
Louisville, KY 40291
502.239.0351
www.harryo.net

Hooker Baits
PO Box 338
West Harwich, MA 02672
508.432.2325
www.hookerbaits.com

H&H Lure Company
10874 N. Dual Street
Baton Rouge, LA 70814
225.275.1471

Illusion Lures
1115 W. Flood
PO Box 721353
Norman, OK 73070
www.illusionlures.com

Kalin's
PO Box 1234
Brawley, CA 92227
760.344.2550
www.kalinlures.com

Ledge Runner Baits
PO Box 462
Halifax, MA 02338
781.293.9752
www.ledgerunnerbaits.com

**Lindy Legendary
Fishing Tackle**
1110 Wright Street
Brainerd, MN 56401
218.829.1714
www.lindyfishingtackle.com

Lucky Strike Bait Works Ltd.
RR #3
2287 Whittington Drive
Peterborough, Ontario
Canada K9J 6X4
705.743.3849
www.luckystrikebaitworks.com

Lunker City Fishing Specialists
PO Box 1807
Meriden, CT 06450
203.237.3474
www.lunkercity.com

Mister Twister Inc.
PO Drawer 1152
Minden, LA 71058
318.377.8818
www.mistertwister.com

Mario's Lures
PO Box 1363
Middletown, CT 06457
860.344.1009

Mann's Bait Company, Inc.
1111 State Docks Road
Eufaula, AL 36027
334.687.5716
www.mannsbait.com

MegaBait
(Pace Products, Inc.)
1050-AS S. Cypress St.
LaHabra, CA 90631
714.773.4132
www.megabait.com

Netters Inc.
PO Box 7242
Gilford, NH 03247
888.883.2673
www.nettersinc.com

Natural Motion Lures, Inc.
PO Box 701990
St. Cloud, FL 34770
877.catch-10
www.naturalmotionlures.com

Newport Lures
PO Box 629
Greenwood, DE 19950
888.468.5447
www.bucktail.com

Nichols Lures, Inc.
PO Box 1928
Jacksonville, TX 75766
903.589.8100
www.nicholslures.com

OutKast Tackle, Inc.
PO Box 385901
Bloomington, MN 55438
www.outkasttackle.com

Panther Martin Lures
19 North Columbia Street
Port Jefferson, NY 11777
1.800.852.0925
www.PantherMartin.com

Reaction Lures
29900 Highway 191
Many, LA 71449
800.256.2075
www.reactionlures.com

Sea Striker
PO Box 459
158 Little Nine Drive
Morehead City, NC 28557
252.247.4113
www.seastriker.com

So Slo Lures
11880 E. 86th Street N.
Owasso, OK 74055
www.soslo.com

SPRO
3900 Kennesaw 75 Parkway
Suite 140
Kennesaw, GA 30144
770.919.1722
www.spro.com

SR Plastics
Santee, CA
619.449.7727
www.srplastics.com

Stamina Inc.
8401 73rd Ave N.
Unit 40
Brooklyn Park, MN 55428
763.253.0450
www.staminainc.com

Stanley Jigs, Inc.
107 North Main Street
Huntington, TX 75949
936.876.5713
www.fishstanlet.com

Storm Lures
10395 Yellow Circle Drive
Minnetonka, MN 55343
952.933.7060
www.stormlures.com

Striper Magnets
43 Eastern Avenue
North Hampton, MA 01060
413.584.2421

Texas Tackle Factory
1085 Northside Drive
Victoria, TX 77904
361.575.4751
www.texastacklefactory.com

Tidal Surge Fishing Lures
603 Pinebrook Lane
Baytown, TX 77521
281.420.7604

TNT Lures
13286 Morning Glory Drive
Lakeside, CA 92040

Uncle Josh Bait Company
525 Jefferson Street
Fort Atkinson, WI 53538
866.BIG-BASS
www.unclejosh.com

Venom Lures
3031 Williams Road #154
Richmond BC V7E 4G1
Canada
www.venomlures.com

Wave Worms
1420 FM 1483
Yantis, TX 75497
903.383.3573
www.WaveFishing.com

WiggleFin, Inc.
2109 Madison Ave
Boise, ID 83702
208.388.8539
www.wigglefin.com

Yum Bait Company
3601 Jenny Lind
Fort Smith, AR 72901
www.yum3x.com

Zoom Bait Company
1581 Jennings Mill Road
Bogart, GA 30622
706.548.1008
www.zoombait.com

Molds And Plastics

Do-It Corporation
501 North State Street
Denver, IA 50622
319.984.6055
www.do-itmolds.com

Zeiner's Bass Shop
737 S. Washington #6
Wichita, KS 67211
316.265.5551
www.zeiners.com

9er's Lures
79 Middleboro Avenue
Taunton, MA 02780
508.822.9650
www.9erslures.com

Scents

Berkley (Pure Fishing)
1900 18th Street
Spirit Lake, IA 51380
712.336.1520
www.purefishing.com

Carolina Lunker Sauce
PO Box 12049
Raleigh, NC 27605
800.242.1671
www.lunkersauce.com

Catcher Company/
Smelly Jelly
5285 N.E. Elam Young Parkway
Suite B-700
Hillsboro, OR 97124
503.648.2643

Eagle Claw Fishing Tackle
PO Box 16011
Denver, CO 80216
720.941.8700
www.eagleclaw.com

Edge Products
9582 Hamilton #255
Huntington Beach, CA 92646
714.965.0750

Fish Formula Company
PO Box 1705
Dickson, TN 37056
800.874.6965
www.fishformula.com

Jack's Juice
PO Box 310
Orchard Hill, GA 30266
800.835.3474
www.jacksjuice.com

O. Mustad & Son, Inc.
PO Box 838
Auburn, NY 13021
315.253.2793
www.mustad.com

Hooks, Weights, Molds & Jigheads ———

Bullet Weights, Inc.
PO Box 187
122 Apollo Drive
Alda, NE 68810
308.382.7436
www.bulletweights.com

Eagle Claw Fishing Tackle
Wright & McGill Co.
PO Box 16011
Denver, CO 80216
720.941.8700
www.eagleclaw.com

Falcon Tackle Co.
1823 West Reno
Broken Arrow, OK 74012
918.251.0020
www.falconrods.com

Gamakatsu U.S.A., Inc.
PO Box 1797
Tacoma, WA 98401
408.730.1377
www.gwdfishing.com

The Gapen Company
17910 87th St
Becker, MN 55308
763.263.3891
www.gapen.com

Hook Up Lures, Inc.
PO Box 1135
Islamorada, FL 33036
305.664.8203
www.hookuplures.com

Jig, Rigs and Stuff
607.739.4303
www.jigsrigsandstuff.com

Matzuo America/APEX
4770-C Forest Street
Denver, CO 80216
720.941.9400
www.matzuo.com

Mojo Lure Company, Inc.
2985 Lincoln Avenue
Suite 404
Banning, CA 92220
800.474.mojo
www.mojolures.com

O. Mustad & Son, Inc.
PO Box 838
241 Grant Avenue
Auburn, NY 13021
315.253.2793
www.mustad.com

Owner American
3199-B Airport Loop Drive
Costa Mesa, CA 92626
714.668.9011
www.ownerhooks.com

Pope's Jigs
PO Box 155
Waynesboro, TN 38485

P & P Rattle
PO Box 6073
Champaign, IL 61826
217.355.5508
www.pprattle.com

Tru-Turn
PO Box 1177
100 Red Eagle Road
Wetumpka, AL 36092
334.567.2011
www.truturnhooks.com

Accessories

Falcon Lures
100 Asma Blvd
Suite 140
Lafayette, LA 70508
337.232.7326
www.falconlures.com

Jann's Netcraft
PO Box 89
3350 Briarfield Blvd
Maumee, OH 43537
419.868.8288
www.jannsnetcraft.com

Plano Molding Company
431 E. South Street
Plano, IL 60545
800.226.9868
www.planomolding.com

ABOUT THE AUTHOR

© Laptew Productions

Capt. Jim White is a U.S. Coast Guard Captain licensed captain operating White Ghost Guide Service, Ltd., along with his son Capt. Justin White out of East Greenwich, RI. They specialize in light tackle and fly fishing charter trips for striped bass, bluefish, summer flounder, weakfish, bonito, and albacore. Jim has fished all over the world and has taken over 68 different species of fish on light tackle and fly rods which makes him an expert in the light tackle circles of saltwater angling.

His father's family came from Portugal and fished for their living. He is a fourth generation seaman, starting at age 4 with his dad. After a 3-year Army hitch during the Vietnam War he began to fish with a rod and reel to support himself. He mated on charter boats in Point Judith and Snug Harbor using his knowledge and expertise to help others catch fish. Twelve years ago he went into business for himself, and later formed a father-and-son team, building one of the finest fly and light-tackle guide businesses on the eastern seaboard.

Jim's clients include the likes of Lefty Kreh, Bob Popovics, Nick Curcione, Bob Clouser, Mike Laptew, Rick Ruoff, Bob Pond, Art Lavallee Jr., Shaw Grigsby, Martin James of BBC Radio Lancaster,

England and Tom Dorsey of Thomas & Thomas Fly Rod Company, one of the worlds greatest rod designers. He's appeared on ESPN-2 on the Orvis Sporting Life, OLN Network for Bass Pro Shops, TNN on One More Cast with Shaw Grigsby, Canadian PBS Television for three shows on saltwater fishing and BBC Radio.

After *The Fisherman* published his first story in 1978, Jim has written for *Saltwater Sportsman*, *Outdoor Life*, *Fly-Fishing in Saltwater*, *Fly Fish America*, *On The Water*, *New England Fly-Fishing*, *Mid Atlantic Fly-Fishing*, *Striped Bass* magazine and *Shallow Water Angler*. He is on the pro-staffs of Quantum/Van Staal, Lowrance Electronics, Ocean Waves Sunglasses, Yo-Zuri Lures, Ande Line, Triton Boats, Honda Marine, Thomas & Thomas Fly Rods, Lunker City Lures, Acme Tackle and Tru-Turn Hooks.

Since the late 1970s, Jim has worked extensively on striped bass conservation issues when he lead a group of anglers who wrote and introduced the first moratorium striped bass fishing legislation introduced by Congresswomen Claudine Schneider. His involvement has been detailed in "Striper Wars" written by Dick Russell. He is now the state chairman for Stripers Forever, a conservation group working to make the striped bass a gamefish and sits on many different committees and boards.

When he is not fishing or writing he is spending time with his grandson, Devon James, teaching him how to fish and be a professional someday.